Changed Lives

Guideposts®

CARMEL, NEW YORK 10512

www.guidepostsbooks.com

Acknowledgments

Material from *Climbing the Mountain* by Kirk Douglas is used by permission of Simon & Schuster. Copyright © 1997 by The Bryna Company.

Scripture quotations, marked (NIV) are taken from *The Holy Bible, New International Version*. Copyright © 1973, 1978, 1984 International Bible Society. Used by permission of Zondervan Bible Publishers.

Scripture quotations marked (KJV) are taken from *The King James Version of the Bible*.

Scripture quotations marked (RSV) are taken from the *Revised Standard Version of the Bible*. Copyright © 1946, 1952, 1971 by Division of Christian Education of the National Council of Churches of Christ in the U.S.A. Used by permission.

www.guidepostsbooks.com
Guideposts Book & Inspirational Media Division
Design by Patricia Tyler
Cover design by Dennis Arnold
Typeset by Westchester Book Composition
Printed in the United States of America

TABLE OF CONTENTS

CONTENTS

CONTENTS

.. ..

CONTENTS

Just Like the Rest of Us

Richard H. Schneider, Senior Editor

In my 33 years with *Guideposts*, I've worked closely with hundreds of people on their stories. Many have been celebrities. In learning their hopes and dreams, troubles they faced, and how their faith sustained them, I've discovered a basic truth.

They're just like the rest of us.

When I first visited Jimmy Stewart many years ago, I was tongue-tied and nervous walking up to his Tudor home in Beverly Hills. Would he be like the rough-hewn gunslinger in *The Man from Laramie*? The tense, resourceful observer in *Rear Window*? The down-home savings & loan man in *It's a Wonderful Life*?

To further rattle me, a big "See the Stars" tour bus pulled up on the street behind me. I could hear the guide pointing out the house on which I was ringing the door bell. (Yes, an ordinary push-button bell; *that* should have told me something.)

The tall silver-haired man who greeted me was quietly gracious. We relaxed on sofas in his comfortable living room; above the fireplace hung a picture of the African veldt. He nodded at it: "Gloria and I like to safari there; we enjoy looking at the animals." At that a big yellow dog ambled into the room making me feel at home.

The man's blue-gray eyes sparkled with interest as he reminisced about growing up in Indiana, Pennsylvania, putting on basement plays with his sisters, making a model of the

Spirit of St. Louis which he moved across his father's hardware-store display window to match the plane's progress on the day Lindberg flew the Atlantic.

In following visits, a humorous and self-deprecating "star" emerged. He chuckled one day about his grandchildren who had just come for a visit. "They got one of those maps of movie-star homes," he said, "and they were all excited about seeing Michael Jackson's place." He smiled. So much for grandpop.

Getting to know Jimmy Stewart reminded me of what my dad used to say: "Every man puts on his pants one leg at a time."

Jimmy Stewart was not uncomfortable talking about his faith. One only had to sit by him in the Beverly Hills Presbyterian Church to sense the comfort he drew from it.

Practically every celebrity I met had a deep personal faith. If not, they didn't have a story for us.

Every morning at the Lloyd Bridges breakfast table with their daughter and two sons, Jeff and Beau, Dad or Mom would read aloud from a devotional.

I remember General Colin Powell telling how he still preferred the 1928 Episcopal prayer book to the one the denomination had revised in later years.

And though Ernest Borgnine prays every morning, he continues expressing his thanks to God anytime he's deeply moved, such as when he's in the cathedral atmosphere of the Redwoods.

Kathie Lee Gifford, who attended Oral Roberts University, has turned down many roles which she felt were not consistent with her Christian faith.

I was surprised when Chi Chi Rodriguez told me how much *The Power of Positive Thinking* had helped him. One of his golfing buddies had been Dr. Smiley Blanton, the famed Christian psychiatrist with whom Norman Vincent Peale worked so closely.

And I'll always remember the deep chortle of James Earl Jones when he told about his grandfather changing from "everyday talk" to fine English when he preached on Sundays.

The more I visited with so-called "stars," the more I learned they were susceptible to the same worries, temptations and despairs as all of us. And knowing this I appreciated them even more when seeing them at work. For I understood the problems they had to overcome, their sacrifices, and hard work to achieve the success they have earned.

Most of all, I appreciated their frankness in telling their stories that would edify and help others, and their willingness to share their faith in God, a faith that links us all together. The ground is level at the foot of the cross.

Changed Lives
.. ..

INTRODUCTION

L ong ago when God's people were walking a wilderness, looking for the Promised Land, God gave them rules and principles to live by. But that's not all. He gave them a dream for what their future could be—if they learned the lessons of faith and focus, if they looked to God for guidance and power. In Deuteronomy 30 God lays it out: "What I am commanding you today is not too difficult for you or beyond your reach. . . . I have set before you life and death. . . . Now choose life" (NIV).

Some things never change. Like God giving us the opportunity and power to choose life.

That's what this book is about. Here you'll find some of the most memorable choices made by some of the most memorable names of the twentieth century. These are men and women of faith, who have learned about the many facets of success—not defined only in glamorous terms but also in godly terms. Celebrated men and women who've excelled in their secular fields: drama, sports, movies, television. Writers, journalists, singers, comedians, politicians, soldiers. What prompted them to step onto their career path? What brought them to success? What gave them courage to persevere through hardship, failure, or loss—to maintain their purpose and rekindle their dream?

In *Changed Lives* they tell of God's intervening ways—how He gave them vision and power to grab hold of the good, the excellent, the right. In these true-life stories, the nudge to choose Life may be a passage of Scripture; sometimes a prayer spoken, remembered, or heard; sometimes a principle embedded in the mind, an insight realized in the quiet . . . or something that makes sense only in the realm of miracles.

But many of these headliner people say the catalyst for change in their lives was a phrase, an action, or an example of an ordinary person: a parent, spouse, mentor, a colleague, even a stranger. In her story "How to Be an Eskimo," Mariette Hartley recalls a story that humorously illustrates this clandestine work of God, so evident in these pages: When a man ice fishing in the Arctic wilderness got lost in a blizzard, he prayed for God to intervene and spare his life. He lived to tell the tale, but he had grown cynical, because he thought his prayer had not been answered. "Did God help you?" a priest asked. "No," the skeptic answered. "God didn't lift a finger. Some Eskimo appeared out of nowhere and showed me the way."

Mariette, who reminds her readers that she is "not Mrs. James Garner," as portrayed in Polaroid commercials, relates her own personal experience of learning that God often answers prayer "in the form of Eskimos"—the people who are part of the ordinary landscape.

We think you'll enjoy the wide variety of stories in this star-studded *Changed Lives* collection. As you read you'll appreciate the truth of Saint Augustine's line: "We do the works, but God works in us the doing of the works."

We choose life but God gives us the power to make that choice.

And like the men and women in these pages, you can learn that making that choice changes not only your life but your world—even if you're walking a wilderness, looking for a Promised Land.

.. ..

PART I

The Power
in a Parent's Lessons

A wise son hears his father's instruction.
Proverbs 13:1 (RSV)

There's no way for a parent to know which particular words or actions a child—young or grown—will remember as a positive life-changing lesson. No parent is perfect, that's for sure. And yet time and again God uses a parent's voice to speak wise words that become embedded in his or her child's mind. An unforgettable lesson that time nurtures until it becomes a grown-up tale that begs to be retold. *I am who I am because my mama told me. . . . I remember the day my father taught me. . . .*

Those are the kind of stories you'll read here, crediting the influential parents of Reba McEntire, Burl Ives, Roger Staubach, Lorne Greene, Marian Anderson, and more.

With a Little Help from Mama

Reba McEntire

It was a beautiful spring morning when Mama and I set off from our ranch in Oklahoma for Nashville, Tennessee, where I was going to audition for a recording contract. I was twenty years old, well prepared vocally, ready to take a chance on the dream of a lifetime.

But as the hillsides rolled by, resplendent with the whites and pinks of dogwood and redbud blossoms, I felt a creeping uneasiness. The closer we got to the country music capital, the more I tried to prolong the trip, making Mama detour for some sightseeing, then for a snack, then for anything I could think of. Finally I yelled, "Stop!" and Mama pulled the big blue Ford into a Dairy Queen on the side of the highway and we went inside.

As I toyed with my mountain of ice cream, I didn't have to explain I was scared. Mama knew me too well. "Reba Nell," she said, adding the Nell for gentle emphasis, "we can turn around right now and go on back home if that's what you want, and I'll understand. The music business is not for every-one."

I looked at Mama across the melting swirl of my sundae. She wasn't pushing me. But when she was my age, Mama would have given just about anything to have had the opportunity I was getting a chance at now. I wondered if that was what was confusing me.

We'd always had a special bond. Maybe it was because of

my singing. Music had gone way back in Mama's life. But right out of high school she had to take a teaching job, working in a two-room schoolhouse. Then she married, worked as an assistant to the school superintendent, and did all the bookkeeping on our ranch while raising four kids.

Mama and I were middle kids, both the third of four children. Being a middle kid, I was always looking for attention. I was a tomboy, doing everything my older brother, Pake, did. "Anything you can do I can do better!" was our sibling motto, whether it was throwing rocks and doing chin-ups, or riding horses and roping. I was out to be the best, to get the attention. Then I learned to sing.

I remember in the second grade my music teacher, pretty Mrs. Kanton, helped me learn "My Favorite Things" from *The Sound of Music*. When I went home and sang it for Mama, her eyes met mine and just sort of glowed. It tickled me to think I could make Mama react like that, and to hear adults say that I was gifted.

That's what my grandmother—Mama's mother and my namesake—used to say when I was growing up. But she called it a special gift, a gift from God. I was almost as close to her as I was to Mama. Grandma used to take me fishing at a pond on her place. We never did catch much, but we liked to throw in our lines and sit on the pond dam while Grandma told stories, mostly from the Bible. She told me about David, Moses and Daniel, and the special gifts that God had given them, like courage and leadership and prophecy. In fact, David was a songwriter.

I probably learned as much of my Bible going fishing with Grandma as I did in Sunday school. She taught me gospel songs and hymns so I could sing to her. "Reba," she'd say,

.. ..

"God gives all of us our own special gifts, and He's given you yours for a reason. Now you have to learn to use it."

The cherry was sliding down the whipped cream peak on my sundae. I looked outside at the glowing Dairy Queen cone rotating slowly, almost as if it were sitting on a record turntable. Mama was nursing a cup of coffee and watching the traffic flash by. She was not about to rush me.

We'd spent many an hour on the road together. Grandpap and Daddy were champion steer ropers. Summers we'd all go with Daddy on the rodeo circuit. We had a two-horse trailer that was so heavy all four of us kids had to stand on the back of it so Daddy could pull the nose up and hitch it to the Ford. Then we'd pile into the backseat and take off for rodeos in Wyoming and Colorado. We'd play road games, like counting mile markers or Volkswagens. We'd see who could spot the most out-of-state license plates.

Then someone struck up a song and everybody joined in. Mama coached. She kept us on pitch and taught us how to harmonize. If the lyrics got lost in the jumble, she announced, "Okay, stop. Reba Nell, *enunciate*. Now go ahead." One word would do it. That was the schoolteacher coming out in her.

When we got older, Pake; my younger sister, Susie; and I formed a country-and-western band at Kiowa High School. We called ourselves the Singing McEntires. We practiced in the living room while Mama was in the kitchen frying potatoes. I remember one day we were singing harmonies and things got a little messed up. I was on Susie's part or Susie was on Pake's— we couldn't tell—but Pake got really aggravated and started bossing us around. Quick enough, Mama marched in, spatula in hand. "All right," she said, "sing it."

We sang it.

"Susie, you're on Reba's part," she said, pointing with her spatula. "Now, just sing the song." We sang it.

"That sounds better. Sing it again." We sang it again.

"That's perfect. Now do it once more." Then she walked back into the kitchen. That was Mama.

Across the Formica tabletop I caught Mama glancing at her watch. I couldn't stall much longer. My ice cream had turned to soup.

After my voice had matured into a real singer's instrument, I started performing at rodeos. I loved singing to the big crowds. I'd listen to my favorite country music stars, like Loretta Lynn and Dolly Parton, and go out there and try to sound just like them and get all that attention. Then one day Mama took me aside for a quiet talk that would turn out to be one of the most important conversations we ever had.

"Reba Nell," she said, "you have a beautiful voice all your own. If people want to hear Dolly or Loretta sing, they'll buy their albums. But now you've got to find your own style. Sing what you feel, sing from your own heart, and you'll discover the voice God intended for you. That's what people will really come to hear."

She was right. After our talk people in the music business started taking a real look at me, and that's why we were now sitting here in this Dairy Queen outside Nashville.

I looked up at Mama. She was fishing in her purse for the keys to the Ford. "Reba," she said, pulling them out, "I'm serious about turning back. But if you get that record deal, I'll be very proud of you. If you don't—I'll be just as proud." Then she reached over and gave me a tight hug, and suddenly I remembered the glow in her eyes when I sang "My Favorite Things."

.. ..

I knew what that glow had meant. All Mama wanted—all any mother wants for her child—was for me to be myself. And she'd seen what I could be. She didn't have to say that if I signed a record deal she'd be living out her dreams a little bit through me. I understood that now and I was proud. Suddenly I wanted to get to Nashville as quick as we could.

And I've been making records ever since, using those gifts that Grandma talked about and Mama helped me find. The gifts God provides to make each of us unique.

The Gift Inside

Burl Ives

Whenever I've had to ask myself, "What makes a gift special?" my mind goes back to one memorable night in my childhood . . . to the tenant farm my father worked in southern Illinois.

That long-ago night a sudden storm shivered the earth, a terrible assault of thunder and lightning. A shattering bolt blazed across the sky, and my father yelled, "That one hit Jim Parr's place!" Father stood six feet and weighed over two-hundred pounds, but he took off like a deer. Jim Parr was a neighbor, and Father believed that you do unto a neighbor what you know he would do unto you.

Father helplessly watched as the flames turned Jim's grange to ashes. He shepherded Jim, his weeping wife and their ten children to our house. Mother built a fire to warm them and dry their clothes, their only remaining worldly goods.

That night we six young Ives children shared our beds with the ten young Parr children. The next day nine were taken to relatives and neighbors. Jim, his wife and their baby stayed in our house.

Within a day or two Father fixed a big hayrack to his wagon, hitched up a team of horses and visited surrounding farms to collect necessities for the Parrs, unaware that two other farmers were doing the same thing.

They learned of each other's efforts at nightfall when they brought their loaded wagons to an untenanted farm, where the

Parrs would start anew. Into the house went furniture and bedding, kitchenware and a stove, clothes, a ham, a can of lard. Into the barn went a hog, a horse, cow and calf, sheep, harness.

And then, finally, from Father's wagon came one last gift, a faded picture of a landscape in an old frame.

Someone sized it up and laughed. "Now what good is that old picture goin' to do the Parrs?"

My father knew where the good was. "Being old don't matter," he said. "It's the gift inside the gift that matters."

What did my father mean? That the gift he was really giving was one of good wishes, of the hope that the Parrs would again be happy—and that through this landscape the Parrs' bare house would have one touch of beauty. The gift inside the gift was loving-kindness.

And that's the gift I'm always hoping will be inside the gifts I offer.

My Rough Road to Obedience

Roger Staubach

L ife took on extra excitement the day they began to build the new house next door to us. I was about seven, an only child, with a yearning for adventure. Aware of my fascination with the construction next door, dad warned me, "You are not to go near that new house."

"Why?"

"Because you might get hurt."

Rebellious, I watched the house develop, floor by floor. The painters came and the house took on real luster. After the workers had mixed cement and carefully spread it on the front walk, the temptation to get a close look was too much. How could I get hurt when the house was almost finished?

Late in the afternoon after the workers had all gone home and while Mother seemed to be quite involved in the basement, I crept stealthily into the forbidden territory and sat down beside the new cement walk. Carefully, I placed the palm of my right hand face down on the wet cement. It felt soft and cool. For a moment I studied the imprint of my hand on the walk. Then I placed my left hand on the cement.

"Hey, kid. Get outa there!"

Startled, I looked up. Striding toward me was a man whom I recognized as the supervisor. Like a startled fawn I bolted back into my house, the man in hot pursuit. From under the bed of my room I heard the doorbell ring, then voices in the living room.

That night I got it. First, a spanking from my father. Then the worst part—I was forbidden to use the playground across the street for two weeks.

Along with the punishment came an explanation that no family could function properly unless children obeyed their parents, and that my disobedience had resulted in damage to property.

There were other times when I was disobedient and needed correction, but my parents, while firm, were always fair and loving about it. And it didn't take many punishments for me to see something very clearly: When I messed up, there was unhappiness in our home and I was miserable. When I obeyed the rules set down by my parents, there was harmony and contentment in our family.

Since my father made a rather unpredictable income as representative for a shoe firm, economy and discipline were essential in our home. Mother took a job when I was nine, so this meant shared duties all around.

And yet, while our rules were important, the more I accepted responsibility the more freedom and flexibility there was for me as I went from junior high on through high school.

Perhaps this is why the strict rules at the Naval Academy were so hard to take when I entered there in 1959. I could accept the need for order and routine, and even the ribbing plebes had to take from upperclassmen. But the time spent on keeping my shoes looking like mirrors and memorizing a lot of wordy regulations seemed so pointless.

My rebellion flared. Soon demerits were being posted in my record book, like points on the scoreboard during a high scoring basketball game. I collected over one-hundred demerits the first six months.

Furthermore, I was having academic problems as well, in metallurgy and mechanical drawing. It began to look as if my stay at Annapolis would be a very short one.

I suppose it was a combination of factors that helped straighten me out. Good advice from my parents. Plus the counsel of a young instructor who had graduated from the academy only a few years before.

"Roger, I know some of these rules seem like nonsense to you," he told me. "You and others think we're behind the times here at the academy. Changes will come—slowly. But the main purpose behind these regulations is to teach obedience. If military men don't learn to obey an order—whether they like it or not—we'll have chaos in our armed forces. In addition to that, I'm convinced that obedience is the key to the contented life."

When I did shape up, it worked out just as the instructor said. My grades went up, the demerits stopped accumulating, and one day I suddenly realized that I loved the place.

What then followed was a great football experience at Navy, but much more important than the awards and honors from football was learning something about that very elusive quality of leadership. To become a leader, I learned that you first have to be willing to accept authority.

But when I finished my stint in the Navy and joined the Dallas Cowboys in 1968, I found that once again, I still had something to learn about obedience. For what I loved so much about being quarterback for the Navy football team back in 1961–63 was the feeling that I was in command of an eleven-man unit.

The quarterback of a football team directs the attack. He usually calls the plays in a huddle after getting advice and information from his teammates. The coach will occasionally send in instructions from the sidelines, but the quarterback is considered the commander of the offensive field unit.

But it didn't work out that way a few years later when Dallas won the professional football championship. At the beginning of the season, two quarterbacks were competing for the Number one position on the Dallas team—Craig Morton and me. Our coach, Tom Landry, alternated us for the first seven games.

One day he told me, "Roger, from now on you're my number one quarterback."

I was elated, of course, but soon found myself chafing at the conditions. As a quarterback of a team of outstanding players, I was only a partial leader. Coach Tom Landry called the plays, sending in his instructions during our huddles. I threw passes only when he said to, used the running plays he called. In an emergency situation, I could change a play on the line of scrimmage if I felt it was right—but I had better be right!

I'll admit it—a lot of the problem here was ego, my ego. With Coach Landry calling the plays, the implication was, of course, that quarterback Staubach was not good enough to know what plays to call.

When I was willing to go through a spiritual struggle to get self out of the way, the real facts emerged. I was darn lucky to be the Number one quarterback of one of the best teams in pro football. I was inexperienced and had a lot to learn about play calling in the pros. Coach Landry had one of the few "genius minds" when it comes to football strategy. We were winning, and I was playing well with our coach sending in the plays.

So again I faced up to the issue of obedience, suddenly aware of how it confronts you in different ways at different times in your life. What then happened was the same thing that happened in my home and at the Naval Academy. Once I learned to obey—harmony, fulfillment, victory.

The point still had to be rammed home in one more area of my life. This occurred at the birth of our fourth child. We were all greatly anticipating this big event—my wife, Marianne, and our three young daughters, Jennifer, Michele and Stephanie Marie.

But during the delivery something went wrong. The baby girl was stillborn.

I'll never forgot that day at the cemetery, when the tiny casket was lowered into the ground over which was the simple inscription "Baby Staubach." This was a real testing period of my life, for my father had passed away a year earlier.

As so many do in such personal crises, I asked the question, "Why, Lord?" Inside me once again were the stirrings of rebellion, this time against the Almighty who had such power over life and death.

It wasn't a long rebellion. Deep down I knew that strength came through my faith. When I prayed for understanding, I felt this sudden sense of peace and comfort. The Lord was Lord. He was with my daughter and my father. This world is not the end, but the beginning. If we believe in Him, there is the promise of eternal life.

Out of this acceptance has come gratitude for all He has given me: a strong body, clear mind, fine parents, a career doing what I like most to do—play football—a wife and three daughters whom I love very much. The old prophet Isaiah was right on target when he said, "If ye be willing and obedient, ye shall eat the good of the land"(Isaiah 1:19, KJV).

.. ..

The Dog Next Door

Jimmy Stewart

as told to Richard H. Schneider

W hen I was about thirteen years old back home in Indiana, Pennsylvania, I had a dog named Bounce. He was just a street dog of indeterminate parentage who had followed me home from school one day. Kind of Airdalish, but of an orange color, Bounce became my close companion. He'd frolic alongside me when I'd go into the woods to hunt arrowheads and snore at my feet when I'd build a model airplane. I loved that dog.

Late one summer I had been away to a Boy Scout camp at Two Lick Creek, and when I got home Bounce wasn't there to greet me. When I asked Mother about him, she gently took me inside. "I'm sorry, Jim, but Bounce is gone."

"Did he run away?"

"No, Son, he's dead."

I couldn't believe it. "What happened?" I choked.

"He was killed."

"How?"

Mom looked over to my father. He cleared his throat. "Well, Jim," he said, "Bogy broke his chain, came over and killed Bounce."

I was aghast. Bogy was the next-door neighbors' English bulldog. Normally he was linked by a chain to a wire that stretched about one-hundred feet across their backyard.

I was grief-stricken and angry. That night I tossed and

turned. The next morning I stepped out to look at the bulldog, hoping to see at least a gash in its speckled hide. But no, there on a heavier chain stood the barrel-chested villain. Every time I saw poor Bounce's empty house, his forlorn blanket, his food dish, I seethed with hatred for the animal that had taken my best friend.

Finally one morning I reached into my closet and pulled out the Remington .22 rifle Dad had given me the past Christmas. I stepped out into our backyard and climbed up into the apple tree. Perched in its upper limbs, I could see the bulldog as he traipsed up and down the length of his wire. With the rifle I followed him in the sights. But every time I got a bead on him, tree foliage got in the way.

Suddenly a gasp sounded from below. "Jim, what are you *doing* up there?"

Mom didn't wait for an answer. Our screen door slammed and I could tell she was on the phone with my father at his hardware store. In a few minutes our Ford chattered into the driveway. Dad climbed out and came over to the apple tree.

"C'mon down, Jim," he said gently. Reluctantly, I put the safety on and let myself down onto the summer-seared grass.

The next morning, Dad, who knew me better than I knew myself, said, "Jim, after you finish school today, I want you to come to the store."

That afternoon I trudged, kicking dust, downtown to Dad's hardware store, figuring he wanted the windows washed or something. He stepped out from behind the counter and led me back to the stockroom. We edged past kegs of nails, coils of garden hose and rolls of screen wire to a corner. There squatted my hated nemesis, Bogy, tied to a post.

"Now here's the bulldog," Dad said. "This is the easy way

to kill him if you still feel that way." He handed me a short-barreled .22-caliber rifle. I glanced at him questioningly. He nodded.

I took the gun, lifted it to my shoulder and sighted down the black barrel. Bogy, brown eyes regarding me, panted happily, pink tongue peeking from tusked jaws. As I began to squeeze the trigger, a thousand thoughts flashed through my mind while Dad stood silently by. But my mind wasn't silent; all of Dad's teaching about our responsibility to defenseless creatures, fair play, right and wrong, welled within me. I thought of Mom loving me after I broke her favorite china serving bowl. There were other voices, our preacher leading us in prayer, asking God to forgive us as we forgave others.

Suddenly the rifle weighed a ton and the sight wavered in my vision. I lowered it and looked up at Dad helplessly. A quiet smile crossed his face and he clasped my shoulder. "I know, Son," he said gently. I realized then: He had never expected me to pull that trigger. In his wise, deep way he let me face my decision on my own. I never did learn how Dad managed to arrange Bogy's presence that afternoon, but I know he had trusted me to make the right choice.

A tremendous relief overwhelmed me as I put down the gun. I knelt down with Dad and helped untie Bogy, who wriggled against us happily, his stub tail wiggling furiously.

That night I slept well for the first time in days. The next morning as I leaped down the back steps, I saw Bogy next door and stopped. Dad ruffled my hair. "Seems you've forgiven him, Son."

I raced off to school. Forgiveness, I found, could be exhilarating.

You Can Talk to the Man

Lorne Greene

When I was playing Ben Cartwright, the father in the *Bonanza* television series, I got talking one afternoon with Joe Reisman—my friend and record producer—about my own father.

Dad was a big, gentle man who had the wonderful gift of being a good listener. I was telling Joe all about this—especially about the time that gift of his helped me make a crucial decision.

I had enrolled in the chemical engineering course at Queen's University in Kingston, Ontario, but I had another love, too. I wanted to be an actor. As soon as I started taking classes, I discovered that only people in non-lab courses could go out for the Drama Guild. Suddenly I wanted to talk this over with Dad. I called him on a pay phone and raced the three-minute limit to get it all said.

"Isn't this a coincidence!" Dad interrupted me. "I'll be passing through Kingston tomorrow on my way to Toronto. Why don't I stop by the school and you can tell me more?"

The next afternoon I poured out my thoughts and dreams for the future, and by the time I finished I had chosen my career—in the theater.

I explained to Joe what I later found out. "My dad didn't have to go to Toronto at all. He made that hundred-mile trip because he knew I needed him to listen. You know, Joe," I added, "I could always talk to the man."

As a record producer, Joe had a sharp ear for new material and he jotted down some of the things I'd said about my father. Eventually his notes found their way to Merle Kilgore, a songwriter. Here's what Merle did with them:

> *Yes, you can talk to the Man;*
> *He's got the time; He'll understand;*
> *He's got shoulders big enough to cry on.*
> *Tell all your troubles, take your time;*
> *He's in no hurry; He doesn't mind.*
> *It matters not how bad you've been,*
> *You can talk to the Man.*

Now I'd been talking about Dad. But by the time Merle set the words to music and we'd made a record of them, "Man" had become capitalized, and the record was about God, the Father of us all.

That's a natural progression, when you think about it, because we depend on the same accessibility, the loving attention of a father on earth, when we pray to our Father in Heaven.

To me, it's one of the most powerful insights a father can give his children about God: **You can talk to the Man.**

Game Plan

Pee Wee Kirkland

Some sounds you never forget. I remember first hearing the slap-slap-slap of a basketball on the streets of Harlem when I was eight years old. I loved it right away, like a great song. My father, Joseph, was into baseball, and he wanted me to be a shortstop. But I couldn't tear my eyes away from the kids shooting hoops, and finally I picked up a ball. It was like magic in my hands. At the playground at Milbank Community Center on 118 Street, I saw guys forever practicing things I got down in ten minutes. That's when I knew I had a gift.

Back then, in the mid 1960s, Roger "Buster" Bryant, the coach at Milbank, was every kid's inspiration, and I wanted to make him proud. "You've got a bright future, Pee Wee," he told me one day. Then he warned me some of the older guys would be after me, trying to lead me astray. "If they do, keep it outside this gate," he said, pointing to the playground entrance. Buster believed the basketball court was sacred ground, a place we could come for refuge from the streets and discover the better parts of ourselves.

My mother, Mary, felt the same way about church, and she made sure to take me and my brothers to services every week. I usually squirmed beside her in the pew, itching to be back outside at Milbank, perfecting my moves. One Sunday she pulled me close. "When you start listening," she whispered, "your whole life will change."

I didn't get what she was trying to tell me, not then. I was too young, and what the older kids had to teach me seemed more interesting at the time. They taught me to play craps for money, and I liked the sound of dice rattling on the sidewalk. Before I knew it, I was hooked.

I was tired of the ghetto life. I wore the same shirt to school every day, saw my parents break their backs to put food on the table, heard my mother crying because they had no presents for us at Christmas. *God,* I used to pray, *if You're as powerful as my mother says, make me a force so I can help my family. I want something bigger and better for them.*

For a boy growing up in Harlem in those days the biggest thing in the world was basketball. We all played at Rucker Park on 155 Street and Frederick Douglass Boulevard. NBA stars came up there to test their skills against the street legends, guys like Joe "The Destroyer" Hammond, "Jumpin" Jackie Jackson and Frank "Shake and Bake" Streety. By the time I was in my teens, Pee Wee Kirkland had become a name, too. I was the only player in high school scoring fifty points in a game. They called me Stickman, because I had so many moves I made the other guys look like they were stuck to the court.

Pretty soon I came to understand the money game as well as I understood basketball. Before I graduated from high school I graduated from petty crime to the big time, lending money for drug deals. It was okay. I told myself, because I was only doing it to get my folks out of the ghetto. And I did. I moved them out of Harlem to a nice house on Long Island.

I thought I had made it. Still, I knew my parents—especially my mother—would be deeply disappointed in me if they ever found out how I came by my money. So I tried to go legit. I was running the fast break at Norfolk State University when the NBA offered me a forty-thousand-dollar contract with the

Chicago Bulls in 1968. I went to Chicago, only to have the coach promote another rookie. Maybe he went to a school with a bigger name, but I knew I was the better player. To me, that wasn't what basketball was about. I quit and went home to New York.

It didn't take long before people from the old days came to me. "Get us a hundred thousand dollars," they said, "and we'll give you a hundred and fifty at the end of the month." I had given up crime when I went to college, but now I didn't have a job and I needed to make a living. So I got into moneylending—and the fast life—again.

In 1970 my wrongdoings caught up with me. I was arrested on charges of conspiracy to sell drugs. If anybody deserved to go to jail, it was Pee Wee Kirkland. I just wasn't guilty in *that* particular case. The warrant had been issued from Boston, where I had never been in my life, but a witness pointed me out in court, and I was sentenced to fifteen years. Later I said to the district attorney, "You know I wasn't guilty." He agreed, then told me, "But it's not like you had a nine to five, Pee Wee."

His words stuck with me after I was sent to Lewisburg Federal Penitentiary in Pennsylvania. There in prison I didn't have the wads of cash, the fancy cars, the expensive houses anymore. I had nothing. Nothing but plenty of time to sit in my cell and think.

I took a long, hard look at myself, and I wasn't proud of what I saw. That D.A. was right. Here I was, a grown man, and I had never bothered to make an honest living. Instead I took the easy way out and let down everyone who believed in me. My old coach, Buster. My father. My mother. Especially Mom.

Then I heard her voice, gentle yet firm, as she said to me in church so long ago, "When you start listening, your whole life will change." Suddenly it was crystal clear what she had been trying to tell me. It wasn't just that she expected better from me. *God* expected better from me. To truly live, I had to listen to Him, to do what He wanted me to do. I had to let Him show me the plan He had for my life.

The best way to gain that wisdom, I figured, was to go back to the beginning, to where I had felt the clearest sense of purpose: the basketball court. I began doing in prison what Buster had done for me on the playground—trying to teach the younger guys not just the game, but also teamwork and self-respect. And I started reading the Bible, as I had seen my mother do all those years. Hearing the slap of the ball as I dribbled downcourt during a prison-yard game and really listening to the Word of God for the first time, I felt like I was headed in the right direction again.

Shortly after I was released from prison in 1988 (after serving a second sentence, for tax evasion), I met and married a wonderful woman, KleoPatra. We made our home in Brooklyn, New York, her old neighborhood, and both of us kept praying for God's design to continue unfolding.

One day I saw a kid shooting baskets with his father at a playground near our house. "You teaching him the game?" I asked.

"I'm trying," his dad admitted, "but I don't really know it myself."

I showed the kid, Sweetwater, the basics. That boy loved basketball. Even when it was freezing he was outside working on his jumper, and I would put on my gloves and join him.

By 1990 my work with Sweetwater had grown into a program called the School of Skillz, with the support of Nike and

Manhattan's Central Baptist Church, whose pastor, Reverend Faulkner, let us use the church gym. I wanted to teach kids from Harlem the skills they needed to do well—on and off the court. If I could help even one of them avoid making the mistakes I had made, then I could feel like I had finally done something to make my mother and Buster proud.

In 1996 I started working with another group of kids. Reverend Faulkner introduced me to Stephen Spahn, chancellor of the Dwight School in Manhattan, who offered me a job as basketball coach. The guys on the Dwight team came from backgrounds different from the ones I worked with in the School of Skillz, but my goals for them were the same: Be good people first, then good ballplayers.

In 1997 our team won the private-school state championship. I was happy for the kids and the school, and sure, I was excited about winning. Still, as the final buzzer went off, I caught my wife's eye across the court, then thought about my mother cheering us on at home, and I knew that as important as basketball was to me, my life went beyond the game. It was like my mother told me: When I started listening, I began to understand what my life was about. It was about God's game plan, God's design. He had merely chosen basketball to teach me.

Grace Before Greatness

Marian Anderson

Failure and frustration are in the unwritten pages of everyone's record. I have had my share of them. But if my mother's gentle hands were not there to guide me, perhaps my life in music would have ended long ago.

The faith my mother taught me is my foundation. It is the only ground on which I stand. With it I have a freedom in life I could not have in any other way. Whatever is in my voice, my faith has put it there.

Her presence runs through everything I ever wanted to be. The particular religion a child echoes is an accident of birth. But I was converted to my mother's faith and patient understanding long before I could define either.

We were poor folk. But there was a wealth in our poverty, a wealth of music, and love and faith. My two sisters, Alice and Ethel, and I were all in the church choir—the junior, not the senior one. There is still a vivid memory of our mother and father, their faces shining with pride, watching us from the front pews. And when I was six I was once fortunate enough to be selected to step out in front of the choir and sing "The Lord Is My Shepherd."

It was a Baptist church we attended in Philadelphia. But my mother taught us early that the form of one's faith is less important than what's in one's heart.

"When you come to Him," she said, "He never asks what you are."

We children never heard her complain about her lot; or criticize those who offended her. One of her guiding precepts has always been: "Never abuse those who abuse you. Bear them no malice, and theirs will disappear."

My sisters still attend the Baptist church in Philadelphia. It is a church and a congregation I hold most fondly in my heart for many reasons. These were the people who, years ago, pooled their pennies into what they grandly called "The Fund for Marian Anderson's Future," a gesture of love and confidence impossible to forget in a lifetime. When I returned to Philadelphia, I always tried to see some of these people who had been so important to me, and though it seldom is possible these days, I love to sing in their choir.

My father died when I was twelve, and my mother's burden became heavier. Before she became a housewife, and the mother of three daughters, she was a schoolteacher. Now she became a father to us as well as a mother, and earned our whole livelihood by taking in washing. It was terribly difficult for her, I know, but she would not even hear of any of us children leaving school for work.

During these years I began to have my first opportunity to earn a little money by singing. Almost entirely they were Sunday evening concerts for the church, or for the YWCA and the YMCA. At these affairs I could sing, perhaps, two or three songs, and my fee was a very grand fifty cents, or once in a great while, one dollar. Sometimes I would dash to four or five of these concerts in one evening.

Many people were kind to me: teachers who took no fees, those who urged me forward when I was discouraged. Gradually I began to sing with glee clubs and churches in other cities. After one minor effort in Harlem, I was hastily sponsored for a concert in Town Hall in New York by a group of well-meaning people.

It seemed at once incredible and wonderful. But I wasn't ready: Indeed, I was far from it either in experience or maturity. On the exciting night of my first real concert I was told Town Hall was sold out. While waiting in a dazed delight to go on, my sponsor said there would be a slight delay. I waited five, ten, fifteen minutes. Then peeked through the curtain.

The house was half empty! I died inside. But when the curtain went up I sang my heart out. And when the concert was over, I knew I had failed. The critics next day agreed with me, but what they said was really not so important. I was shattered, because within me I felt I had let down all those people who had had faith and confidence in me. It seemed irrevocable.

"I'd better forget all about singing and do something else," I told my mother.

"Why don't you think about it a little, and pray a lot, first?" she cautioned.

She had taught me to make my own decisions when I could, and pray for the right ones when I could not. But I did not heed her now. I refused a few offers to sing at other concerts. I avoided my music teacher. For a whole year I brooded in silence. My mother suffered because I was not expressing myself in the only way I knew happiness. But she knew I had to find my own way back alone. From time to time she just prodded me, gently:

"Have you prayed, Marian? Have you prayed?"

No, I hadn't. Nothing would help. I embraced my grief. It was sufficient. But in those tearful hours there slowly came the thought that there is a time when even the most self-sufficient cannot find enough strength to stand alone. Then, one prays with a fervor one never had before. From my torment I prayed with the sure knowledge there was Someone to whom I could pour out the greatest need of my heart and soul. It did not matter if He answered. It was enough to pray.

Slowly I came out of my despair. My mind began to clear. No one was to blame for my failure. Self-pity left me. In a burst of exuberance I told my mother, "I want to study again. I want to be the best, and be loved by everyone, and be perfect in everything."

"That's a wonderful goal," she chided. "But our dear Lord walked this earth as the most perfect of all beings, yet not everybody loved Him."

Subdued, I decided to return to my music, to seek humbleness before perfection.

One day I came home from my teacher unaware that I was humming. It was the first music I had uttered at home in a whole year. My mother heard it, and she rushed to meet me, and put her arms around me and kissed me. It was her way of saying, "Your prayers have been answered, and mine have, too."

For a brief moment we stood there silently. Then my mother defined the sweet spell of our gratitude, "Prayer begins where human capacity ends," she said.

The golden echo of that moment has always been with me through the years of struggle that followed. I have been blessed with an active career, and the worldly goods that come with it. If sometimes I do not hear the echo of that moment but listen only to the applause, my mother reminds me quickly of what should come first, "Grace must always come before greatness."

Be Careful of Gray

Walter Cronkite

There came a time when I was growing up in Houston, Texas, that I wanted to own a watch. In fact, I had a particular watch picked out, an Ingersoll on display in our local drugstore. It cost a dollar. Since I had no money, and no prospects for raising a dollar quickly, I asked the druggist if I could take the watch and pay for it little by little. He agreed, and the next day, when my mother happened to come into the store, he casually mentioned the arrangement we'd made.

My mother would have none of it. She was a woman of scrupulous honesty, and to her, I'd taken advantage of another person's willingness to trust me. She paid the druggist the dollar and hurried home to confront me.

"Don't you see?" she said. "Your intentions are honorable, but even you admit you don't know how you're going to earn the money for that watch. There's no outright dishonesty here, but you're flirting with it. It's one of those risky gray areas, Walter. Be careful of gray—it might be grime."

Then she took the watch and kept it until I earned the money to retrieve it.

Throughout the years since that experience, I've had plenty of reasons to remember my mother's admonition. As a newscaster I've always had to be on guard against gray—a presentation of only half the facts, a story that didn't ring quite true. And there have been such occasions in my personal life as well. One time, for instance, some speculators offered to give me a large parcel of land. There was no suggestion that I talk about their property on the air. They were not being dishonest; they just wanted to be able to say that I owned land in the area that they were trying to promote. But it seemed like a gray area to me. I didn't accept the offer.

I believe that most of the people in this world are honest, and want to be honest. But honesty, like all other virtues, requires vigilance. My mother, Helen Lena Cronkite, knew this. This is what she had in mind as she helped me to stay clear of ambiguity—the gray areas that might be grime.

PART 2

The Power in Dreams and Determination

By wisdom a house is built,
and by understanding it is established.
                              Proverbs 24:3 (RSV)

G *o for it.* Sometimes God imparts to human hearts a dream, a vision of what is possible for us if we persevere, work hard, see and accept opportunities.

For some people that steady focused dream comes as young children. Such was the case for astronaut Neil Armstrong who as a boy was obsessed with airplanes. Others gradually envision their place and purpose—their particular talent—and then with gritty determination follow the inner voice that tells them to overcome obstacles to reach their highest potential.

Dreams and determination. It's a powerful pair of nouns when activated to become verbs. Go for it. Dream and do.

Neil Armstrong's Boyhood Crisis

Mrs. Stephen Armstrong

as told to Lorraine Wetzel

Most people think Neil Armstrong took the most important step in his life when he set foot on the moon. But as his mother, I remember an even greater step taken in our old home on Pearl Street in Wapakoneta, Ohio, on another July day—twenty-three years earlier.

The story begins when Neil was two and his father and I lived in Cleveland, not far from the airport. Like many families during the Depression days of the early thirties, one of our inexpensive Sunday-afternoon pastimes was airplane watching. Neil stood between us, his little face pressed so intently against the fence that it often left red marks. We were always ready to leave long before he was, and his plea was always the same: "Can't we see just *one* more airplane?"

I was often uneasy about Neil's obvious fascination with planes. And I had to admit to myself that this child, our firstborn, was very special to me. After Stephen and I married, I was haunted by the fear that maybe I couldn't conceive. I had been an only child and often thought, *What if I can't have even one baby?*

Then finally the day came when our doctor assured me I was pregnant. The minute I got home I went down on my knees and thanked God for His blessing to us and, in the fullness of my heart, I dedicated this child-to-be to Him. In the months that followed, I prayed steadily that this child would be given a thirst for knowledge, and the capacity for learning that someday would accomplish noble deeds—hopefully to serve the work of the Lord.

One Sunday morning, when Neil was five or six, he and my husband left for Sunday school. When they returned, both had peculiar expressions on their faces. Stephen was a bit white-faced, but Neil was beaming from ear to ear.

"What is wrong with you two?" I asked. There was utter silence.

Suddenly a thought came to me. "Did you go up in that airplane I read about in the paper?"

Now they looked relieved. Yes, that is exactly what they had done. A pilot was barnstorming in town, and Stephen said rates were cheaper in the morning. He had not really enjoyed the flight, but little Neil had loved every minute of it.

One morning Neil and I were walking down the cluttered aisles of a dime store looking for cereal bowls. My husband and I now had a wonderful family of three active children who consumed vast quantities of cereal. Somehow the bowls were always getting chipped or broken. I was selecting five shiny new ones when I felt a tug at my arm. "Mom, will you buy this for me?" Neil held up a gaily colored box.

"What is it?" I asked cautiously.

"It's a model-airplane kit." The eagerness in his voice betrayed his excitement. "Mom, this way I could learn how to make airplanes. It's twenty cents."

Quickly I thought how twenty cents would buy two cereal bowls, but how could I resist the urgency and enthusiasm in my son's voice?

"Honey," I said gently, "could you find a kit for ten cents?"

"Sure, Mom!" His face radiant, he raced back to the toy counter.

.. ..

Although Neil was then only eight years old, that was the beginning of two important occupations in his life. The first was his meticulous assembly line for many model airplanes. We put a table in one corner of the living room, and it was never moved—even when company came.

The second occupation made the first one possible. Beginning with his first model plane, Neil was never without a job, no matter how small. First he cut grass in a cemetery for ten cents an hour. Later he cleaned out the bread mixer at Neumeister's Bakery every night. After we moved to Wapakoneta, Neil delivered orders for the neighborhood grocery, swept out the hardware store and opened cartons at Rhine and Brading's Pharmacy.

When Neil wasn't working or studying, he rode his bicycle three miles north on a gravel road to the Wapak Flying Service Airport. Today this field isn't used, but in 1944 it bustled with activity. A young instructor, Charles Finkenbine, kept three light airplanes busy as trainers. Budding pilots came from surrounding counties to learn to fly, and Neil at fourteen was a familiar figure sitting on the sidelines, his eyes glued to every takeoff and landing. One afternoon I was making grape jelly when the screen door banged as he rushed into the kitchen.

"Mom," he shouted, "Mr. Finkenbine let me *touch* one of the airplanes!"

"That's fine, son," I said.

"He says from now on I can be a grease monkey and one of these days he'll teach me to fly!"

"Are you sure you're old enough, Neil?" I tried to hide the anxiety in my voice.

He flashed his wide, confident grin. "Don't worry. I'll be careful."

The screen door banged again, and he was gone. I'm afraid his assurance did little to comfort me. By now I was beginning to wonder how the Lord could be served by a youngster so completely captivated by airplanes.

From then on every penny Neil earned went for flying lessons. At forty cents an hour at the pharmacy it took him between twenty-two and twenty-three hours of work to pay for one nine-dollar lesson. But both Dick Brading and Charles Finkenbine were generous men: The first often let Neil off early to go to the airport, the latter managed free flying time for our son in exchange for odd jobs around the hangar. Neil's goal was to get his flying license as soon as he reached his sixteenth birthday in August.

In July our two boys, Neil and Dean, with their father as scoutmaster, attended Boy Scout camp in Defiance Ohio. The evening they were due back I planned a special homecoming supper. They thought they'd be home at five o'clock, so I peeled potatoes and put them on to boil at 4:30, then started to set the table.

At 5:15 I picked up my darning basket and started to mend some of Dean's socks. An hour dragged by. I finished the socks and walked to the window. They were more than an hour overdue, and I knew something was wrong.

Then looking through the grape arbor, I saw our car drive into the garage. My husband appeared in the doorway, his face pale and drawn. Fear clutched my throat.

"What's wrong, Stephen? Has something happened to the boys?"

"No, they're all right. Dean is here with me, and Neil will be along soon. But there has been an accident."

"What do you mean?"

.. ..

"Viola, come into the living room, and I'll tell you all about it." He put his arm around me, and together we walked to the sofa.

"We were on our way home this afternoon," he continued, "when we noticed an airplane flying parallel to us. Neil recognized it immediately as one of the trainers from the Wapak Flying Service. Some student was practicing takeoffs and landings in a field near the road. Then he must have dipped too low over the telephone wires, because suddenly the airplane was in trouble."

"Oh, no!" I whispered.

"It nosedived into the field, and at the same time Neil yelled, 'Stop the car!' and before I knew it, he had climbed over the fence and was running toward the plane. Then we all got out and ran over to help, too. Neil was lifting a young fellow out of the cockpit, and just as we got there he died in Neil's arms."

"Oh, Stephen, how awful! That poor boy and his family." Then a terrifying new thought seared my brain. "It might have been Neil."

"Yes, Viola, it could have been." My husband's voice roughened with emotion. "Instead it was a young man from Lima whom Neil knew. Neil is staying with him until the ambulance comes."

A car door slammed, and I heard slow footsteps coming up the front-porch steps. Then suddenly Neil and I were in each other's arms, tears streaming down our faces.

"He was my friend, Mom. And he was *only* twenty!" I could hardly bear the anguish in his voice.

"I know, honey." I released him, with a mother's sudden awareness that her son was no longer a boy. I forced my voice to sound cheerful. "Do you want some supper?"

.. ..

"No, thanks, I'm going up to my room." He stopped on the landing and tried to smile. "Don't worry, Mom. I'll be all right."

"I know you will, Neil." I watched him walk up the stairs and quietly close the door as dry sobs tore through me.

Stephen and I both thought it best to let him alone for a while. But we could not help wondering if Neil would want to keep flying. Both of us agreed he must fight this battle himself.

The next two days were the hardest of my life. As all mothers know, whatever hurts your children hurts you twice as much. And yet I knew he had to make this decision himself. Had our closeness with the Creator and the nightly prayers through the years prepared him to find the help he needed so desperately now? At this stage, it was out of my hands. All I could do was wait.

I tried to carry on a normal family life, but my heart and mind were always in that back bedroom with the iron bed, yellow wallpaper, the single overhead light fixture and the bureau covered with model airplanes. What was he thinking? What would he decide?

Finally, near dusk on the second day, I couldn't stand the silence and separation any longer. I baked oatmeal and raisin cookies and took a plate of them and a glass of cold milk upstairs.

"Neil, may I come in, please? Here are some cookies still warm from the oven."

He opened the door, and I walked into the stuffy little room and put the cookies on the bureau. What I saw made my heart leap. Next to a model airplane was an old Sunday-school notebook with a picture of Jesus on the cover. It was now turned to the page where years before Neil had written in his large childish hand, "The Character of Jesus," and had listed ten qualities of His. Among those that caught my eye were: He was sinless, He was humble, He championed the poor, He was unselfish. But the one that struck me the most was number eight—He was close to God.

Suddenly I felt like singing hosanna. "Honey, what have you decided about flying?" I asked him.

Neil's eyes held mine in a steady gaze, then he said firmly, "Mom, I hope you and Dad will understand, but with God's help, I *must* go on flying."

For a minute I was jolted as I thought of that other mother only a few miles away in Lima, brokenhearted and perhaps standing in her son's empty room at this very minute. I asked God for strength and the right words, and He gave them to me.

"All right, son. Dad and I will go along with your decision." My heart was pounding. "And, Neil," I said, "when you get your license in a few weeks, may I be your first passenger?"

What I've Learned from Weary Willie

Emmett Kelly

What's the hardest thing in the world to be? I can tell you in one word: yourself. Especially if what you are is different from the crowd. But I'll guarantee this: If you can find the courage to be yourself, to be the person God intended you to be, you're going to come out all right.

Let me tell you how this old clown found out about all this. Back in the Depression days of the 1930s, work in the circus (or anywhere else) was tough to come by, so when I landed a job as a clown with the Sells-Floto Circus in 1933, I was over-joyed. Before then I'd done some trapeze work, but the idea of being a clown had been germinating in my mind for a long time. While performing high above the audience, I'd watched the clowns with secret envy; now I had my chance.

Right away I knew that I had found my niche—clowning was for me. Trying to cheer people up, making wide-eyed kids and their long-faced parents laugh, gave me a deep feeling of satisfaction and made me want to do a creative job.

Within a few weeks, however, my creativity turned out to be a problem. When I tried to add a few new touches to my act, the head clown gave me a dressing down. "No freelancing, Kelly. Stay in line."

At that time clowns all looked pretty much the same: pow-der-white faces, silly white wigs, zany Harpo Marx smiles and

baggy white suits with ruffled collars. We had prescribed uni-
forms and a prescribed routine. Trained monkeys could have
done the job. One day I decided I had to do something original
or burst.

In my mind's eye I had this picture of a sad-faced, woebe-
gone hobo clown. He didn't jump into being all at once,
though; I dreamed him into reality bit by bit.

As a kid, I loved to draw and when I wasn't doing chores
for Dad on our farm in Texas County, Missouri, I was off
under a tree sketching. Mother encouraged me and persuaded
Dad to pay for a correspondence course in cartooning that I
took. At age twenty I went off to Kansas City to make my
mark. Unfortunately, no one had told Kansas City and the art
world that I was coming. As a result, I wound up cutting butter
in a creamery. What a career! I'd gone from milking Dad's
cows in the country to cutting butter in the city.

Eventually, I did get work as a pen-and-ink cartoonist for a
film company that made motion picture trailer ads and lantern
slides for movie theaters. One of the characters I created was a
baggy pants hobo.

My career took another track when I joined the circus. Still,
the joy of creating things never left me, and when I was searching for some innovative way to develop a new type of clown,
that old hobo drawing popped into my mind.

Dusting off my pad and pencils, I began trying to draw the
hobo I wanted to bring to life. I knew he was a mournful
tramp, rather pathetic, with a six-day beard and ragtag clothes.
But there was something about him with which everyone could
identify. An underdog, down on his luck, but still trying, still
hoping that his ship would come in.

To get the character I wanted, I added a bulbous nose,

arched eyebrows and a sad-sack, turned-down smile. I was getting close.

When the circus played in New York, I went to a costume shop looking for a hat. There I found a battered brown one with dirty splotches on it.

"How much for this one?" I asked.

"Gimme a buck," the proprietor answered. (It was the best buy I ever made.) Then I went to a shoemaker and had him construct the biggest, floppiest shoes I could imagine.

Back in the privacy of my own room, I put on the raggedy clothes and makeup. Looking in the mirror, I saw for the first time the character I'd been dreaming about for so long, and as I looked at him his name came to me. "Willie. Weary Willie," I said, and now everything was ready for his debut.

The circus moved west, and I waited, trying to work up courage to introduce Willie. Finally, in Mason City, Iowa, I donned the clothing and waited until all the others in Clown Alley had entered the Big Top. I followed, and it was love at first sight. The audience took one look at Weary Willie and loved him.

Only the clown master was unsmiling. Afterward, he told me to forget the hobo—"too grubby, too scruffy for the circus." So begrudgingly I went back to my all-white costume and finished out the year. But something kept whispering, "Be yourself, Kelly. Don't be like that fellow in the Bible who buried his talent in the ground." When we struck our tents in the last town, I gave notice I was quitting.

It was a big decision. I had a wife and a new son to support, and there was no guarantee I could find another job, but I knew I had to try.

You see, I believed in my Weary Willie creation with all my

heart, and when you really believe in something you are filled
with a faith that can move mountains, just like it says in the
Bible. The Lord made each of us unique, I believe, and we are
truest to Him when we are true to ourselves. Anyway, that was
the conviction I had about Willie and my future.

A few weeks later, I heard about a job opening and went for
an interview.

"Well, show me your act," the boss said.

So I put on my costume and makeup and introduced him to
Willie. Willie didn't have his whole act together yet; there was
no sledgehammer to crack peanuts with and no broom to
sweep up the circle of lights made on the floor by a spotlight,
but otherwise he was complete.

The circus boss sat through my routine poker-faced, and my
heart was right down in my floppy shoes. But finally, when I
was through he shook his head resignedly and laughed out
loud.

"I never saw an act like this one," he said, "but I think
they'll like you."

He was right. Forty-five years later people still seemed to
enjoy Willie's unorthodox antics.

So if you ever worry about being different from the crowd,
stop worrying. Weary Willie's had almost half a century of fun
just being himself. And so have I.

My Search for The Apostle

Robert Duvall

I've been an actor all my working life, and learning a part has always meant more than just memorizing my lines. I immerse myself in the character I am to play. I find out everything I can about who he is, the world he comes from, his dreams, his fears, his passion, his humanity. I try to transform myself. A remarkable thing can happen in this process. Many times I discover something new about myself. Sometimes it is a discovery that changes my life.

In my recent movie, which I also wrote and directed, I play a troubled preacher who calls himself The Apostle. For years I have wanted to make this film. It's been a labor of love, and it began in 1962 when I prepared to play a character from the rural South in an off-Broadway play. To research the role I traveled to Hughes, Arkansas. Wandering the streets of the sleepy Delta town, hanging out in the coffee shop and the post office, I hoped to learn something about my character—from the way a man tipped his hat or drawled the directions to the local hotel. But what I never expected to find was something that would change how I looked at religion.

One Sunday as I strolled down the main drag I noticed people flocking to a simple white clapboard building, the local Pentecostal church. All sorts of folks, young and old, were going inside, where I could hear the clink of tambourines, the rap of a snare drum and organ music rising. *Might as well check this out*, I thought. I slipped in and sat in back.

I grew up in a churchgoing Navy family. During World War II we lived in Annapolis, Maryland, while Dad commanded a destroyer escort in the North Atlantic, playing a deadly game of cat and mouse with German U-boats. Occasionally Mom woke up in the middle of the night with the overwhelming urge to pray for him. One morning at the breakfast table, she told us of the trouble she had sensed Dad was in. Later, we learned he had narrowly escaped being blown sky-high by a German torpedo during the night.

So I knew about the inner life of the Spirit, but I had never seen such an extraordinary outward expression of faith as I witnessed in that Pentecostal church. I had never seen church like that. People could barely contain the joy of their faith. Their faces were alive with it, imbued. Folks were on their feet, singing praise and clapping, shouting to God! The air crackled with the Spirit. It was nearly impossible to be a mere observer. I wanted to sing and shout with them. I couldn't explain it, but I knew the people in that church had a gift, a story to share. Somehow, someday, I would tell that story.

Soon after, my career boomed. I started working in movies, dozens of them, from *To Kill a Mockingbird* to *The Godfather*. I was fortunate to get some excellent roles. I wrote and directed a couple of films. Yet my interest in Pentecostalism never waned, incubating until I could figure out what to do with it. Then in 1981 I was cast as an evangelical preacher in a movie called *The Kingdom*. Again I immersed myself in my role. I made trips to small country churches all over the heartland, seeking out the incredible power of expressed faith I had felt in Hughes, soaking up all I could. But after months of preparation the film was canceled. I wondered what I would do with all I had learned.

In 1983 I won an Oscar for my portrayal of a down-and-out country singer who finds salvation in the film *Tender Mercies*. After I was named Best Actor I expected the offers to flood in. But my telephone was surprisingly quiet. There was a lull in my usually busy schedule.

I went home to Virginia, where my parents had retired and where I live when I'm not shooting a movie. My father had died and Mom was ailing. My two brothers and I were trying to figure out what would be best for her, and I needed to be there. I kept thinking of my mother's faith and how it had sustained her all the years Dad was at sea, how it had sustained all of us, how she prayed for me when I went off to New York to study acting. I was not a tortured artist from a troubled family; I had strong parents and a solid childhood. It seemed like only yesterday when we kids were fishing soft-shell crabs out of the bay, laughing and one-upping each other.

One day I sat at the desk in my father's wood-paneled den. Studying the walls, I was struck by his innate modesty. A rear admiral in the Navy, he had no plaques or medals displayed, none of his citations or awards for bravery. Everyone knew he was a hero. His career had spoken for itself. He believed in his country. I sat and wondered what I would be remembered for. Looking around my father's study and suddenly sensing the unyielding passage of time, I felt I needed to do something that had real meaning for me, before it was too late. Something I believed in. I took out a legal pad and began writing a story, the one I had wanted to write for many years.

A story of a preacher. A good man but a flawed one—flawed as we all are. Called by God at the age of twelve, he becomes a respected minister with a rousing gift for charismatic preaching. But his family is torn apart by marital infi-

.. ..

delity. In a dreadful moment of jealous rage he injures a man and runs. His flight becomes a journey toward a redeemed faith, a return to God's saving grace. Assuming a new identity, he starts a church deep in the Louisiana bayou. Again his gift for preaching sweeps up a congregation, returning faith to a town where it had lagged, but his own redemption can come only when he faces the truth of his transgressions.

What was most important to me was to make a movie where Christianity was treated on its own terms, with the respect it deserves. Hollywood usually shows preachers as hucksters and hypocrites, and I was sick and tired of that. I wanted to show the joy and vitality I had seen with my own eyes and felt in my heart and in my life, the sheer, extraordinary excitement of faith. I especially wanted to capture the rich flavor, the infectious cadences and rhythm of good, down-home, no-holds-barred preaching.

The story seemed to flow from me. I wrote everywhere, in airports and hotels, on set between scenes, even in meetings. But writing a screenplay is one thing. Getting it produced is something else altogether. I took my script to Hollywood producers, and was met with the same response: "Bob, religion is not a subject our audiences want to watch." I disagreed. Why wouldn't audiences want to watch a movie about something that is foremost in so many people's lives?

I kept gathering material for the film and reworking the script. Near my house in Virginia I met an astounding ninety-three-year-old preacher named Isham Williams. "If I was any younger I'd make that movie with you," he declared. I was even more impressed when preachers I met said I could use anything I wanted from their sermons. No squabbles about copyright or screen credit. James Robison, one of the greatest, gave me free run. I adapted one of his most powerful sermons for the penultimate scene.

I called the film *The Apostle*—what my protagonist, Sonny, calls himself when he sets up his new church. In my research I was drawn several times to Memphis. Once, I attended a conference of believers, where I overheard the phrase I used when Sonny prays: "I always call You Jesus, and You always call me Sonny."

I wasn't getting anywhere with Hollywood, yet my work on the movie filled my soul. One Sunday in New York I visited six churches, ending up at Harlem's vast Abyssinian Baptist Church. There in a packed congregation before a huge choir, when we all began to sing "What a Friend We Have in Jesus," I found myself connected to the Lord in a way I had never felt before, deep within me. *Yes*, I thought, *we're all kin through Jesus.* Not just what we read about Him in the Bible, but who He *is*. That was the secret to powerful faith, the power I wanted to convey in my movie.

I told anybody who would listen, "Even if I can't get some big money from a studio, I've got to make this movie." The next thing I knew my accountant called me up and said, "I know this is an important project for you, Bob. I've been poring over your finances and you've finally gotten to the point where you can afford to spend a chunk of your money." He is a very conservative accountant, so I knew I was getting the green light!

In the end, that's what I did. Some of my Pentecostal friends tell me my urgings were the Holy Spirit's doing. I'm inclined to agree with them. In an amazingly swift seven-week period we filmed *The Apostle*, all on location in Louisiana. The things I worried about never came to pass. Generators didn't break

.. ..

down, the weather was good, people showed up on time, no one got sick.

I'm proud of the film. Many of the parts are played by real people and real preachers, not professional actors, because true faith is something that's hard to duplicate. I think some viewers might be shocked—pleasantly so, I hope—to hear Jesus' name mentioned so often, or startled by the unironic tone of the church scenes and worship services. They might be surprised to see blacks and whites worshiping together as equals even in the deepest rural South. Mostly, I hope they will be moved— moved the way I was when I happened upon that small church in Hughes, Arkansas, and with no warning something awakened within me that had always been there, dormant and untouched until that day. It was the greatest discovery I ever made.

The Talent I Didn't Know I Had

Michael Landon

If there's one thing I can't stand people saying, it's "I'm no good at anything . . . I don't have any talent." I just don't buy that at all. To me, everyone has at least one talent, and while it sometimes takes you a lifetime to find, it *does* exist.

There was a time, of course, when I didn't believe that. What changed my mind was a seemingly small event that took place back in 1953.

At that time I was a skinny little high school sophomore in Collingswood, New Jersey, a town just across the Delaware River from Philadelphia. At Collingswood High I was a good student, but as far as I was concerned, in just about every other department I was a loser. As a funny-looking pip-squeak named Eugene Orowitz, who weighed barely a hundred pounds, I desperately wanted to fit in, to be something and do something well. But because I hadn't found anything I was good at, I looked upon myself as being a total flop.

One sunny afternoon during the spring of that year, our gym class went out to the school's running track. The teacher was going to acquaint us all with various track and field events. We were shown hurdles, the broad jump, the pole vault. I stumbled weakly through them all.

"Now we'll try the javelin," the teacher said.

I watched as he picked up a gleaming metal spear about six feet long and gave it a short toss. Suddenly I was captivated and didn't know why. Something inside me began saying, "Try it! Try it!"

I had to wait my turn, though, because several others wanted a crack at the javelin too. Shy and scared, I watched them, trying not to look too eager. Finally, when everyone had had a chance to throw—the longest heave going about thirty yards—I looked at the teacher.

"Hey, Orowitz, you want to try?" he asked.

Embarrassed, I looked down, but managed to nod my head.

"Well, come on then," he said impatiently, and handed me the javelin. Behind me I could hear some of my classmates chuckling.

"Think you can lift it, Ugy?" one said.

"Don't stab yourself," another added, laughing.

As I grasped the javelin in my hand, I was seized with a strange feeling—a new-found excitement. Seeing myself as a Roman warrior about to do battle, my fears vanished. For some crazy reason, I was relaxed over what I was about to do, even though I'd never done it before.

I raised the javelin over my head, took six quick steps and let the thing go. The same voice that had urged me into throwing it, now told me it was a good throw. I watched as the spear took off. While other students' throws had wobbled or turned cockeyed in the air, to my surprise, my throw was traveling straight and true.

My heart quickened as I saw it continue to sail, thirty yards out, then forty. As it went past the fifty-yard mark, it was still going when it went crashing down beyond some empty bleachers.

For a minute nothing was said. Then someone whispered,

"Holy cow!" and others began cheering and slapping me on the back. Nobody could believe what little Orowitz had just done. Neither could I, really. And when I think back on it, the whole scene must have resembled something out of a grade-B movie.

I ran to retrieve the javelin and when I found it, I saw the tip had been broken off in landing. Expecting a real bawling out, I took the javelin back to the gym teacher.

"Don't worry about it," he said, still shaking his head in wonder. "You keep the thing."

That night I took the javelin home with me and, much to my parents' astonishment, never let it out of my sight. The very next day I began practicing with it, and every day that summer—for six hours or more—I would throw it in a nearby schoolyard. The joy of finding something I could do made me determined to do as well in it as I could.

By the time I was a senior and a member of the track team, all my practice paid off. I threw the javelin 211 feet that year, the best throw by any high school boy in the country.

That record gave me a track scholarship to the University of Southern California. With my eye on the Olympics, I continued to work out until one day in college, after not warming up properly, I tore some ligaments in my left shoulder. While I still could throw, I was never able to achieve the distance I once could, and so I gave up my track scholarship and my dream of the Olympics.

Though that was a terrible disappointment, I've learned since then that as we are developing one talent, others seem to spring from it without our realizing it. While the javelin gave me a chance to go to college, it also provided me with a new-found confidence and the ability to shed my inferiority complex. I was able to see the importance of that when later, after I dropped out of U.S.C., I took a job in a Los Angeles warehouse. There, a co-worker, an aspiring actor, asked my help in learning his part in a small playhouse production of *Home of the Brave*.

When I began reading the script, I became mesmerized. The same kind of fascination that took hold of me when I picked up the javelin now turned me on to dramatics. Immediately I enrolled in acting school. That led to small parts in movies, which in turn brought me the role of Little Joe Cartwright in *Bonanza*. That TV series lasted fourteen years and it led me to still another area—directing *Little House on the Prairie*.

I'm convinced that everyone has some kind of hidden talent. God sees to it—it's that simple. The difficult part for some of us is in finding the talent. That's why I feel strongly that we must keep our minds open; we can't let ourselves be discouraged or depressed when the talent doesn't readily appear. Yet when it does, we must be prepared to grab hold of it right away.

Whenever I think about what made that scrawny kid pick up that javelin, I know there was a reason. God was on that high school field whispering to me, "Here's an opportunity. Take it." And am I glad I listened to Him—glad I trusted my enthusiasm—for I not only found my talent, but I truly found myself.

Someone Is Watching

Colin L. Powell

In 1991 I faced an enjoyable yet formidable challenge. I was returning to my old neighborhood in the South Bronx to speak to the students of my old school, Morris High. As we drove down streets where my friend Gene Norman and I used to race bicycles, I thought of the pitfalls awaiting the kids living here. The drugs, the temptations, the crime. What could I say to encourage them?

As we passed the hamburger place that I used to haunt, I remembered my growing-up years here, the joys, the sorrows, the choices. Even then kids faced choices. There were drugs in my neighborhood and a youngster could gain easy access to them if tempted. But in my family, the decision was simple: You just didn't do it. We knew it was stupid and the most self-destructive thing you could do with the life God had given you.

Dad and Mom had moved to America from Jamaica. They both worked hard in the garment district, Dad as a shipping clerk, Mom as a seamstress. Our folks gave my sister and me structure and direction; they made it clear they had high expectations for us. And kids usually live up to expectations.

Moreover, their guidance was buttressed by an extended family of aunts, uncles and cousins all living in the area, keeping an eye on us. Someone was always watching. But that "someone" would be far more than just family, I was to learn.

At age seventeen I found a summer job in a local soft-drink bottling plant at ninety cents an hour. I was thrilled. On my first day of work, having joined the ranks of other newly hired teenagers, I was full of enthusiasm. The bottling machines caught my eye, but only the white boys worked there. I was hired as a porter and my foreman handed me a mop.

I got to work. I mopped what seemed like acres of sticky, cola-stained floor. Today as I talk to young people who may face the same frustrations, I tell a story that mirrors my experience.

It seems there were three men who were ditchdiggers. They'd be out there every day, except that one guy would be leaning on his shovel talking about how one day he was going to own the company. The second guy leaned on his shovel and complained they didn't pay him enough. But the third guy just kept on digging.

Years went by, and the first guy was still leaning on that shovel telling how one of these days he was going to own the company. The second guy was still complaining about the hours and pay. But the third guy was now driving a forklift truck.

More years passed; the first guy, now gray-headed, still leaned on that shovel, saying, "One of these days I'm going to own this company." The second guy had retired on disability after a phony injury. And the third guy? He owned the company.

For me, that story has a moral to it. It says that in whatever you do, someone is always watching. Perhaps I was conscious of that fact as a teenager, for I decided to be the best mop wielder there ever was. Right to left, left to right. One day someone let fifty cases of cola crash to the cement, and brown sticky foam cascaded across the floor. It was almost more than I could bear. But I kept on mopping. Right to left, left to right.

.. ..

At summer's end the foreman said, "You mop floors pretty good."

"You sure gave me enough opportunity to learn, sir," I said.

Next summer he put me to work loading bottles on the filling machine. The third summer I was deputy foreman.

Someone far more important was also watching, I learned. We Powells faithfully attended St. Margaret's Episcopal Church in the Bronx, where Dad was senior warden. I'll never forget when I was confirmed, the bishop laying his hands on my head and intoning, "Defend, O Lord, this Thy child with Thy heavenly grace; that he may continue Thine forever; and daily increase in Thy Holy Spirit more and more, until he comes unto Thy everlasting kingdom. Amen."

Those words gave me a deep assurance, and every year thereafter when I heard this supplication, that feeling of God watching over me was reaffirmed. Along with it was a sense of needing to live up to His expectations, and my family made it clear this involved getting all the education we could. Dad had never finished high school. "I want you to do better than I have," he emphasized.

Though I was in the "slow" class as a fourth-grader at P.S. 39 and a C student in high school, I managed to squeeze into City College of New York. Its main attraction was the tuition, $10 a year. My grades weren't the best, but I did well in the Reserve Officers' Training Corps. In fact, had it not been for ROTC, I might not have had the grades to graduate. The Army felt right to me, and when I graduated I was commissioned as a second lieutenant. Some folks in my family wondered: "Cousin Johnny went into law, cousin Cecilia is studying medicine, and here Colin, of all things, is going into the Army. He isn't in trouble or anything?" But Dad and Mom gave me their blessing.

Within four years of my 1958 graduation from college, I was assigned to Vietnam, where I began to find the truth in the adage that even when necessary, war is a terrible thing.

In 1963 I went to Fort Benning, Georgia, followed by further studies at the Army Command and General Staff College located at Fort Leavenworth, Kansas. There I became interested in opportunities for an advanced degree in graduate school. This became a shining goal, and I decided I would apply despite only average college grades.

I'd come to recognize the value of striving to learn as much in and about life as I could. In fact, by that time I clearly recognized that one had to work especially hard for the things that were of value and importance. Out of a graduating class of 1,244 at Command and General State College, I ranked second. Upon graduation in 1968, I was sent back to Vietnam.

Not long afterward, the *Army Times* ran an article about the staff college's top five students. Again someone was watching. When my division commander in Vietnam saw the story, he pulled me in from the field to be his operations chief.

In 1969 my opportunity for graduate school finally came. I entered George Washington University, where I earned a master's degree in business administration.

In the twenty years that followed I held many military commands and served in the Pentagon and at the White House. In 1989 President George Bush appointed me chairman of the Joint Chiefs of Staff. I held that position when I returned to the Bronx.

My old school hadn't changed much. As I walked up its familiar stone steps, I remembered racing up them to beat the bell. The setting for my talk to the student body was the gymnasium.

"I remember this place," I told the students. "I remember it all. I remember running through Van Cortlandt Park with the track team, the route I used to take each day from my home on Kelly Street to school.

"I also remember, upon occasion, experiencing the feeling 'You can't make it,' " I continued. "But you can. When I was coming up, opportunities were limited. But now the opportunities are there to be anything you want to be. But wanting to be isn't enough, dreaming about it isn't enough. You've got to study for it, work for it, fight for it with all your heart, energy and soul, so that nothing will be denied you."

I wanted them to make the right choices, to work hard and not lose sight of a dream. And I wanted them to know that someone is always watching.

PART 3

The Power
in a Goodly Heritage

The lines are fallen unto me in pleasant
places; yea, I have a goodly heritage.
                    Psalm 16:6 (KJV)

The celebrities who tell their stories in this section have seen God's power to mold their lives as they wrestled with and answered the big questions: Who are we? Where do we come from? What is important to us? Answers of those questions defined them, particularly in terms of their family and cultural heritage. Perry Como, Billy Mills, Victor Borge, Joe Carcione . . . may have left their hometowns or homelands, but they never walked away from the good and godly heritage they received. A heritage they wanted to pass on to their children and grandchildren, wherever they would roam.

No Tax on My Heritage

Perry Como

My father was a mill hand, and during the last fifteen years of his life he was a hopeless invalid. Always vigorous and active he suddenly became sick, and could not work. It was his heart. A little group of friends would come to visit him every evening. Plain people. This is Canonsburg, Pennsylvania, a mill and mining town. These men, with the lined faces and bent backs and gnarled hands, who worked every day from sunup to sundown, were brought together by my father's illness. Before, they had spent their free hours in noisy play, freeing themselves from the monotonous drudgery of the mill and mine. Now, sitting there, clustered around my father, they all asked themselves: Who are we? Where do we come from?

They all had heard of God. They all believed. But they didn't work at it. They never really listened hard. Now they came within earshot of Him. There was a new light in all their faces, including my father's. It shone when he said: "Become poor in spirit and share the light with me."

At the time I didn't understand all this. I was fourteen. But I knew that my father was showing me how to believe in many ways. His last fifteen years were years of pain, but they were the happiest years of his life.

They couldn't have been made so happy because of what he owned. Pop never made more than $175 a month. But he raised thirteen kids, and not one of them a black sheep. We all worked. It was natural for me to start at the age of eleven in a barber shop. Before school I opened the shop and lit the stoves. After school I swept the hair off the floors, polished the mirrors, and the owner taught me how to cut hair. My pay was fifty cents a week. My ambition then was to be the best barber between Canonsburg and Cleveland.

When I was fourteen, my father set me up in my own shop. If things got slow, I'd pick up my guitar and sing. You put someone with Italian blood down in the bleak mine country, and his only defense against the bleakness is to sing. The singing was also a reflection of the joy that came from a happy home.

By the time I was twenty, I was making a big fat forty dollars a week. My mother and father thought that was the height of prosperity. To Pop, prosperity meant "enough to remind you to be thankful." My mother even predicted that some day I'd be making sixty dollars a week.

Later, much later, my father never could understand what they call success in the singing business. He was always puzzled by how a man standing in front of a microphone could earn a lot of money. The first time he heard me sing was in a theater where I was appearing. After the show I rushed to him, asking silently for his approval.

"Bravo," was all he said.

At first I was hurt. But when Pop added: "The audience . . . do all your audiences cheer you so loud and crazy?" I realized what he meant: applause every day keeps feeding your vanity and pride and greed. And that's no way to become poor in spirit.

Besides, to people like Pop, singers meant Caruso, Martinelli, Scotti. And you know, maybe they're right.

Anyway, I wouldn't have had my father different.

And my mother, she's still teaching me how to be poor in spirit. I'd like her to come and stay with me and my wife Roselle and our three kids. But she won't. At her house in Canonsburg, with all her grandchildren, it's like a big party all the time. She sits on the porch and everybody who comes by says hello.

Up here in New York nobody says hello in quite the same way. She's probably right. To people like Mom, a little conversation with a friend is more important than running around for big things. Mom still can't figure out what I do for a living. When we bring her a gift, and it's a little expensive, she looks at me suspiciously, and asks: "Where did you get the money?"

I wouldn't have her different either.

Sure, I got the things money can buy now. But the things money can't buy my mother and my father gave me.

My wife, Roselle, gives them to me too. A year after we were married, we went off for a week's vacation to Cleveland, and there Roselle talked me into singing for a band leader named Fred Carlone.

He offered me twenty-five dollars a week. That was the end of my making an honest living. But it began seven years of one-night stands, climbing on and off buses, living in fleabag hotels. Three years with Carlone, and four with another band leader named Ted Weems. Roselle traveled with me. It was like the foreign legion. We couldn't get out. No, I take that back. Going from twenty-five dollars to one hundred twenty-five dollars a week was a lot of money. I didn't want to get out—until our son Ronnie was on the way.

We went back home, and I was all ready to open a barber shop when I got a phone call from New York. Columbia

Broadcasting offered me seventy-six dollars a week on a sustaining show of my own. I hesitated. But Roselle said: "Honey, you can always open up a barber shop." I went to New York.

It was the time of the Frank Sinatra bonfire. Anyone with some hair, a set of his own teeth, and a voice that could stay in key had plenty of chances. They gave me the jackpot; theatres, night clubs, records. Then they signed me to a big radio show, and I even got a movie contract. All within a few months. And then television.

It was crazy, but it was the singing business. A barber can work from 8:00 a.m. to 10:00 p.m. to make fifty dollars a week—maybe. An engineer, a scientist, a doctor, a writer, they sweat and study long and hard before they can even start earning a buck. But in this business a guy makes one record and gets $50,000.

Somewhere along the line Someone sure put His hand on my head. I keep trying to deserve it.

We've got reason to be thankful, Roselle and I. But we never talk about it. That kind of gratitude isn't for conversation. Faith is a word for doing, not talking.

I pray just like my kids, before they climb into bed every night. Were my prayers ever answered? If you believe, anything you think, do, or have is an answer to prayer. If you believe, you know that without anybody having to tell it to you. Then your heart's at peace. If your heart's at peace, everything else is. If it isn't, everything else is wrong. That's the way it always is.

Everything that's ever happened to me has been the result of faith. The faith I found in my father's house, and now find in my own house, and in my world. Sure, there are different beliefs, but as long as men believe, they believe basically the same thing. The lyrics may be different, but the music is always the same.

I know now that with his illness and poverty, my father had wealth beyond money. His heritage to his children was greater than any fortune.

That's the only heritage a man can give his children while he's alive.

It's the only one that becomes more precious after his death.

All of Us Need to Belong

Billy Mills

In the spring of 1974 I went back to Pine Ridge looking for answers. I stood on the dusty road that runs through the prairie town into the rolling Black Hills of South Dakota, and squinted in the morning sun at the tiny ramshackle house where I'd spent the first twelve years of my life. I had fought hard to leave the poverty of our reservation, and I had. Like other members of minority groups who make it outside their home turf, I was truly grateful for what I now had: a loving wife, three precious daughters and a comfortable home. Yet, like others, I still felt a restlessness at the core of my being. This had driven me here, back to my heritage, to look for something to ease the loneliness I was feeling.

This sleepy South Dakota town on the Pine Ridge Indian Reservation had not changed much in twenty years. The small board houses were still dwarfed by the wealth of nature surrounding them. I'd lived here with my mother, who was three-quarters French and one-quarter Indian; my father, a Lakota (Sioux) man; and my brothers and sisters and relatives. Sometimes we numbered as many as fifteen in our four-room house. I hardly remember my mother, who died when I was small, but I can never forget my father, a stocky muscular man with straight dark hair and a gentle, weathered face.

Dad had a fierce love for all of his children, but I felt there was a special connection between him and me. Now, standing in front of this small house, I pictured the year I was twelve

years old. I saw the two of us as we walked home from church
in the early morning: him broad-shouldered and proud in a
dark tie and a white shirt, and me, a barely awake youngster in
T-shirt and jeans. Since his stroke, he'd run a barbershop out of
our house, and my favorite time of day was helping him set up
for the day's business. I'd sweep the floor while he sharpened
his shiny barber's scissors. And we'd talk. There wasn't anything I couldn't tell him.

All of us need to belong, yet even as a child I felt I didn't fit
anywhere. "The white people don't want me," I'd complain to
Dad. "To them I'm an Indian, and they have signs up in their
town: 'No dogs or Indians allowed,' and they won't serve us in
their restaurants. And my Lakota classmates, well . . ." I
paused, embarrassed, "they say the only thing worse than a
Wasicu [white man] is an Ieska [half blood]. I wish I was one
thing or the other. But I'm nothing. I don't fit anywhere."

Dad never tried to placate me. Instead he'd try to find practical solutions for my feeling of not belonging. "Billy," he said
to me more than once, "you can learn to be good at sports. It's
a way to compete in white society." He must have seen the
look on my face. We both knew I wasn't a natural athlete.

Or he would say, "It will be a struggle, son, to find a place
in the white world—or to earn the respect of your father's people—but it is possible to walk in two worlds with one spirit.
This, however, you must always remember: You are my son,
and you belong. You belong to me."

I believed that I belonged to him and took strength from
that knowledge. But that frail cord of acceptance snapped one
morning several weeks later while Dad was cutting hair. He
suffered another stroke and was taken to the hospital. That
night when my sister told me he was dead, I ran out the creak-

.. ..

ing back door, over the hills, as far as my legs could carry me. I don't remember anything about the next two days.

But two things had changed: I now felt completely alone. And I'd started running.

I continued running at Haskell, one of the Indian boarding schools where my brothers and sisters and I were sent, as there was no one at home to care for us. I would run five or ten miles on weekends, because it allowed me to get away from everybody else. And I just cried. I'd be crying while I was running. A half blood and an orphan—you couldn't feel much lonelier than that.

Before long, running, my means of escape, became my means of acceptance. I won a track scholarship to a predominantly white university. After graduation I earned a commission in the Marine Corps. Eventually, on October 14, 1964, the world was astounded at the Tokyo Olympics when I won the gold medal for the 10,000-meter race.

Dad had been right, that day thirteen years earlier. Through sports I'd won acceptance and respect. The Lakota people gave me Warrior status and an Indian name. Makocé Terila ("Respects-the-Earth"). These were honors usually reserved for full-bloods. I'd married Pat, the woman I loved, who was white, and we settled in a beautiful community outside Sacramento, California. I had a good job selling insurance. I wanted to make sure that others wouldn't be left destitute because of a death, the way my own family had been. Things were going well. I should have been content.

So why was I standing here in front of this now-dilapidated house in Pine Ridge? I had thought that this long-sought acceptance would finally give me a sense of belonging. Instead there was a vacuum in the center of me. Was it that, even though two cultures accepted me, I knew I wasn't truly one or the other? *I* knew I didn't belong. Somehow I hoped that by coming back to my roots, back to where I was born, that I could find some answer to my restlessness. So Respects-the-Earth had come back.

As had happened before, when I first arrived at the reservation, I felt a fleeting sense of peace. At first I saw what I wanted to see: the ancestral land of a proud, strong people. So much of what I'd learned here was right: respect for the earth, for one's elders, for wisdom, for the culture of hundreds of generations now gone. But when my eyes adjusted, I saw the struggle of Pine Ridge: Once, we had been a people at home here. We had a spiritual grounding in this country and knew that the Black Hills was "the heart of everything there is." But promises had shattered, treaties had been broken. The Black Hills had been illegally taken away. Now the reservation meant inadequate housing, improper medical care, splintered families. The spirit of our people was imprisoned. There was poverty and despair.

Like other Lakota facing this struggle, I knew this place itself was not the answer to my heart's cry to belong.

I had come to the end of my resources. I needed someone wiser than myself. "Oh, Dad," I said, "you had such wisdom. Why aren't you here to tell me the secret of your serenity? How did you find peace in the face of need and ill health?"

Of course, Dad wasn't here. But another very wise man was—Fools Crow, an elder and spiritual leader of our tribe. I felt a new hope mixed with trepidation at the idea of an audience with him, but I knew I had to go.

While the honored citizens of many cultures have mansions and fancy cars, Fools Crow chose to live simply in a log cabin, miles from anywhere.

.. ..

There was a tranquillity inside the small house. Fools Crow was past seventy, his chestnut skin was weathered, but he still stood tall and his eyes shone with an ageless vitality. He received me and invited me to sit down. "I am troubled," I started. "There are questions to which I cannot find answers."

All of my frustrations came pouring out: my need to know where I truly belonged. How I'd looked everywhere and hoped to find my answer here. How the yearning still hadn't gone away.

"Billy," he started, speaking in Lakota, "I think you are still troubled that you are Ieska. But that is not the cause of your restlessness. Many of our people, full-bloods, go to the city as you did. Look what happens: Many of them drink, fight, become lost—lost souls. So they come back here, and what are they doing? Fighting, drinking. Their souls are lost here as well. The reservation is not the answer. A place does not give peace. So, what is the answer to this yearning?"

He paused and looked squarely at me. "The answer you seek lies with your Creator. Lakota, white, black; the Great Mysterious Creator made us all. There are two roads in life, the black road and the red road—the spiritual road. We are made with a yearning to walk the spirit road with our Creator. When you are on the spirit road, you may journey through any country in peace."

The burning in my chest told me he was right. This was his secret and this had been Dad's secret as well. God, the Great Mysterious Creator, had been Dad's strength, his center. This is why he had taken me to church, why he began each day in worship. Dad had counseled me to "walk in two worlds with one Spirit." Yet, I hadn't taken much time for God, for the "red road."

.. ..

"Fools Crow," I said, "my father worshiped the Christian God. My daughters are in Catholic school. Am I turning my back on my heritage to worship this way?"

"Billy," he said gently, "there is one God. You honor your people in worshiping Him the way you know to be true."

A chilly wind parted the grasses as I left Fools Crow's cabin. But as I stood in the silence of the prairie, looking toward the Black Hills, I heard a familiar answer to my plea for acceptance, this time from a Father even greater than my own: *You are My son, and you belong. You belong to Me.*

I started down the dirt road. For the first time, I wasn't running away from, or toward, anything. I was running *with* my God, my Creator. And no matter where my earthly journey takes me, I know Billy Mills is already home.

A Sanctuary in Copenhagen, A Chapel in Stockholm

Victor Borge

W hen I grew up in Denmark, my family was bound together by love for one another and our intense interest in music. For thirty-five years my father was a violinist in the Royal Philharmonic Orchestra, and he wanted me to take up the violin, too. My mother, however, loved the piano. And that did it!

In the 1920s and '30s I became immensely busy on the stage, radio and in the movies. But in the 1930s something else was happening in Europe. We in Denmark despised the Nazis, and it was natural for me to make them the butt of much of my satirical humor. That they were not in love with me either was obvious from the letters and threatening phone calls I received.

My father, who at my birth in 1909 was sixty-two years old, had died in 1932. By the spring of 1940, just as I had left for Sweden to star in a musical revue, Mother grew gravely ill. Then, on April 9th, the Germans swept into Denmark. In my absence Mother was immediately brought to a private hospital and admitted under an assumed name to save her from being held hostage in retaliation for my disappearance, because I had been placed on the most-wanted list by the Nazis.

Known as I was by every Dane, I nevertheless managed to slip back into Denmark undetected. Fully aware of the danger involved, I had to see my mother, who had not been told of the Nazi invasion. Pale and weak, she held out her arms to greet me and drew me close. "You see," she whispered, "I'm getting better, and soon . . ." Her strength had gone. At that moment, desperate to find a way to cheer her, I told her that I had just received an incredible offer from Hollywood, and that—as soon as she was well enough—together we would go to America. It was a tremendous lie. At that time I had not the slightest notion of going to America. But I would have done or said anything just to see her smile again. She did . . . and whispered barely audibly, ". . . don't let it go to your head. . . ."

We talked a little until it was time to leave. I leaned down and kissed her. "Good-bye, Mother," and as the sound of the last word echoed in my ears, I knew that I should never see her again.

That evening I returned across the Sound to Sweden. How was it possible to perform those nights in a musical comedy revue? A week later the cablegram came: Mother had died in her sleep. At 10 o'clock on Friday morning there would be a service for her.

I wanted desperately to get back, but it was impossible. The dangers were now too hazardous to overcome, and no longer could I offer comfort to my mother. In my hotel room in Stockholm I read the cable again—"Service at 10 o'clock," it said. What sort of service would there be? As a student, I'd earned extra money playing the organ at many funeral services. The ritual I knew by heart.

On the day of the funeral, at 9:30 in the morning, I climbed the steps leading to a cemetery in a Stockholm suburb. I knocked on the door of the caretaker's office. Yes, he understood what I wanted to do, and led me to a small stone chapel, opened the door, walked away, and left me alone.

For a moment I stood in the aisle of the little church. A soft light filtered down from the stained-glass windows. Then I went to the organ and sat down. I looked at my watch. It was almost 10 o'clock.

Five hundred miles south in Copenhagen, the people who knew and loved my mother were filing into the sanctuary where her body rested. I began by playing a simple lullaby that Mother had sung to me. My hands dropped to my lap. After a few moments had passed, I could almost hear the voice of someone in that distant chapel speaking about my mother's dedication to her family and friends, and her devotion to decency and to dignity. I played again, improvising upon some music we had shared.

Strange, I thought, *that the walls of the little chapel could withstand the surge of my emotions.*

There I was, far from home in another country, forbidden to be at my mother's side even during the last hours of her life.

But she was now freed from the horrors of war and the holocaust—and so was I. For her death made it possible for me to escape the tragic fate that I would have been dealt by the enemy.

That's the way my mother would have chosen it. I know. . . .

And, by miraculous circumstances, I was able to reach America, where soon after I went to Hollywood and was virtually absolved from my great lie.

Light the Candles

Kirk Douglas

*A*ctor *Kirk Douglas, star of movie classics including* Champion, Spartacus, *and* Paths of Glory, *was born as Issur Danielovitch in Amsterdam, New York. He fondly remembers his mother and the centrality of her Jewish faith and heritage. Memory of her example took center stage in his life at the end of his career, the night he accepted a lifetime achievement award by the John F. Kennedy Center for the Performing Arts. The turning point came as Kirk's son, actor Michael Douglas, addressed the gala event in Washington, D.C. That evening Kirk shared the presidential box with First Lady Hillary Rodham Clinton.*

It was the name my father never called her; to him she was always "Hey you," or "the missus." But Bryna was the name I taught her to write. Before that she always signed my report cards from school with an X.

My mother was illiterate—in English. But I remember how on the Sabbath she would make our whirlwind family stand still, and sit on the porch reading her Hebrew prayer book.

After the Bryna Company had become famous producing hits like *Paths of Glory* and *The Vikings* (and later *Spartacus, Lonely are the Brave* and *Seven Days in May*), I took her to Times Square one night in a big limo and pointed out a sign that covered the whole building. "You see, Ma, in lights, BRYNA

PRESENTS . . ." My mother shook her head and sighed, "America, such a wonderful land." I agreed with my mother.

It is no coincidence that when I formed the Bryna Company, I also started a charitable foundation. I should have named it after my mother as well, because it was clearly her influence that was playing out in me.

I remember that in our home we had a small tin box—a *pushke*—nailed to the wall. *Pushke* in Yiddish means tin can but this one was more like a piggy bank. It was where we placed coins to be given to charity. Of course, we had barely enough to eat so our *pushke* was never bulging. But my mother made sure that something was always in it. The Torah commands us to give to the poor. Charity is called *tzedaka*—justice. And even a beggar must give *tzedaka*—because there is always someone who has less.

We lived near the railroad tracks, and often hobos would come to the door begging for food. My mother always found something to give them.

A lot of people in the neighborhood thought she was a *tzaddikes*—a saint. They would bring her a handkerchief to bless and then place it on the head of some sick person, convinced that her blessing would make the sick well. Maybe it did.

My freshman year in college, I became ill with the flu, and was lying in my dormitory room with a high fever. There was a knock on the door. "Your mother's on the phone." I was startled—we didn't have a telephone at home. She never called. I threw on a robe and walked down the hall.

My mother was calling me from a neighbor's home. "I had a feeling you were sick," she said. After assuring her that I would be fine, I went back to my bed perplexed. How could she have known?

I never gave her credit for so many things she did and was responsible for. Only now I realize the profound influence she had on me.

Most of all, I remember vividly how she died. She had been in the hospital some time, unable to fight off pneumonia because of her weak heart and complications from her diabetes. My sisters and I stayed at her side as she got weaker and weaker, drifted in and out of consciousness. At dusk one day she roused herself. "What day is it?"

"Friday, Mama."

"Don't forget to light the candles for the Sabbath."

We quickly brought four candles to the room and started to light them. The nurses came in screaming. With the oxygen in the room, we could have blown up the hospital. So we went to my sister Betty's house to do it there. Afterward, I came back alone.

I was overwhelmed by my mother's composure and dignity. My father had died some years before, and the look in his dying eyes was unmistakable—sheer terror.

Watching my mother in that hospital bed. I must have seemed pretty scared myself, because she looked up at me and smiled a clear, serene smile. It was the same kind of smile she used to have every Sabbath when she sat on the porch with her prayer book. "Don't be afraid, Issur. It happens to all of us," she said.

I choked. Holding my own breath, I watched my mother breathe so slowly in, then out, each breath causing her pain. Until a long, deflating exhale followed by . . . nothing.

That's how the *tzaddikim* die. I have been told. It is called "dying by the kiss of God." The same God who created man breathing life into him now kisses him and takes that breath away. It is a sign from God that someone is very special. . . .

[Years later on receiving a lifetime Achievement Award] Michael began by saying warm things about me. And a funny feeling started to creep over me. Take it easy, Kirk, I said to myself. Spartacus doesn't cry. And I held it back. Michael talked about a lullaby that my mother sang to me in Yiddish, *"Rozhinkes mit Mandlen"* ("Raisins and Almonds"), a song that brings sweet dreams. I had visions of blubbering all over the First Lady's velvet gown. I was determined not to give in. But then I heard a flute playing the tune, and about fifty children walked out onstage singing. Listening to the song that I had heard so often many many years ago, I suddenly knew the meaning of "voices of angels." Those sweet sounds seemed to fill every part of me. I closed my eyes to hold back the tears and saw visions of my mother blessing the Friday-evening Shabbat candles.

On Saturday morning, she would be so neatly dressed her hair combed perfectly, as she'd sit in a rocking chair on the front porch with her arms folded. She looked so peaceful. It was an unusual sight. There was a holiness about my mother. And as that song about raisins and almonds floated up to me, I thought, *My God, how far away I've strayed.* Right then and there, I made a promise to start lighting candles every Friday night.

The Greengrocer

Joe Carcione

The American Dream. Its bright hope drew my parents to this country from Sicily. Its challenge inspired me to reach for the stars in building my own produce company. And then one day my dream got squashed.

Ever since high school, when I started out in January 1933 working in San Francisco's produce terminal sweeping floors and lugging crates, among other duties, the fresh fruit and vegetable wholesale business has been my life. I'd learned it from my father, who could almost tell what an orange was thinking. He knew when produce was at its best and when to avoid it. "Pepino," he'd tell me, "buy the ripe strawberries, not the ones with the green shoulders. The red ones have all the sweetness that the good Lord said they should have."

Every night I'd fall into bed almost too tired to say my prayers. But I loved the work, the dark misty dawn when farm trucks groaned up to the sidewalks of the old San Francisco market under dew-glistening loads of iceberg lettuce, Santa Rosa plums, Valencia oranges.

I learned to pick out the best quality. I loved the cheerful haggling with produce buyers and the deals you closed with a handshake; and the afternoons I'd be phoning growers: "You *sure* our load of asparagus is coming in tomorrow?"

Finally, in 1958, I was able to start my own company, Best Fruit and Produce.

For many years I would get up every morning between one

and two to be at the market on time. It was providing a good living for my wife Madeline, three children and me.

In order to increase the sale of my produce, I bought advertising on radio station KCBS in San Francisco. In time, the program director of the station asked me to make a report every Monday through Friday about what was fresh and good in the market that day. I was surprised. I told him I had never been on radio before. He suggested that I try it. I did. And I have been on that radio station every day since 1967.

I am not a sophisticated man; my voice is pure North Beach Italian-American and somewhat raspy. But then, God made me like I am. So I figured I would just be myself. I found myself talking by telephone direct from the terminal on an informational spot called "The Man on the Produce Market."

I spoke to listeners just like I'd talk to a friend. I told them how to spot spoiled or unripe fruit, how to test vegetables for freshness, quality; finding good buys and tips on serving them.

People liked it and soon San Francisco's *Chronicle* asked me to write a daily column, which became known as "The Greengrocer."

It helped people become even more aware of the value of fresh fruits and vegetables. But then one morning I was checking a load of Tokay grapes. They were flame red and sweet. I was sampling one when someone shouted: "Hey Joe, telephone."

My bank was calling. "Could you come in this afternoon, Mr. Carcione?"

In the bank's quiet office I had my answer. After closing the door behind them, two bank officials sat down with me.

"Joe, it's not just that your account is overdrawn, but . . ."

"Overdrawn?" I stared at them. "By how much?"

"Somewhere around a hundred thousand dollars."

I shot forward in my chair. I couldn't believe it. There had to be a mistake. My accountant. He handled all my company's complex finances. The payroll records, bank deposits, taxes. He would know. Then I remembered. He had not been in the office the past two days. Someone said he had called in sick. I called him. There was no answer.

When I finally got home I could hardly talk to Madeline about it. But even I had no idea of how bad things were.

Within a week I knew. Our Social Security and Federal withholding taxes had not been paid. On top of that, over a hundred-fifty-thousand dollars had been siphoned off. We were short a half-million dollars!

The accountant? A man I had known and trusted. He had simply disappeared.

For six months I struggled to keep Best Fruit and Produce going. But it had been dealt a fatal blow. "Joe," my lawyer said sadly, "I know it's tough, but there's only one thing you can do."

"Not bankruptcy?"

He nodded.

Late that night when I stumbled into the house, I told Madeline all about it. "Babe," I quavered, my voice breaking, "I don't understand how it all happened, but . . . but we may lose our house."

Madeline gave me a long hug and said softly: "Don't worry, Joe; we've lived in worse places."

Without her encouragement I don't know what I would have done. Even so, I was not prepared for the trauma of bankruptcy proceedings, the court appearances, the deep shame. It killed me to see everything I'd struggled for sold under the auctioneer's hammer: all our trucks, dock equipment, office furniture.

The last day I walked alone through the packing shed. It was still redolent with the tangy scent of oranges, the fragrance of bell peppers and green beans. It was also full of memories.

Now everything was gone. Even the radio program and newspaper column seemed meaningless.

I went home, walked past Madeline directly into our bedroom where I fell onto the bed. Thirty-four years down the drain. I thought of my family, my parents, who were so proud of me. Now what would they think of the one who had to declare bankruptcy?

As I lay there thinking of my family, I remembered my grandmother. I could again see her in her black satin dress, slowly working her way up the street to attend mass at Saint Peter and Paul. After her sight gave out, neighbors gently guided her. But every morning she went, no matter the weather.

I couldn't understand her tenacity and asked my mother, "Isn't it about time she took a rest from all that?"

My mother's brown eyes became thoughtful and she said: "She is an old woman, yes. Her husband is gone and she lives with memories. But she goes to give God what she has: her prayers, her faith, her gratefulness."

She gently squeezed my shoulder. "Every day she thanks Him for making the dream come true."

I lay there in the bedroom thinking of that dream; the American Dream they called it, the dream that brought them to this country.

I remembered my father looking at me levelly. "You know, Joe, back in the old country some people thought gold could be picked up in the streets here." He chuckled. "They soon found out that things were different. But the dream, the real American Dream, was that over here you . . ." He looked out toward the Bay. "Well, I'll tell you; back there whatever your father did, you followed in his footsteps, whether he was a fisherman or ran a fruit stand. But, over here, if you work hard enough, you have the freedom and the opportunity to make of yourself anything you want."

Lying on the bed, I thought of the man who came to this country with nothing, nothing but hope, determination and a deep trust in God.

Suddenly, I felt ashamed for lying on my back like a defeated man when I already had so much. A wonderful wife, fine children and a knowledge of fruits and vegetables that nobody could take away from me. And all the while here I was acting as though money was the American Dream. "Well, it's not," I said, almost out loud, "it's not."

I jumped up, ran into the kitchen where Madeline was stirring spaghetti sauce and grabbed her around the waist. "Hey, Babe," I shouted, "to heck with bankruptcy, to heck with the past. There's nothing anyone can do about it. We're going to fight back and we're going to come out all right!"

Her blue eyes shone and she kissed me, spilling spaghetti sauce down my shirt. I felt like a boy again.

Maybe I had lost the produce business, but I still had the radio program and newspaper column. And through them, I could help others.

When I did my next radio program from the market and wrote my newspaper column, I completely forgot the past.

"Folks," I waxed enthusiastic, "you gotta believe me, we have pineapples in here this morning that are out of this world. They'll be in your supermarket later today. You know, folks, a golden ripe pineapple has a marvelous fragrance. If you put it in the trunk of your car, in a very short while it will fill your car with its wonderful aroma. That's one way the pineapple tells you it's ripe and ready for eating. Most of the time a green pineapple has no aroma at all."

When something needed criticizing, I called a spade a spade. "The price of iceberg lettuce is out of sight today, folks," I'd warn. "Don't buy it; buy cabbage. It's cheap and plentiful and it has more vitamins and minerals."

"More and more people are tuning in, Joe," said the program director, "and research shows that listeners love you."

Not everybody loved me. Marketing produce is a rough and tumble business, and I had my share of critics among growers, wholesalers and retailers.

Then I overheard a wholesaler: "So he puts the knock on a bad shipment of tomatoes. But he can turn around and rave about grapes and the buyer impact is felt almost immediately. So we hate him one day and love him the next."

Two years after my radio debut, I was asked to make a television appearance. From that developed a regular weekly show on San Francisco's Channel 4, KRON-TV. Again I was scared. I'm not the most handsome guy in the world.

It worked. Within a few years the television spot was syndicated. By 1984 my *Greengrocer* show was seen regularly by more than seven-million people in sixty-five different cities across the nation.

At age sixty-nine I'm having more fun and excitement than ever. I run a small fruit exporting business. But with the growing demand for fresh, natural goods, I'm having the time of my life helping folks pick the finest fruits and vegetables for the money and giving out my favorite old-country recipes. I even found time to write two books, *The Consumers Guide to Fruits & Vegetables* and *The Greengrocer*.

That accountant? I don't know what happened to him. *Vengeance is mine; I will repay, saith the Lord* (Romans 12:19, KJV). And I have long left him to God. In fact, when I think of all the fun I'm having today, I wonder. Maybe the guy even did me a favor?

So let me tell you something. The American Dream is as true today as when it attracted our forefathers. It is the freedom to grow as much as we're able. It is the opportunity to rise up when we are flat on our backs and begin again. And it works best when we concentrate on our God-given talents. Mine is to tell people about radishes and cauliflowers. Yours may be being a housewife, typing letters, or helping build houses.

But when we concentrate on the *giving* and the *trusting*, it puts us in the best position to reap His blessings. So remember. *Buon appetito. Salute per cento anni!* (Good health for one-hundred years.)

My Path of Prayer

Duke Ellington

When my mother died in 1935, I lost all ambition. I did nothing but brood. And when my father died a couple of years later, the bottom just dropped out.

The grief was so great because I kept remembering everything my parents had left me. There was the memory of my mother playing the Rosary on the piano when I was four. It was so beautiful I burst out crying. Afterward, she had me take some piano lessons on a new upright. Later I worked and pounded the piano keys until I was all music.

My father was a caterer and sometimes worked at the White House. He later became a blueprint technician for the Navy Department. My mother, my sister, myself, we never wanted for anything. He was a good provider. He was also a man of rectitude and faith.

My parents loved us, fed us, cleaned us, took us to church. Two churches. Every Sunday we first went to my father's church, Methodist. Then my mother took us to her church, Baptist. Their respect for each other was a lesson itself. You don't forget that kind of teaching.

They left me such a heritage of belief that after they were gone it was natural I should turn to the Bible for help, again. I read it through four times. That took over two years. What did I get out of it? I thought that I knew something about life and living, about a good sound and grief and joy. But after studying the Scriptures, I found a new awareness of how to meet my problems, how to deal with my fellowman, and how to bring God further into my work.

There's really nothing new under the sun. "One generation passeth away, and another generation comes, but the earth abideth forever" (Ecclesiastes 1:4, KJV.) So there's nothing to get uptight about. If you know that, you don't have to jump at every trouble. I wrote a piece, *There Ain't But the One*, which said it all. So leave it to God.

One sure way I know to meet my problems is prayer. I pray regularly, when I arise, when I retire. I pray my thanks for whatever He gives me: a thought, a bar of music, food. I believe I am helped by prayer. It makes me aware of my total dependence on Him.

We all belong to Him in the first place. I figure that when we're born we are only given a lease, that's all. We're accountable to Him at the end of the lease time. We're not supposed to arrive at the end all scarred up by anger and hurt and self-pity. My grief left when it came to me that past a certain point, it's a sin to grieve.

The light that shows us how to deal with our neighbors and ourselves and God is easy to find: the Ten Commandments. Beautiful poetry, but they're a whole way of life, too. There's a natural inclination to break them, but we are shown the way back if we allow ourselves to be.

One of the great things the Bible gave me was to try and look inside a man instead of at the cut of his clothes. It makes you aware of what you lack. My manager has always said that my band has no boss. He's right. I won't argue with anybody, in the band or out of it. I accept my fellowmen. I love them, or try to. That gives me an inner peace of my own. Arguing with anyone brings me to the point of anger and then to judging others. I can't and won't do that. That's pitting my puny strength against the great Power that runs the universe.

My feeling is that God gives each of us a role to play in life. Mine is music. The first piece I ever wrote was *Soda Fountain Rag*. I was fifteen and jerking soda in the Poodle Dog Cafe in Washington, D.C., my home town. Since then there have been many thousands of pieces, many of them called sacred music.

Where do they come from? God fills your mind and heart with them. All you have to do is believe and wait until they come and use them, whether it's laying brick a new way or writing a song. The ideas come to me anytime, anyplace. So I accept the blessings and write them. I write on trains, planes, ships, in cabs, buses—at night, in the morning, in the din and fury of the music world and the frenzy of a thousand one-night stands.

Way back, years ago, Mahalia Jackson did one of my things, *Come Sunday*, and my version of Psalm 23. Later, we did an album together. It attracted the attention of various church people. Dean C. Julian Bartlett and the Rev. John Yaryan, canon of Grace Cathedral in San Francisco, asked me to present a concert of sacred music there. When you get that kind of invitation, you're not in show business. You think to yourself, *It all has to be kind of right. You have to go out there and make a noise that tells the truth.*

I had to stop and figure out my eligibility. I prayed.

Every man prays in his own language, and I believe there is no language that God does not understand. Every time his children have thrown away fear in the pursuit of His word, miracles have happened.

When I went out to Grace Cathedral in 1965, there was a

shout that it was all new. It wasn't. The sacred music began a way back, in the Thirties, and earlier inside me.

At that first concert in San Francisco I told the 2,500 people present, "In this program you hear a statement without words, but I think you should know that it is a statement with six tones symbolizing the six syllables in the first four words of the Bible, 'In the beginning God. . . . ' "

We opened and closed with *Praise God*. It was based on Psalm 150. In the program, I tried new songs and new instrumental works, *Supreme Being* and *Something About Believing* and *Almighty God*. The trumpet preached a solo. A fire-and-brimstone sermonette came from the percussion section. When we reached the closing, *Praise God*, the audience was on its feet and stayed there through a whole *a capella* rendition of *The Lord's Prayer*.

The response to that first sacred concert was completely unexpected. One news story began: "Duke Ellington talked to the Lord in Grace Cathedral last night." All of us, every listener, every member of the band and chorus were talking to the Lord that night.

Since then we have done sacred concerts in more than fifty houses of worship in America and Europe. When the church is too small we go into a hall. One church found the two-hundred voices in the chorus too much, so the church rented a ballpark. The chorus need be only twenty voices. In a church, the band and chorus are arranged in the sanctuary. The bishop, minister, priest or rabbi usually address the congregation before we begin.

The sacred concerts do not take the place of worship in the ordinary manner. But the music I write for them is and always was an act of worship. From the very beginning it was a response to a growing sense of obligation to myself in self-defense through the Almighty. It continues to be an expression of God in my life.

I am only saying in music what I have been saying on my knees for a long time.

My Best Investment

Bob Hope

"I t's a long way from Cleveland," I said to myself on twenty-two different Christmas mornings, when I found myself far from the United States entertaining U.S. troops stationed overseas.

It sure was a long way from Cleveland, where the Christmases of my childhood and my early years were spent. Every year, like clockwork, reporters would say to me, "How can you leave home? How can you be away from your family at Christmas?"

The truth is that my Christmas travels were always an affirmation of family, not a denial. Both Dolores and I—despite my heavy travel commitments—consider ourselves to be "family people." She understood, maybe because she came from a big family herself, that those Christmas trips represented a gift, rather than a sacrifice. A gift to me, not just from me.

Wherever I went—to Berlin or Korea or Vietnam—I always took my Cleveland memories with me. It's no secret that the Hope clan was a big one . . . seven boys (Ivor, Jim, Fred, Leslie—that's me—Jack, Sid and George) . . . and not exactly rich. Still, while the presents at Christmas weren't lavish, they were exciting to us. So was the big turkey my mother always cooked, and the plum pudding, which reminded Mother and Dad of England, where the family had started.

On Christmas morning without fail the whole family would go to the Euclid Avenue Presbyterian Church. The kids went to

Sunday school, but Mother and Dad attended the regular church service. (One Christmas they sat in the same pew with President Woodrow Wilson and Mrs. Galt, whom he later married. Let me tell you that resulted in some excited conversation at Christmas dinner!)

Christmas was family day, just the way it is in thousands of homes across the United States. I loved it especially because of the laughter, the big family meal, the presents, everything.

When I went into vaudeville in the late 1920s, it wasn't always possible to get home for Christmas, although I used to try to fix my bookings so I could be in Cleveland. Making a long-distance Christmas phone call to the folks was better than nothing if I couldn't be there. Being away from home really bothered me. I'd look at the audiences out front and wonder if a lot of them weren't lonesome, too.

Later, of course, with Dolores and the kids, Christmas was a beautiful time. But I never forgot what it was like to be in a strange place away from the family.

So in 1948, Senator Stuart Symington asked me to go to Berlin to entertain the troops, I said yes, and that marked the beginning of a big increase in the size of my "Christmas family." When I stepped out on that stage in front of all those homesick servicemen and heard the first laugh come rolling back, I had the feeling I was back in the living room of our house in Cleveland. (You told a joke to my brothers and you really got a laugh.)

I looked at those young people in uniform and I thought, *Why hello there family! You're glad to see me. I'm glad to see you, and that's what family reunions are all about.* Their folks couldn't be there, so I tried to stand in and express to them all the love and laughter that was waiting for them back home.

.. ..

Although I didn't know it at first, going to those bleak, remote bases overseas was a kind of investment in Christmas, and ever since dividends have been flowing back to me in the friendship and love and gratitude of those lonely G.I.'s. Maybe that's a good thing for all of us to remember when we put a lot of ourselves into Christmas preparations, Christmas festivities, Christmas meals, Christmas hospitality. Sometimes it seems like a big investment of time and effort, but the dividends surely will come back to you, just as they have to me. You're not just investing in a holiday; you're investing in the greatest event since time began.

In my travels around the United States, I run into hundreds of people who were there on those lonely overseas Christmases. Many of them make a point of reminding me, and they say, "Thank you." There's only one way to reply to that, and so I'll say it now: "Merry Christmas to all of you! You're always in my heart."

PART 4

The Power in a Stranger's Work and Word

I was a stranger and you welcomed me.
Matthew 25:35

God sure knows how to surprise His children. It can be a poor wayfaring traveler or a generous prospective benefactor. A circus actor or a jail keeper . . . These stories by Carol Burnett, Lloyd Bridges, Ray Bradbury, Johnny Cash, Danny Thomas . . . show how God can powerfully work when a stranger, someone never met before, steps on the stage of life for a brief moment and changes the course of a day—or of the whole career-play.

Ready for the surprise?

The Secret Behind My Success

Carol Burnett

My career—TV, stage, movies, all of it—was founded on a strange event that was to be a deep mystery to me for years. Only after my life had changed drastically, did I begin to solve the puzzle I was confronted with one long-ago June evening in California.

In those days I was one of a group of stage-struck drama-school students at UCLA, living on hopes and dreams and not much else. As school ended, one of our professors was leaving for a vacation in Europe. He had a house near San Diego, and a bon voyage party was planned. It was suggested that some of us drama students might drive down and entertain his supper guests with scenes from musical comedies.

Nine of us agreed to go. One of the boys and I had rehearsed a scene from *Annie Get Your Gun*, I remember, and that was our part of the program. Everything went well. The guests seemed to enjoy our singing, and we enjoyed it, too.

After our performance, supper was announced. I was standing at the buffet when a man I had never seen before spoke to me pleasantly. He said he had admired our performance. Then he asked me what I intended to do with my life.

I told him that I hoped to go to New York some day and make a career for myself on the stage. When he asked what was stopping me, I told him truthfully that I barely had enough money to get back to Los Angeles, let alone New York. I might have added, but didn't, that at times my grandmother, my mother, my sister and I had been on welfare. The man smiled and said that he would be happy to lend me the money to go to New York. A thousand dollars, he added, should be enough to get me started.

Well, in those days I was pretty innocent, but not that innocent. So I refused his offer politely. He went away, but in a few moments he was back with a pleasant-faced lady whom he introduced as his wife. Then he made his offer all over again. He was quite serious, he said. There were only three conditions. First, if I did meet with success, I was to repay the loan without interest in five years. Next, I was never to reveal his identity to anyone. Finally, if I accepted his offer, I was eventually to pass the kindness along, to help some other person in similar circumstances when I was able to do so.

He told me to think it over and telephone him when I got back to Los Angeles. He added that he was prepared to make a similar offer to my partner in the scene from *Annie Get Your Gun*, and he gave me his telephone number.

The next day, half convinced I had dreamed the whole thing, I called the number. I was told that if I had decided to accept the conditions, I could drive down on Monday morning and pick up my check. Still unbelieving, I told my mother and grandmother. Their reaction, not surprisingly, was to urge me strongly not to have anything to do with my mysterious benefactor. But somehow I was convinced that the man was sincere, and I believed, furthermore, that the good Lord was giving me, Carol Burnett, a strong and unmistakable push. I was *supposed* to accept the offer. I was being guided. And if I didn't go, I would regret it for the rest of my life.

At sunup on Monday morning my partner and I were on

the road. We drove for three hours. At nine o'clock, we were at the man's office. We had to wait perhaps half an hour—and believe me, that was the longest half hour of my life! But finally we were ushered in. Our friend was crisp, serious, business-like. He reminded us of the conditions, especially the one about not revealing his identity. Then he had his secretary bring in the checks. I watched as he signed them. I had never seen so many beautiful zeros in my life.

We tried to thank him, but he just smiled and ushered us out. When we came to the car, still dazed, we realized we didn't have enough gasoline to get back to Los Angeles—and not enough cash to buy any. We had to go to a bank, present one of the thousand-dollar checks, then wait while the astonished bank officials telephoned our friend's office to make sure that we weren't a pair of international forgers. But finally they did cash it for us.

Back in Los Angeles, I wasted no time. I spent a little of the money on a visit to the dentist where I had two teeth filled and one extracted—I hadn't been able to afford a dentist for years. Then, with my family's anxious admonitions ringing in my ears, I headed for New York.

In all of that vast city I knew just one soul, a girl named Eleanore Ebe. I called her up and found that she was staying at the Rehearsal Club, where in those days young theatrical hope-fuls could find room and board for eighteen dollars a week. So I moved in with Ellie, and settled down to the long grind of finding work on the New York stage.

It was the old story. No experience? Then no work. But how can you get experience if you can't get work? My funds got lower and lower. I went to work as a hat check girl in a restaurant. Unfortunately, it catered mostly to ladies who had no desire or reason to check their hats. Still, I managed to make about thirty dollars a week from tips—enough to get by.

My grandmother wrote me sternly that if I hadn't found a job on the stage by Christmas I had better come home. So I redoubled my visits to theatrical agencies. Finally one agent said wearily, "Why don't you put on your own show? Maybe then you'd stop bothering us!"

That sparked an idea. Back at the Rehearsal Club I talked to all my jobless friends. If we were really bursting with talent, as we were sure we were, why not hire a hall, send out invitations to all the agents and critics in town, and put on our own revue?

Everyone agreed that it was a great idea. We started chipping in fifty cents apiece each night for a fund to hire the hall. Talented youngsters took on the task of creating scenery, writing music and lyrics, doing the choreography. When our first act was ready, we performed it for the board of directors of the Club who then gave us some additional help. When the "Rehearsal Club Revue" finally opened and ran for three nights, it seemed to us that everyone in New York show business was in the audience. The day after it closed, three agents called me with offers of jobs. From that point on, the magic doors swung open and I was on my way.

I reported all my progress to my benefactor back on the West Coast, but I heard very little from him. He continued to insist upon his anonymity. He showed no desire to share any spotlights, take any credit.

Five years to the day after I accepted his loan, I paid him back, and since then I've kept my pledge never to reveal his identity. He never told me his reasons for helping me in the manner he did, but as the years have gone by I've been able to

.. ..

unravel the mystery of this man, at least to my own satisfaction, and in the process I've discovered a powerful spiritual principle to use in my own life.

I stumbled upon the key clue one day when I was glancing through a copy of the Living Bible. I had turned to Matthew 6 because I wanted to see how the Lord's Prayer had been translated. Suddenly, some verses seemed to leap out of the page: "When you give a gift to a beggar, don't shout about it as the hypocrites do . . . When you do a kindness to someone, do it secretly . . . And your Father Who knows all secrets will reward you . . ." (Matthew 6:2–4, TLB).

Do it secretly, the passage read, and at once I thought of my secretive friend. From that moment, what he had done and how he had done it began to make sense.

I began to see that when he made his offer to me, my benefactor had employed the spiritual principle of giving-in-secret-without-seeking-credit. He had done it partly to be kind, of course, but also because he knew that great dividends flow back to anyone who is wise enough to practice this kind of giving.

I believe that, as the Bible says, there is a great liberating force in not trying to take credit for one's good deeds. It tames the ego. It moves us away from petty vanity—and I'm convinced that the further we move away from ourselves, the closer we come to God.

So that's the story of how my career began. I shall always be grateful to my anonymous friend. With pride I repaid his loan, and with pride I have kept his name secret. As for his stipulation about passing the kindness along to others—well, that's my secret!

Strangers on the Road

Lloyd Bridges

My wife, Dorothy, and I often enjoy the company of our grandchildren at breakfast in our sunny kitchen in Los Angeles. And when they're with us they take part in our regular morning devotions, as did their parents before them. The other morning as Dotty was reading aloud the parable of the Good Samaritan, I saw a little hand tentatively reach for a sugared doughnut. At that moment I caught myself wondering just how much children remember of the things we read and teach them. Do seeds really sprout and take root in their minds, and influence their lives?

Later, I was thinking about the parable Dotty read that morning and my mind drifted back to a day when I was a traveler on my own road to Jericho. Only it was near Eureka, California, on a rainy Christmas morning over forty years ago.

I remember how the sleet slashed at our windshield as I drove our old Dodge sedan down a twisting wilderness road along the Eel River. There were six of us crowded in that car—Dotty and me, our three-year-old son Beau, my sister and her two small children. We were on our way to spend Christmas with my mother.

As we nosed down a steep curve, my brakes suddenly gave out and we began to slide out of control. "Hold on!" I yelled to the others as I steered the car into the metal guardrail where, thank God, the car lurched to a stop.

After checking that we were all safe, I tried to back the car on to the road. I felt that if I could drive in low gear I'd have enough control to make it to a repair garage. But on shifting into reverse, the car wouldn't budge. The front bumper was locked into the guardrail.

For a moment I sat silent, the rain drumming on the metal roof above us.

"Lloyd, what can we do?" asked Dotty.

"I don't know," I sighed. "But we can't stay in the car." Other autos occasionally splashed around us and I feared that in the mist we might not be seen and some car might crash into us, toppling us into the river below.

The cold rain soaked us all as we climbed out. The rest of the family huddled under a tree while I tried to pry the bumper loose from the guardrail with a tire iron. But it was in vain.

My only hope was to flag a ride to a garage and get a tow-truck.

Squinting into the rain, I stepped out and waved at a passing car. It veered and disappeared around the curve. Hunched in my soggy coat collar, I waved at car after car. But all of them swished past, with only the faces of the little children peering curiously out the back windows at me. I realized how dangerous it would be for anyone to stop on that hairpin turn. Who would want to jeopardize his life for a stranger?

In despair, I was about to begin slogging down the road when a car slowed, U-turned and came back to me. The driver rolled down a fogged window.

"What's wrong?" he asked. From their clothes, it was obvious that he, his wife and little girl were dressed up for Christmas or church—or both.

"My car is locked into the guardrail," I said, "and I need a lift to a garage."

He studied his steering wheel for a moment, said something to his wife, and climbed out into the rain.

"No, please." I urged. "You're getting all wet."

"That's okay," he said, sloshing to the guardrail. After examining it, he went to his trunk and pulled out giant cutting shears. "I'm a tinsmith," he said. "Maybe these will help."

I followed him back to my car, feeling terribly guilty as his good dark blue suit got soaked. Grunting with effort, he slowly cut the heavy metal with the powerful shears. As he cut through the last of the rail, the bumper popped free.

"There," he exhaled, stepping back.

"Thank you, thank you!" I exclaimed, reaching for my wallet.

He waved it away and climbed back into his car. "Hey," he said, "you needed help. I was glad to give it. After all, we're all brothers, aren't we?" Putting his car in gear, he called out the window, "Merry Christmas!" and drove away.

"Merry Christmas, and God bless you," I echoed quietly, as I watched his taillights disappear into the mist.

Many years later, on a crisp fall evening, Dotty and I were in New York on business, during the days when I was playing the part of Mike Nelson the skin-diver adventurer in the television series, *Sea Hunt*. That evening we were window shopping our way across town.

As we neared Sixth Avenue, we noticed a commotion taking place on the next corner. An excited crowd stood watching something at the intersection.

I was appalled to see what was going on. A large man, obviously drunk and in a rage, was hurling huge chunks of concrete and other rubble from a construction site into the street. Roaring foul language, he narrowly missed the cars passing by.

.. ..

A woman was pleading from a nearby parked car: "Somebody help my husband! He doesn't know what he's doing!"

It was obvious that before the police could arrive someone could be terribly hurt. There were exclamations and a snicker here and there among the onlookers, but no one was doing anything. Yet it was understandable. Who would want to reason with a madman?

I was about to suggest to Dotty that we go the other way when it seemed that out of the distant past I heard those words again. *Hey, we're all brothers, aren't we?* Suddenly, over Dotty's anguished protests, I found myself stepping forward through the crowd to the enraged man. Grasping his powerful shoulders under a sweat-dampened blue suit, I pleaded: "Come on, your wife is calling you."

He twisted free and lunged for another chunk of concrete.

I grabbed his arm. "You don't want to hurt someone, or hurt yourself."

With an angry roar, he swung around to face me, and then his jaw dropped. Staring at me wide-eyed, he exclaimed, "Mike Nelson!"

"Yeah," I said, gently guiding him, "let's go to your car."

But he was already a step ahead of me. Pulling me to his wife, he exclaimed, "Look, honey, I found Mike Nelson. Mike Nelson is here!"

The rage had left him and soon he was slumped in the backseat where he promptly fell asleep.

His wife looked up through tear-filled eyes. "He's a good man, but tonight he was badly insulted by someone and he started drinking to try to escape his hurt. He was so angry he just seemed to lose his mind. I don't know how to thank you."

She reached through the driver's window and grasped my hand. "God bless you," she said, then drove off.

As I watched the car's taillights disappear into the night, I remembered that rainy morning on the road by the Eel River and thought about seeds being planted.

And so at our breakfast table as I listen with the little ones to the old, old stories, I pray that Jesus' words will fall on good soil, to be held fast in honest and good hearts, and bring forth much fruit (Luke 8:15).

Mr. Electrico

Ray Bradbury

The longer I live the more I see how God often touches our lives through other people. I'll never forget that magical autumn afternoon when He used Mr. Electrico to touch mine. It happened when I was twelve, in my hometown of Waukegan, Illinois, on Lake Michigan's shore.

It was the kind of golden September day when farewell summer touched the land while the autumn wind promised winter. It was also the day when the Dill Brothers Combined Traveling Shows came to town.

To me, the Dill Brothers Shows might well have come from Katmandu, the other side of the moon or the outer rings of Saturn. As soon as their gasoline generators coughed awake and the calliope's chords drifted over the seared fields, I dashed headlong toward this faded and patched canvas wonderland.

I ran so hard I tasted iron, and my heart exploded as I arrived at the sideshow where I stared openmouthed at Mr. Electrico. A towering hawk-nosed figure with a fiery stare that put out your eyes, he spoke in tones I felt proclaimed God's truth. With a flourish of his black cape, he ensconced himself in a wondrous electric chair, and an assistant threw a switch and proclaimed, "Here go ten million volts of pure fire, ten million volts of electricity into the flesh of Mr. Electrico!"

As the current surged through his body, his white hair billowed into a bright halo, his body seemed to glow and incandescent fire danced at his fingertips. I watched mesmerized as he picked up a silver sword, leaned down and with it touched *me* on both shoulders, then the tip of my nose. The electricity surged through me, making *my* hair stand on end. He shouted, *"Live forever!"*

I fell back stunned. His words brimmed my ears like a divine command. I did not know that the electricity used in such performances was of low amperage and harmless, but I did know that something incredible was happening to me.

The next day, even while attending an uncle's funeral, I could not forget Mr. Electrico. As our car headed home for the family's post-funeral wake, to my parent's consternation I leaped out and raced down the hill to the carnival. I carried with me a ball-in-vase trick I had ordered through the mail from Johnson Smith & Co. as an excuse to see Mr. Electrico. I *had* to find out just how to "Live forever!" How did it fit with what I'd learned Sundays at my Baptist church? I sensed that we could live on with God after we died, but Mr. Electrico's proclamation indicated something different.

I found him wandering thoughtfully among the tents. He seemed happy to see me and offered to introduce me to his fellow performers. Before we entered he slapped the side of the faded tent with his cane and cried, "Clean up your language!"

The sideshow folks "cleaned up their language" and he ushered me in and introduced me to the Skeleton Man, the Fat Woman, the Illustrated Man and the Bearded Lady. Then we walked out to the sandy shore of Lake Michigan, where we sat on a log. He talked his small philosophies and let me talk my big ones.

It was a long conversation that lasted until the lake horizon melted into dusk. What were my goals? What was the meaning of my life? As we talked, I discovered he had been a Presbyterian minister. As I was to learn, he was still ministering.

He spoke of how important it was for us to be true to what we had been given to do in life. And on that log I began to realize just what he meant by "Live forever!" He wasn't referring to salvation. His emphasis was on the word *live*. He was saying that this life too was sacred and must be lived to the fullest. Each day, each hour was precious. Each of us must make the most of every moment to use the gifts God had given us.

As I listened to Mr. Electrico, I realized that a few years before, I had almost discarded the gift God had given me. At age nine the call of distant planets had excited my imagination. I had carefully cut out Buck Rogers comic strips from our local newspaper. But when the kids in school learned about it they made fun of me. I tore them up in embarrassment. A month later I burst into tears and wondered why I was crying. Who had died? *Me!* For I had listened to those fools who couldn't understand my gift or my need for the influence of Buck Rogers in shaping my future. I went back to collecting him. I was made whole again.

Something happened to me as Mr. Electrico and I talked through that warm autumn afternoon. His blazing sword had truly fired my imagination, to make me fully realize what my calling in life was.

Though I had done some writing, after my encounter with Mr. Electrico I began to write faithfully every day. I asked for and got a Simplex toy typewriter from my parents for Christmas. It took hours to compose a single paragraph on the machine, dialing letters on a rubber disc and pressing them one by one against the paper. But I wrote all of my first stories with the wondrous gift.

Since that one bright afternoon with Mr. Electrico I have
never stopped writing. Thus I celebrate the gift God has given
me. I believe each of us has such a talent to put to work to find
ourselves and in the finding help others. Some ignore their talents, some let friends talk them out of their gifts as not being
"practical." Sadly, too many forgo their inherent genetic ability
in the mindless pursuit of money.

I'll never forget the taxi driver I once met in New York; he
took great joy in celebrating his gift. He was a joy to ride with
because he madly loved his cab. It must have been thirty years
old but he kept it polished so that it blazed. When we reached
our destination, he jumped out to lift the hood and proudly
displayed its motor. It was all silver-chromed; he had burnished
every part by hand. As the engine purred between us like a
huge contented cat, I looked up at him to see a delighted, fulfilled man.

He knew how to live. Somewhere, long ago, he had met *his*
Mr. Electrico!

I'm a Free Man Now

Johnny Cash

Now I looked at the old man. He looked like he was behind bars. But I knew that I was the one behind the bars, only I didn't know where the jail was or how I got there.

The old man said, "Let me know when you're ready."

I forced myself to sit up. "I'm ready now."

Ready for what? I wasn't sure why I'd been arrested. I figured it had something to do with the pills. Once before, the pills had put me behind bars, but that time I was lucky.

That was in 1965. I had gone into Mexico to get a supply of the pills I felt I needed to stay alive. As I was re-entering at El Paso, the customs inspector found the pills. That time I spent a day in jail. Because it was my first arrest, the judge let me off with a year's suspended sentence. There was a newspaper reporter in the courtroom; his story went out on the wires, and that's how people found out I was an addict.

A lot of people already knew. By then, I had been on pills five years. I took pep pills to turn me on enough to do a show. Then I took depressants to calm down enough to get some sleep. That, at least, was what my friends said. They said I was working too hard and traveling too much and trying to squeeze too much out of every day. They said maybe I should take some time off.

I knew better. I tried pep pills the first time because they happened to be available one day when I was in the mood for a new kick. The high they gave me was beautiful. I felt I owned the world, and the world was perfect during those lofty moments. I couldn't believe that a couple of little pills could contain so much beauty and joy. I stayed on pills because they made me feel great. If people wanted to give excuses for my habit, I let them.

Then I began to realize that the highs were getting lower. The few pills I was on every day weren't enough anymore. I had to go from a few to several, then to dozens. Still that old feeling wasn't there. I was always nervous and tense and irritable. I didn't want to eat. I couldn't sleep. I started losing weight.

So I went on depressants, looking for lows, looking for peace. When I found peace, I couldn't trust it because I knew it was a fleeting peace. Soon I would crave to get high, and the highs would not come to me.

After the El Paso mess, I took an apartment with a friend who was also on pills. One day when my supply ran out, I remembered that he had some in his car. He was asleep and I couldn't find his keys, so I went out and broke into the car. When he later accused me of this, I denied it violently and we almost fought. He knew I was lying, and I knew he did. Next day, I admitted it, and he said he understood. We were like two cowardly kids forgiving each other for being afraid of the dark.

In time, I became afraid of everything. I would be a nervous wreck before a show; I was never sure of myself during a performance; I didn't believe people when they said things had gone all right. Sometimes I was too sick to work. Sometimes I didn't even show up. It didn't take booking agents long to stop risking their money on me. Even though I knew this meant a loss of income to others in the show, people who were good friends, I didn't care. I didn't care about anything.

.. ..

I knew I was killing myself. I had seen drugs kill others. Whatever drug an addict is hooked on, he has to keep increasing his daily dosage to feel anywhere near normal. This is the nature of addiction. The day comes when he takes the overdose that kills him. Knowing this, I accepted early death as the inescapable fate of addicts: There was just no other way out. Even when I thought of all the things I had to be thankful for, I could find no hope for myself, no chance for change.

I was twelve, I remembered, when electricity came to the small Arkansas farm where I was raised. Dad bought a radio, and I'll never forget the first Saturday night I heard the exciting country music from the Grand Ole Opry, in Nashville. That moment, I discovered my future. Right away, I started writing my own country songs, and I told everybody I was going to become an entertainer. I guess only my mother believed me. We were poor, and so she took in laundry to pay for a few voice lessons. At seventeen, I earned my first money at performing: the fifteen-dollar first prize in an amateur contest. Then I learned to play the guitar.

In 1954, I attended a radio-announcing school, hoping that becoming a disc jockey might open doors to performing. To earn a living, I sold housewares door-to-door. I got to know guitarist Luther Perkins and bassist Marshall Grant. We put together an act; we rehearsed a lot; we worked whenever we could, whether or not we got paid. After a year, we agreed that the only way we could find out if we were ready for the Big Time was to audition for somebody big.

We auditioned for Sun Records, which led to our first recording. This led to a two-year contract at the Grand Ole Opry.

We made more recordings. We went on the road. We

became known. By 1960 we had advanced enough to put together a show of our own. Then I moved on to the high of pills.

By 1967, I was on the verge of a nervous breakdown, and I knew it. I was usually on a hundred pills a day, but I got no pleasure from them, no peace. I couldn't stand my life, but I couldn't find my way out of it. One day my friends talked to me about entering a mental institution, and the thought of that completely shattered me. I got into my car, well supplied with pills, and headed south. I remember crossing the Georgia border. Next thing I knew, I was staring at a ceiling and an elderly jailer was asking me if I felt better.

I got up. He unlocked the door. I asked, "How did I get here?"

He said, "One of the night men found you stumbling around the streets. He brought you in so you wouldn't hurt yourself."

I followed him down a corridor and into his office, and I asked, "How much time do you think I'll get for this?"

He shook his head. "You're doing time right now, Johnny, the worst kind." He handed me an envelope. "Here are your things." As I was putting things into my pockets, he said, "I'm a fan of yours, Johnny. I've always admired you. It's a shame to see you ruining yourself. I didn't know you were this bad off."

I'd heard that sad song before, from concerned friends. I said, "Yeah. Sure."

He said, "I don't know where you think you got your talent from, Johnny, but if you think it came from God, then you're sure wrecking the body He put it in."

I said, "Yeah. Sure. Thanks. Can I go now?" He nodded.

That morning, as I stepped into the warm sunshine, I took a

quick but deep look at my life over the past seven years, and I knew that I was a better man than that.

Maybe it was the reference to God that suddenly cleared my mind. I had been raised by religious parents; faith had always meant a lot to me; I have tried to express it in some of my songs. But until that morning it hadn't occurred to me to turn to God for help in kicking my habit.

I remembered this: "Know ye not that your body is the temple of the Holy Spirit which is in you, which ye have of God, and ye are not your own?" 1 Corinthians 6:19 (KJV). This helped convince me that I must try to break my habit. But how?

And I remembered this: God had given me a free will, and I had freely used it in deciding to experiment with the drugs, which had now robbed me of it. I realized that to be free again I would need all the will power I could acquire, and I knew this power could come only from God, who had created me free. I asked Him to go to work on me, then and there.

Back in Nashville, I went to June Carter and Marshall Grant, and I told them, "I'm kicking pills, as of now. I don't expect it to be easy, so I'll need your help. See to it that I eat regular meals. See to it that I keep regular hours. If I can't sleep, sit and talk to me. If we run out of talk, then let's pray."

We prayed a lot. I am a free man now, as I have been since that morning when I discovered that I could be once again.

Because of the kind of work I do, it is difficult to sweep past mistakes under the rug. Every once in a while, I meet some youngster who knows I used to be an addict, as he is now, and he asks me what he can do to kick his habit. I tell him what I learned, "Give God's temple back to Him. The alternative is death."

The Vow I Almost Forgot

Danny Thomas

Many people seem to know that I once vowed to Saint
Jude that I'd build a shrine in his name if he'd help
me through a difficult time in my life. Yet the fascinating part
of that story is how, when I failed to keep my part of the bar-
gain, that saint resolutely refused to let me off the hook.

If you're not a Catholic, as I am, such talk of shrines and
vows and saints might sound a bit strange, but when I was
growing up in a deeply religious family in Toledo, Ohio, these
things were familiar matters. My parents had come from
Lebanon, a country where shrines dedicated to favorite patron
saints are familiar sights. Often these shrines are simply stat-
ues, or little places where you can stop to meditate and pray.

We Catholics, of course, do not worship these patron
saints—we worship only God—but we do look upon them as
special intercessors with God, and we choose them as our
guardians and protectors. And, believe me, as one of nine kids
in a very poor immigrant family, I was grateful for all the protection I could get!

My mother did not hesitate to make her own spiritual vows.
I remember especially a solemn promise she made shortly after
the birth of my youngest brother. His name was Danny. At that
time my name was Amos—Amos Jacobs—but early in my
show business career, I took the names of my youngest and
oldest brothers and became Danny Thomas.

When the first Danny was a few months old, he was badly

bitten by a rat that jumped into his crib. He screamed and went into convulsions. At the hospital the doctors told my mother that Danny was dying, but she wouldn't accept that. She went to her knees in prayer, promising God that if her baby's life were saved she'd beg alms for the poor for a year.

Danny got well, and every day for twelve months my mother, herself one of the poorest of the poor, living in shabby, cramped quarters over a pool hall, went out and begged pennies from door to door.

My mother's faith in God was so strong that she could not possibly give in to fear or hopelessness. To her, despair was a tool of the devil—it was doubting God, and that was a sin. As each of us children was born, she turned us over to God and after that she would not let herself, or us, forget that we had Him to turn to.

When I was ten years old, I landed a job hawking soda pop in the old Columbia burlesque theater in Toledo, which meant that I wouldn't get home until 2:30 in the morning. One day I heard a neighbor asking my mother if she wasn't worried about the things that might happen to her little boy, but my mother's reply rang with certainty "Amos is safe," she said. "I've given him into the care of the Blessed Mother." She knew that I was in good hands, and so did I.

I always had my heart set on being an entertainer, and during the seven years I spent at the burlesque theater, I studied some of the best comedians in the business and grew all the more determined to be one, too. I quit school at sixteen and worked as a busboy, a night watchman, a drill-press operator's assistant, all the while picking up odd jobs singing and clowning at local banquets. Eventually I went to Detroit and sang for a while on a radio program. That's where I met and married

Rosemarie, who's been my wife ever since. And that's where I faced the first real crisis of my life.

In June 1940, a baby was on the way. I was making two dollars a night as an M.C. at a Detroit supper club called the Club Morocco. Then it was announced that on Saturday night the club would close for good. I had no job to go to, and no prospects.

Rosemarie was urging me to consider looking for a more reliable line of work, but all I myself wanted was show business. I wasn't worried about our future. I wasn't in despair— my mother had taught me too well for that—but the time had come when I had to choose a realistic career, for me and for my family.

Rosemarie talked about my going into the grocery business. I had to consider her wishes. Maybe she was right, maybe I could never make my way—and ours—as an entertainer. I was in an agony of indecision.

On Tuesday night a man came into the Club Morocco. He was celebrating something. His pockets were filled with little cards that he was handing out to people as he tried to tell them about an incredible thing that had just happened to him. His wife was in a hospital where she'd been facing an operation for a deadly cancer. All night long this man had knelt on the cold marble floor of the hospital and prayed the same prayer over and over again. When the sun came up in the morning, the doctors called him in to report that, inexplicably, miraculously, his wife's cancer had disappeared.

"This is the prayer that did it," he said, handing me one of the cards. It was the prayer to Saint Jude.

All that night I thought about this man and his appeal to a saint whom I knew only slightly as "Patron of the Hopeless" or "The Forgotten Saint." Though an apostle of Jesus, Jude was not one of the saints whom many Catholics turned to, probably because of his name, which was really Judas Thaddeus, far too similar to that of the hated Judas Iscariot.

The next day I went into a church to pray, and when I reached into my pocket for a coin, I found the card the man had given me. Then and there I felt moved to make my vow. I did not ask for anything specific like money or fame, but I promised Saint Jude that if he would help me find some clear course for my life, I would build him a shrine.

The day after the Club Morocco closed, I drove my old Buick down to Toledo and left Rosemarie with my parents while I took one last stab at looking for work in show business. My plan was to go to Cleveland where I had a number of contacts, but at the last moment, I turned the other way and went to Chicago. It was almost as though I was being drawn there.

Chicago became my town. Very quickly one little radio job led to another, and in a short time I was flourishing as a character actor. Then I tried my hand again as a stand-up entertainer. I opened before eighteen customers in a converted automobile showroom called the 5100 Club; in a few months there were that many people waiting outside trying to get in. Success simply piled upon success.

And what happened to my vow to Saint Jude? Nothing. I was so busy that for two years I had forgotten about it. But Saint Jude had not.

On the way home after a night at the 5100 Club, I used to go to the 5:00 a.m. mass at St. Clement's Church. One morning I picked up a little pamphlet that lay beside me in the pew and, to my surprise, read about a novena—a nine-day period of devotion—about to be offered to none other than my old friend Saint Jude. Even more surprising was the information that there, on the south side of Chicago, was the first national shrine to Saint Jude. Chicago was Saint Jude's town, too! He wanted me to know it.

I did not forget Saint Jude again. I knew I had to do something about fulfilling my vow, but I couldn't make up my mind what kind of a shrine I should build. Rosemarie suggested that I think about a statue, or perhaps a side altar, but somehow nothing seemed right to me. Time went by. I moved on to New York. My career progressed to movies and TV. Still I could not make up my mind.

And then came the dream.

I dreamed one night about a little boy being injured in a car accident. He was rushed to the hospital, but for some reason the doctors were reluctant to treat him and the boy bled to death. The dream was so vivid, so horrifying, that it troubled me for days. But out of that dream came an idea, an idea born of a lifetime of experiences. I thought about the man who had prayed for his wife all night on the cold hospital floor. I thought of my infant brother Danny grabbing hold of life just when the doctors said he was dying, and slowly I began to see Saint Jude's shrine as a hospital. And what better way to honor the Patron Saint of the Hopeless than with a place where "dying" children, children with "incurable" diseases could come to be healed?

That, of course, was the beginning of Saint Jude's Children's Research Hospital in Memphis, Tennessee. It is the only institution on this earth dedicated solely to the conquest of catastrophic diseases. It is open to children of all faiths and races regardless of their parents' ability to pay. No family ever pays for the services rendered there. They are free.

It took me ten years to raise the money to get the hospital started. I did it mainly through benefit performances, going all over the country raising money from Catholics and Protestants and Jews—and Moslems, too—and especially getting help from people of my own Lebanese heritage. I never went before one of those benefit audiences that I didn't think about my mother going door to door begging pennies; for, in my own way, I was doing the same thing, for the same reason.

Today when I look at the hospital that Saint Jude brought into being, when I see the hope that the Saint of the Hopeless has brought to thousands of parents and their youngsters, I am as certain as my mother was certain, that to fight despair is to affirm our faith in God and in the love He has for all of us.

PART 5

The Power in Prayer

God has heard your prayer
and remembered your gifts to the poor.
Acts 10:31

B ack in the days of silent movies . . . So much has changed since then. But nothing has changed in terms of the "tip" Rudolph Valentino gave to actress Dagmar Godowsky: the secret to success that transformed her life.

You may not think of the notable men and women in this section as being people of prayer, but each of them knew the power of God, working through His children's prayers—asking for His blessing, His guidance, His healing, His protection and peace.

You are coming to a King,
Large petitions with you bring
For His grace and power are such
None can ever ask too much.
John Newton

The Secret Rudolph Valentino Taught Me

Dagmar Godowsky

T he other night I watched a revival of a Rudolph
Valentino movie, and I sat there with tears in my eyes
through the whole film. Valentino is remembered mostly as a
great ladies' man; but one day, many years ago, I saw a side of
him that few people knew existed, and the experience changed
my life.

I became stage-struck at an early age, and with it came a
case of excruciating stage fright. When I began to perform, my
blood would grow increasingly colder as curtain time neared
every night, and I'd be sure I couldn't go on.

Once on stage, however, I always regained my composure
and could proceed through the performance without any problems. Even though I knew my fears were temporary, I could
never avoid them and I always dreaded going to the theater for
the nightly suffering.

In making movies, my fears were worse. The "takes" were
short, and there was always much waiting around as the camera crew and the light crew rearranged their equipment. For
me, those waiting periods were like waiting for the curtain to
go up, and I spent most of the day in a state of absolute terror.

In 1924, I was cast in the title role of *A Sainted Devil*, playing opposite Rudolph Valentino. The picture was being made
at the Famous Players-Lasky Studio on Long Island. The morn-

ing I headed for the studio for the first day's work, I could feel the fears and the nausea rising inside me, and by the time I walked on to the set, I was actually ill. And I went on like that, day after day.

Making matters worse was the fact that we had to shoot many of the scenes twice, for the American and European versions. This meant the picture would take longer to make than usual, and I was sure I would never survive.

This time, the fright was greater than ever before. I wondered if working with a superstar like Valentino was the reason. But I had worked with superstars before—Lionel Barrymore, Wallace Reid, Alla Nazimova. I couldn't understand my panic, and I thought seriously of giving up acting if it was going to keep having this effect on me.

We had been working on *A Sainted Devil* for a month when, at the end of a day, Valentino came to my dressing room and asked, "Daggie, did you bring your car to the studio today?"

"I don't have a car, Rudy. I don't like to drive. I use taxis," I replied.

"Then let me give you a lift into town," he said. "I want to talk to you about something."

Minutes later, Valentino was driving us into the city, and we chatted idly about nothing special. I wondered what was on his mind and when we would get to it. We entered Manhattan on the 59th Street Bridge, and, after a few blocks, Rudy drew the car up to a curb and parked.

"I make this stop twice a day, going to work and coming back. Let's go in," Rudy said.

I looked at the building. It was a Catholic church. Although I am not a Catholic, I had been educated in Catholic convents in Europe, so I knew how I should act. We went into the church, Rudy chose a pew, we genuflected together, then entered the pew and knelt. From the movement of his lips, I could tell that Rudy was praying. Since he was an Italian, I had assumed he was a Catholic, but I had no idea that he was devout.

Then he startled me by turning to me suddenly and saying, "Daggie, I'm worried about you. We all are. Why do you always seem to be on your deathbed all day? What's wrong?"

Frustrated, I said, "I don't know, Rudy. I have been like this ever since I started acting. I'm all right once I get going, but it kills me to get started. I am always so afraid."

"I used to be like that," he said.

I couldn't believe it. "You were?"

He nodded. "Yes. You at least attended acting school before you went to work. I didn't. I fell into this business because a few of the right people thought I photographed well. At first I was terrified that the other actors—the directors, the crews—would see how lousy I was, and I got sick as a dog every day."

"How did you get over it?"

He pointed at the altar, then said, "I decided that God was my only audience. I decided that if I had any acting ability, it was because He gave it to me. God became the only Person I had to satisfy. Since then, every morning on the way to work I stop off in a church and ask God for a good day. Going home, I stop off again, thanking Him or asking Him why the day had gone badly. He's always told me."

"How?" I asked.

"He tells my heart," Rudy said, "usually by reminding me that my troubles are my own because I have been unkind or thoughtless or shortsighted. I ask Him to help me change. Anyway, in time I lost my fears about what others thought of me and cared only about what God thought of me, not only as an actor but as a man. And I stopped getting sick."

"I wish I could," I said.

"You can," he said, "and I will help you. As long as we are working on this movie, I'm going to pick you up every morning and we are going to make a stop here. And we will stop off again on our way back. Daggie, you've got to learn to trust God before you can know how to love Him. And once you love Him, He will take care of all your problems."

Going to work the next morning, Valentino and I stopped at the church, and I asked God for a good day. On the set, as we were awaiting the day's first take, Rudy said, "Now, Daggie, remember who your audience is." I kept remembering all day. That evening in the church, I was able to thank God for the least troubled day of my career. Gradually I learned that all aspects of my life became less troubled as long as I kept remembering that I had an unseen audience who was always watching over me, and that brought me an inner peace that has lasted over the years.

People tell me that I must have many wonderful memories about the golden era of the silent movies. I do, and my favorite memory is that the screen's greatest lover taught me how to love God.

Life after Baseball

Dave Dravecky

You may remember the video picture of me breaking my left arm as a result of a pitch I threw in Montreal on August 15, 1989. It seemed at the time as if the whole country saw the gruesome replay that kept showing on television. It was a big story. It was also the end of my baseball career.

Looking at the picture now, I can still feel the pain that seared through the whole left side of my body like a lightning bolt. I remember a collective gasp rising from the stands as I tumbled over in a writhing heap on the hard, blue-green Astro Turf, and the horrified looks of my teammates on the San Francisco Giants who raced to the mound—first baseman Will Clark, catcher Terry Kennedy, trainer Mark Letendre, manager Roger Craig. Even the Expos batter, Tim Raines, trotted out. He'd heard the sharp crack of my arm snapping, like a pistol shot, all the way at home plate, 60 feet 6 inches away. And I remember closing my eyes and asking, "What can You possibly have in store for me now, Lord?"

It was a good question. That last pitch was more than the end of a playing career: It was the end of a sports drama that had played out over the previous weeks in front of a rapt national audience. It had culminated five days earlier, on August 10, in San Francisco's Candlestick Park, amid a deluge of media coverage, when I pitched—and won—my first major league game nearly a year after surgery for removal of a cancerous tumor in my pitching arm.

I will never forget the day Dr. George Muschler at the Cleveland Clinic diagnosed the tumor. It was September 23, 1988. My wife, Janice, was with me in the examining room as Dr. Muschler explained the surgery that would remove half of the deltoid muscle in my left arm, the large muscle that runs from your shoulder to your humerus bone.

Janice wanted to be very clear about what the doctors were telling us. "In other words," she said, her voice wavering slightly, "short of a miracle, Dave will never pitch again."

"That's right," Dr. Muschler replied sadly but absolutely. "Short of a miracle, he'll *never* pitch again."

God gave us that miracle. In the face of all odds, and without most of my deltoid muscle, I came back. The doctors couldn't figure out how I was doing it. They thought that after surgery I'd be lucky to be able to pull my wallet out of my back pocket. Just lifting my arm over my head would signal a remarkable recovery. Far from worrying about saving my career, they were focused on saving the *arm*. Yet in less than a year I was striking out major league hitters. Everyone called it unexplainable, but the explanation was clear to me. Dr. Muschler had said so himself: It could only be God answering prayer.

Why then, I wondered as I was carried off the field in Montreal that day, with players from both sides looking on in tears, had God done so much and brought me so far just to take back the miracle He'd given?

I'd been pitching baseball competitively since high school back in Boardman, Ohio, a quiet suburb of Youngstown. I did my hard time in the minor leagues, where pitching instructors gave me little chance of making the bigs. I endured dysentery and loneliness throwing winter ball in South America. It was there, in Barranquilla, Colombia, during the darkest days of my career, that I began to develop a spiritual yearning for something more in my life than the baseball diamond. There had to be a greater plan.

A year later, struggling in lowly Double A ball in Amarillo, Texas, I met someone who helped me start to find an answer. He was my roommate, Byron Ballard, a likable young pitcher. The first thing I noticed about Byron was that he had hair the color of saffron, with freckles to match, and size fifteen feet. The other thing was that he spent most of his spare time reading and talking about the Bible. For a long time I listened and asked questions. Pretty soon I was reading the Bible too—devouring it. All that hot summer, while other players around me were cursing the hard, scorched infields and brutal game temperatures, the meager meal money and run-down motels, a change I had never dreamed was transfiguring my life and putting the world in an entirely new and startling perspective.

So seven years later, when the bad news about my arm came from Dr. Muschler at the Cleveland Clinic, it had been the most natural thing in the world for Janice and me to pray for a healing. As painful as the thought was of giving up baseball in mid-career, a career I'd worked so hard to build and was just beginning to enjoy the fruits of, we understood it would be completely up to God if I made it back. When the doctors insisted it was impossible, Janice and I knew better and said so. We trusted in the Lord's plan, whatever it was.

When my arm broke after my big comeback game, I was disappointed—all that sweat and pain just to pitch a handful of innings. But angry, no. I knew that God must have something else in mind. What, I wasn't sure. But like any athlete, the prospect of retirement was tough. The career of a ballplayer is relatively short. For most of us it is over way too soon. You grow up being a ballplayer; walking away from it in the prime of your life is the hardest thing you'll do, no matter how successful you've been. In the movie *Field of Dreams* one of the phantom old-time ballplayers who vanishes mysteriously into the cornfield after each "imaginary" game cries out in a joking imitation of *The Wizard of Oz's* Wicked Witch: "Help me! I'm melting!" Melting away—that's how the thought of leaving baseball sounds to those of us who have been fortunate enough to play the game.

On November 13, 1989, I announced my retirement, at the age of thirty-three. I'd broken my arm a second time that fall when I was inadvertently knocked to the field in the wild celebration that followed the Giants clinching the National League pennant. It was clear that without the deltoid muscle to help support it, my humerus bone was acutely vulnerable to stress fractures.

Not long after, doctors informed us that the tumor had returned. I would undergo another operation along with a new treatment that involved surgical implantation of "spikes" containing a small amount of radioactive material. This time I would lose the remainder of my deltoid muscle. In fact losing the whole arm was now a real and frightening possibility.

In the face of such an uncertain future, other things began happening in my life. I'd never particularly cared for all the media attention I got during my comeback. But the one good thing it did give me was a chance to say a few words publicly about my faith, and to set an example for other cancer patients, many of whom suffered far more serious forms of the disease than I. Now people were asking me to speak all over the country—at churches, hospitals, business meetings. I was a bit embarrassed at how much in demand I was. I wrote a book. Movie producers contacted me about doing my story. I was busier than ever.

It dawned on Janice and me that none of this could have happened if a small mysterious lump on my arm had not turned into something else. Which is not to say God gave me cancer—He didn't. But it was only through the love of God that I was led to find good in tragedy. The real miracle in my life was not that I came back from an impossible situation and played ball again. The real miracle in my life—in everyone's life—is that the Son of God came down to earth to suffer and die for our sins and redeem our souls. And that His love is always ready for us.

Inevitably there are times when I miss baseball, when I can practically hear the hum of the crowd as the players take the field. I see a game on television and immediately I am drawn into thinking how I would pitch the batter: slider on the out-side corner of the plate, a change-up out of the strike zone, then *boom*, a fastball in on the hands. Keep 'em guessing. Sometimes it's just a feeling in the air on a humid summer night, the kind of night when a pitcher's arm can get warm and loose and great things might happen.

In the spring of 1991 Janice and I returned to Scottsdale, Arizona, where the Giants train. Actually I was just along for the ride. Janice was speaking to a group of the baseball wives.

For a moment, when I first stepped into camp and heard the crack of wood on hard leather and saw a ball arc lazily into the deep desert sky, it was as if nothing had changed. I felt almost as if I could lace on my cleats again and go nine. But then just as quickly, before that ball smacked into the outstretched glove of a rookie outfielder, my separation from the game became crystallized and final, and I was at peace. It is a chapter of my life that's closed now. I am grateful for every second of it, especially those last few miraculous innings no one ever dreamed I'd get.

I've had several surgeries since my retirement. After each one there seems to be a little less of my left arm to save.

One thing I know. God never takes back a miracle. He just uses miracles in our lives to point the way.

A Medal for Freddie

Rosalind Russell

Lanky, graying Hans Christian Adamson was visiting us in Hollywood when we noticed the first strange turn in our old battle. We were at dinner, back in 1942. It was a long table; I sat at the head of it, Hans Adamson was at my right, and my husband, Freddie Brisson, sat at my left. We were all chatting, when suddenly Hans reached into his pocket and fished among his coins.

Now, Hans and my husband were close friends in spite of the twenty years difference in their ages. They were both officers in the Air Force. Hans Adamson was one of the best-read men I have ever known, which is why Freddie and I took so seriously his views on religion.

Hans was also an agnostic.

Not antireligious; he was interested in religion, but there were things he could not accept with his rational mind. Back at his home on the East Coast, he used to attend church occasionally with his wife, Helen, who was an Episcopalian. But we had the feeling it was more out of respect for her than for her beliefs. Hans often said he envied people who could believe without understanding. "But that's as far as I can go," he would tell us. "I try to understand your churches and your little medals and things. But I cannot. So I cannot believe."

That's why it struck us as so peculiar when Hans fished among his change that night and brought out a medal.

"Freddie," Hans said, and it seemed that his voice pitched a note higher than usual, "Freddie, I stopped at the PX and got you one of those new flying medals, St. Joseph of Copertino. I think he flew or something. You're going to do a lot of flying, and I want you to have this."

With that, the second strange turn occurred. I grabbed Hans's sleeve. I spoke impulsively.

"No. Keep that yourself."

"Why?" Hans asked. "I don't want any medals. I got it for Freddie. He's a Catholic and he believes in these things."

I realized I had spoken sharply, and I tried to soften it down. "What I mean is, you keep it for now, Hans. You just keep it for now."

I tried to change the subject. The dinner party was ruined. But in my mind, I sensed a premonition that actually I had done the right thing . . . that Hans was trying to tell us something with that medal.

Three months later Hans phoned my husband that he was going on a secret mission across the Pacific, and that he would be coming out to California for a visit.

We spent the day together in Beverly Hills. Hans kept saying that he felt nervous. He had never talked that way before. There is not a bit of cowardice in Hans Adamson, yet he kept saying the trip had a fatality about it.

At six the next morning the phone rang.

It was Hans.

"Will you do something for me? Will you call Helen and say good-bye again?"

I was puzzled why Hans didn't call his wife himself. At first I thought he was afraid of alarming her by calling so early. But I answered, "Of course I will."

Then, once more, Hans said something about the trip. Right out of the blue I sat bolt upright in bed.

"Hans, do you have that medal that you tried to give Freddie some time ago?"

Hans was silent for a moment, as if he didn't want to answer.

"Yes," he finally admitted, "I've got it in my pocket with my change."

"Now, mind you I don't think anything is going to happen. But if it does, you take that medal out and put it in your hand and hold on to it."

There was a prolonged silence. I thought I had offended Hans. When he did answer, it was with a single word:

"Yes . . ."

After he hung up, I couldn't get back to sleep. "What's the matter?" Freddie asked.

I told him I felt something was going to happen. I wished I had explained more to Hans about the Catholic use of medals, how we don't claim special powers for the medal itself, how the medal helps us focus our prayers, reminds us of our need for prayer. But I had missed my chance.

We were about to get up when Freddie mentioned: "Oh, by the way, Roz, Hans has a rather famous companion for his trip across the Pacific."

"Yes?"

"Captain Eddie Rickenbacker . . ."

It was perhaps the most famous airplane crash in history. Captain Eddie Rickenbacker, Hans, and six others went down in the Pacific.

Twenty-one days were to pass before their rubber rafts were finally spotted. Twenty-one days of torture for us too . . . waiting.

When the headlines shouted the rafts were spotted, we felt strangely quiet. As if we were being drained of the last of some sort of strength. We learned that Hans was still alive, although from the very first reports he was on the critical list. The men were kept in overseas hospitals for five weeks before they could be moved.

Then, just before Christmas, I got a call at the studio. It was from my husband, at the air base. The hospital plane was coming into San Francisco. Hans had sent a message that he wanted me to be there, that he had something that he wanted to tell me.

We saw Captain Rickenbacker first. He stepped off the plane, perhaps the thinnest man I have ever seen. His shirt stuck out inches, literally, from his neck. His eighty-year-old mother was there to greet him. He walked toward her and she toward him for a few paces. Then they stopped. You could feel the pulses of emotion between them. I had to turn away.

Then I was told to get on the plane. Freddie and I climbed a ladder and were inside. Hans was in bed. He looked worse than Rickenbacker.

I was so upset seeing him that I tried to keep the conversation on trivial things: Welcome home, how good it was to see him alive.

Freddie said: "I don't remember hearing about your hand."

The hand was bandaged.

"It's hurt a bit," Hans answered.

And with that he slowly removed the bandage.

There, cupped in his hand, was the medal.

From holding it in the same position for weeks, his hand muscles had frozen so that he could not straighten his fingers. The medal had worked its way into his flesh. Hans looked up to me.

"I didn't even let them take it away in the hospital."

The plane was silent while with his other hand Hans pried the medal loose. Then softly, he spoke again.

"It's all right, Roz. I understand at last . . . May I give Freddie the medal now?"

The Power of Prayer

Ed Sullivan

W hen I was a kid of eighteen, I was a twelve-dollars-a-week sports editor of the Port Chester, N.Y. *Daily Item*. When the *Hartford Post* offered me a fifty-dollars-a-week job, there was a farewell banquet and speeches—glowing speeches about the bright future in Hartford.

Four days after I started work with the *Hartford Post*, the owner announced he was selling the paper. All employees would be given two weeks' pay.

My whole, big, important world crashed. How could I go back to Port Chester? My successor at the *Item* was already at work. At eighteen a lot of false pride can confuse your thinking. And at eighteen every setback is a major calamity.

I got a job in a Hartford department store, wrapping bundles. Everybody in Connecticut was buying pots and pans that week. And wrapping paper neatly around the handles of pans requires artistry not possessed by an ex-sportswriter.

Then an infection developed on the right side of my lower jaw. The pain became so bad I couldn't sleep. I was alone, too proud to go home, in pain and discouraged.

Just a few years before, when a student at St. Mary's School in Port Chester, we would recite the Rosary, rattling off the responses so rapidly that it became a sing-song, devoid of meaning. But when you're in trouble and kneel in prayer by your bed, the "Hail Mary" becomes a very personal salutation.

And your plea: "Pray for us sinners" is the complete recognition of your helplessness—and your faith.

Every young man comes to one crossroad where he is tested for manhood. At this point in Hartford prayer helped me grow up. I quit feeling sorry for myself, stuck with the job I didn't like, went on my own to the Hartford Hospital Clinic, where a young, cheerful doctor cleaned out the infection in my jaw.

Several days later I returned from the department store to find a letter for me on the hallway table. The upper left-hand corner had the imprint, *New York Evening Mail*. I tore it open. It was from Sam Murphy, Sports Editor of the *Mail* and one of my job contacts.

"Dear Sullivan," he wrote. "I have recommended you to our school-page editor, Jack Jacowitz, to cover sports for him. Can you be in New York Monday morning?"

Could I! I wrapped my last pot and pan that Saturday night, caught an express train to Port Chester and home. That same night I was proudly showing to my mother, father, three sisters, and brother that letter and its offer of a job on a big New York daily.

On Monday morning, I went to work on the *Mail*, and for weeks afterward was staring open-mouthed at all the big-name newspaper byliners along Park Row.

All of my life I've been blessed, first with a wonderful father and mother, sisters and brothers. Later with an exceptional wife, special daughter and splendid son-in-law. My TV show dropped into my lap by complete accident. It is my deepest belief that all of these things have resulted from prayer— not so much my own—but prayers of priests and nuns I have known and with whom I've been privileged to work. And certainly the prayers and intercession of those close to me who have died.

So I know about the power of prayer. I know it keeps you steady, unshaken and able to take pain. I know it will guide you to your place—the place that will best help you grow.

The New Year's Eve
I Won't Forget

Buddy Ebsen

The year 1945 was fading fast as my wife, Nancy, and I trudged home that evening in mid-Manhattan. Nancy had met me at a Broadway theater, where I had been rehearsing for my role in a revival of *Show Boat*. With heads lowered against the swirling snow, we headed back to our apartment.

Traffic sounds were muffled in that special hush which snow lends to harsh city streets. Nancy's boots crunched beside mine as we walked in silence, both lost in the kind of thoughts that the year's end brings.

It was a poignant time for us, as it was, I'm sure, for most people during the early post-World War II days when we all seemed to be finding our way again. In my case I was trying to pick up the pieces of a career interrupted three years earlier, when I had volunteered for Coast Guard service.

Serving aboard a ship in the forlorn reaches of the northern Pacific was a far cry from the singing and dancing I had been doing most of my life. And now, beginning all over again found me wondering what the future held. With war memories still churning within me, I felt unsettled, uneasy. Tap dancing on a stage didn't seem to make sense anymore.

I shook my head and squinted as wind whipped snow into my eyes. A clock in a jewelry-store window indicated 11:30 p.m.

We had no plans for a New Year's Eve celebration. However, I did feel hungry. "Why don't we get a bite to eat before we go home?" I said, taking Nancy's arm.

My wife looked up over the muffler covering her face and nodded. A short distance ahead on 54th Street was a little place called Al & Dick's Steak House, where we had often dined. We quickened our steps, but when we reached the restaurant door, it was locked. Nancy and I glanced at each other in disappointment. But then, behind the curtained plate-glass window I could see shadows of people moving. I knocked on the door. It opened a bit and Al Green, one of the owners, peered out. A former pugilist with a broken nose, Al broke into a grin. "Hey, Buddy, Nancy, c'mon in," and he swung the door back.

It turned out that he and his partner, Dick, had invited all of their employees and spouses to a private New Year's Eve gathering. "Join us," urged Al, "you're part of the family."

And so we stepped into the warmth of the restaurant where couples laughed and chatted and loaded their plates with food from a mammoth buffet. Somewhere a piano tinkled. Nancy and I sat at a table and soon found ourselves caught up in the friendly atmosphere.

Suddenly, a hush fell over the restaurant.

I glanced at my watch; almost midnight. Soon the revelry would begin, I thought, expecting to see horns and noisemakers distributed. Instead, Al Green stepped to the center of the room and stood there as others settled at tables or against the wall.

"It's a tradition," whispered one of his waiters leaning over to us. "He does this every New Year's Eve."

As the big wall clock's hands lifted straight up, Al began to sing without accompaniment.

.. ..
146

I was surprised by his rich, resonant voice; it didn't seem to go with his cauliflower ear and broken nose.

Our Father, which art in Heaven, he sang, *hallowed be Thy Name . . .*

I was transfixed. Al, a Jew, was singing to the Father of us all.

. . . . Thy kingdom come . . . he sang.

I was taken back to the little white-frame church in Belleville, Illinois, where I first learned this prayer.

. . . Thy will be done on earth, as it is in Heaven . . . Give us this day our daily bread . . . And forgive us our debts, as we forgive our debtors. . . .

In a rush my thoughts turned back to my growing-up days in Orlando, Florida; to the dancing school my father ran; to our minister telling me after a school play that I *must* go into show business; to my sister Vilma and me whirling to "Tea for Two," dancing our way across the country in shows and movies in those innocent-seeming years before the world was torn apart.

. . . And lead us not into temptation; but deliver us from evil . . .

"Peace, dear Lord . . ." I silently prayed for the conciliation of all nations.

. . . . For Thine is the kingdom, and the power, and the glory, forever.

Al's voice rose powerfully; his words rang with conviction; and then, as the last firm note drifted away, Al lowered his head and sang the last word as a benediction:

Amen.

Tears streamed down my face. Without taking my eyes off Al Green, I said to Nancy, "Never let me lose faith in God, in myself, or in people."

I could hear the noise outside of a city gone wild with celebration, but inside the restaurant there was a deep silence. It lasted only a moment, a moment in which I seemed to hear the noise and feel the confusion of the past three years. And then, as I came back to the present, back to a restaurant on 54th Street in New York City, the war seemed to fade. I felt calm, reassured. I felt God's serenity.

When it was time for us to leave, Nancy and I put on our coats, and amid hearty good wishes from Al, Dick and our "family," we walked out to the street. The snow had stopped. Everything was still, frosted with a neon iridescence. Tall buildings soared above us like church spires. The stars were like tiny sapphires winking in the deep blue.

"Happy New Year," I said to my wife.

"Yes, *Happy* New Year!" she said in reply as we stepped out confidently into a new year and a new world and a new beginning . . .

Panic

Al Kasha

Our bags had already been checked on board. My wife and I were just about to enter the plane to fly from Los Angeles to New York for a vacation. Then the flight attendant asked to see our boarding passes.

Terror swept through me. I felt nauseous. "I, I can't do it!" I said. I turned to my wife, Ceil. "I can't go on the flight."

Ceil tried to calm me down. "Come on, Al," she said. "You can do it. I'll be right next to you. Just *try* to get on. You can listen to the music or watch the movie. It won't last very long. It'll be over in no time."

Instead of calming down I began to panic. "No! No!" I exclaimed. "I just can't do it! I'm sorry, but I can't." We drove back home to Beverly Hills. Our luggage arrived safely in New York.

How had this happened to me—an American success story? From childhood in a small, cluttered apartment in Brooklyn, I had become a successful songwriter, record producer and writer of movie themes. With my partner, Joel Hirschhorn, I had won two Oscars. Now everything seemed to be coming apart. I was unable to get on a plane, go into a store or even leave the house without being gripped by a paralyzing fear. There's a medical name for this. It's called agoraphobia. But then I had no idea what was happening to me. And even less of an idea that I wasn't alone.

Ironically, some of the very things that had pushed me to

succeed were now pulling me down. In the beginning I'd thrived on competition, and much of that competitiveness was born in my own family. I had always felt a driving need to please my parents and I'd come to look upon my older brother, Larry, who had become a Broadway producer, as a rival. Each successful song I wrote made it necessary to write another. Instead of giving me satisfaction, all my achievements only made me press on.

The first attack occurred at a most unexpected time.

The day after Joel and I won our first Oscar for the song "The Morning After," my mother called to congratulate me. "An Oscar is fine," she said, "but when you win a Tony on Broadway, like your brother, then you really have made it."

Those words caused a startling reaction in me. Standing there, holding the phone, I felt my heart begin to pound so hard that I could barely breathe. My palms were drenched and my legs buckled under me. I felt as if I were going to faint, as though I were going to die. The attack didn't last long, but it bewildered me. And frightened me. I didn't want to mention it to anyone, even Ceil.

Before long however, I began to experience moments when fear would take over without warning. Soon I was unable to drive on a freeway without hyperventilating. The first time this happened, Ceil and I were taking our six-year-old daughter, Dana, to Disneyland. I pulled over and grabbed for the door, desperate to escape the confinement of the car. I asked Ceil to drive and told her to go back home.

A few weeks later Joel and I were having lunch in a restaurant. Just as our sandwiches were arriving, I stood up and said, "We've got to leave!" Joel tried to calm me down, but I tore outside. Even though I tried, I couldn't enter another restaurant for two years.

My world kept narrowing. Panic swept over me at the thought of going into a supermarket, even the one right across the street from my house. Once I made the effort to go, only to leave all my packages in the cart in the middle of the aisle. Eventually I couldn't even step outside the front door. I spent all my time in my study.

I began to turn down work because it was impossible for me to have meetings in anyone's office. I rejected an offer to score a film in England, and persuaded the stars of a Broadway musical Joel and I were writing to come to my home to rehearse the songs.

Joel made excuses for me each time I ducked out of an appointment, telling people I was "under the weather." My work as a freelance songwriter made it possible for me to cover up my phobias, but I was in constant fear that my secret would come out.

One of the worst things about my panic attacks was that I didn't know what was causing them. I went to several analysts, but they seemed as puzzled as I was. It was only three years after my first attack when I heard the word *agoraphobia* on a television program.

Shortly afterward, I saw a behavioral therapist who was willing to come to my home. She confirmed that I was indeed a victim of agoraphobia,* the paralyzing anxiety brought on by tension and repressed hostility. She said I wasn't alone: The National Institute of Mental Health estimates that one adult in every twenty suffers from it.

I began attending group therapy sessions, but the meetings

*Also called Panic Attack Syndrome

only frustrated me when I was unable to overcome my fears. I started taking tranquilizers. Home life became an endless series of fights as Ceil grew unable to understand why I couldn't cope, and my anger increased at her inability to help me.

Finally one night Ceil had had enough. She packed my bag and told me to leave. "You've stopped going to the meetings," she cried. "You won't go to a psychiatrist. You won't help yourself, so how can I help you?"

I was hurt and angry. "Nobody can help me," I snapped, and left.

I spent the next three weeks in a friend's apartment. One night I was still awake at three in the morning. Instead of taking a tranquilizer, I picked up the remote control for the television and pushed the button. I could hear the set in the next room come on.

A rerun of a Robert Schuller program was being broadcast. As I lay sprawled out on the bed, I heard Dr. Schuller say, "Love casts out all fear."

My heart started to pound. My hands grew sweaty. *How ironic*, I thought. *With me it's the opposite—fear casts out all love.*

Then Dr. Schuller said, "Only Jesus Christ can set you free from your bondage." I was soaked with sweat and felt a tremendous pressure on my chest. Once more I was afraid—of dying, of losing control. Whatever happened, I had to be in control. Nobody could help me, not even God.

Or could He?

Without knowing why, I slid out of bed and crawled on hands and knees into the next room. "Jesus," I cried as I approached the television set. Then I saw a tremendous light streaming in through the side window. I turned and looked into what appeared to be childlike eyes.

Then a voice said. *You are My son, and I love you.*

It was as if God Himself was talking to me, telling me, *I love you just as you are. You don't have to prove yourself to Me. All I want is for you to trust Me, and let Me take over.*

I blacked out. When I woke up almost three hours later, the television was still on. I got up and shut it off. Intuitively I sensed that something was different in me. As I moved through the apartment I realized my shoulders were taller, my step was lighter. Something was missing, and I laughed when I discovered what it was. That constant weight of having to be in control, of being on top of things, was gone. In its place was peace; for the first time in a long time, I felt at peace.

Yet even though the need for control was gone—what about the fear?

I wanted to see my wife and daughter. I'd swung out the front door and gotten into the car before it hit me—I was outside! I didn't need to call Ceil and ask her to pick me up; I could drive to see her all by myself. I opened the glove compartment. The Valium tablets were there, but I didn't need them.

By the time I got to the house, I was shaking—but with laughter, not fear. I ran up to the door, rang the bell, and grabbed a very startled Ceil Kasha.

"I'm home!" I shouted. "I love you, honey!"

Poor Ceil didn't know whether to laugh or cry. She wasn't sure whether I was cured or had cracked up altogether!

Turning my life over to Christ didn't immediately solve my problems. It took months of hard work and help from family and friends to conquer the symptoms of agoraphobia, and to deal with its root causes. My greatest help came from knowing that God loved me and was with me. I didn't need to fight the battle on my own. Philippians 4:13 became one of my favorite Bible verses: "I can do all things through Christ which strengtheneth me" (KJV).

It had taken me forty-one years of life to finally find God—or to let Him find me—on October 8, 1978. Since that night, I've gone back to writing songs with Joel, and have started an organization called Faith Over Fear to help other agoraphobia victims. If you are one, I want you to know that you are not alone—in one week I received over one thousand eight hundred pieces of mail from other sufferers.

For those people who saw me accepting the Oscar in 1973 and who thought, *That guy has everything*, my answer is, "Yes, I had everything—but it was really nothing without God."

PART 6

The Power in Exemplary Faith

I have not found so great faith,
no, not in Israel.

MATTHEW 8:10

S aint Francis said that we should preach the gospel at all times. "If necessary use words." Some of us are fortunate to work or live with a person whose demeanor, day-in and day-out, exudes the grace and peace of God. The example of that person's faith and goodness is so strong that we search out for ourselves that "something" that makes them tick. Mike Schmidt, Jahja Ling, Tony Dorsett, and Sal Bando were blessed to know such a person, whose very life preached the Good News of salvation.

Something More

Mike Schmidt

The best and the worst year of my life started with a telephone call. From that moment on, a whole series of
strange things went into motion; I haven't been the same person since.

The call came just after baseball season ended in the fall of
1977. Andre Thornton was on the line. "How about getting
together sometime?" he said. I was surprised to hear from him.
Andy was the first baseman for the Cleveland Indians—a real
first-class fellow. We'd been in the minors together, but now we
were playing in different leagues, and I hadn't seen much of
him. I did remember seeing him at batting practice one day the
year before, when he'd come around the batting cage to talk to
me. The unusual glow on his face that day sort of stuck in my
mind.

I learned the reason for Andy's call a week later, when he
and his wife, Gert, came to dinner with Donna and me at our
house in Cherry Hill, New Jersey. Andy was a very religious
man, something I was not and he'd seen something in one of
the sports columns where I'd mentioned God. Well, the press is
always putting words into players' mouths, and I couldn't
remember having said anything about God to any reporter.

It was true that recently I had started dropping in to Baseball Chapel before the game on Sundays. Maybe that's how the
item got in the sports column. However, the weird thing about
it was that I *had* been doing some thinking that you might call

"spiritual." Something was happening to me; something was making me feel uneasy. As we sat down to dinner I wondered if Andy had sensed that.

Actually, things were going so well for me in those days that it seemed silly to feel uneasy. My life had been charmed ever since college when I was all-American in baseball at Ohio University. The Phillies had drafted me in 1971, and except for a rotten rookie year, my career had been on a steady upswing. I'd been the National League's home-run leader in '74, '75 and '76, and I knew I was on my way to becoming the highest-paid player in the league. Still, I couldn't forget the afternoon a few weeks back when I was outside our house casually shooting baskets in the driveway hoop. There was a moment when I looked over at the Mercedes and Corvette parked there. Out back was our swimming pool; inside the house, my beautiful Donna was busy in the kitchen. *What did I do to deserve all this?* I said to myself. *Why am I so blessed?* It's a strange thing to say, but success was bothering me.

We had a good time that night, two baseball players and our wives sharing a meal and lively talk. Gradually the conversation turned serious, and Andy brought up some of the very things that had been on *my* mind, such as why we should have been singled out for baseball stardom, and what it all meant: the prestige, the money, the sports cars, the mansions. It didn't surprise me that Andy related everything to faith in God, and I was impressed with his knowledge of the Bible, yet the memorable part of the evening was still to come. We turned to the subject of families.

Gert and Andy began telling us about their two children, little Theresa and Andy Junior. From across the table Donna and I looked at each other. We each knew what the other was thinking. "Well," I said out loud, "we talk about having it all, but there's one thing Donna and I don't have, something we've been denied—a child."

Andy Thornton was very moved by this, and right then and there, while we were still at the table, he said a prayer for us in simple, direct, beautiful words he asked God to give Donna and me patience and understanding—and a child of our own.

The evening came to a close. Gert and Andy climbed into their van, waved good-bye and drove away.

One week later, Gert and Andy were riding in that same van with their two children. There was a sleet storm. The van skidded and crashed. Andy and their son escaped with minor injuries. Gert and their daughter were killed.

And one week after that, Donna learned she was pregnant.

This was just the start of that best, and worst, year of my life. The grace with which Andy met and survived his heartbreak inspired everyone in baseball, and the public as well. It led me to think deeply about the kind of faith Andy had. I pictured again the glow I'd seen on his face the day he'd called me over by the batting cage. I remembered now how he'd told me about his having given "the reins" of his life to Christ. I thought, at the time, he'd gone off the deep end.

The winter set in. Donna was doing well. But I was still wrestling with my own uneasy thoughts about life, when I happened to come across a calling card in my wallet. It read: Dr. Wendell Kempton, President of the Association of Baptists for World Evangelism.

Kempton had been a speaker at one of those Sunday Baseball Chapels and he'd talked about having been a heavy drinker, "a real party animal," before his conversion. I'd been impressed by his dynamism. Now I didn't even telephone; I drove right to his office in New Jersey. When he seemed pleased to see me, I sat down and said, "Can we just talk?"

Before I left his office, Wendell suggested getting together for dinner and a short session of Bible study at his house. "Why not bring your wife along?" he said. "And any players who might want to come."

Some "short session"! What was supposed to be a half-hour Bible lesson turned into a six-hour marathon in which Wendell traced God's plan of salvation from Genesis through Revelation. We were spellbound. In awe. And so eager to hear more that we decided to meet again in ten days, this time at my house.

By then things were really churning inside me. *Am I living for the Corvette and Mercedes out there in the driveway?* I asked myself. *There has to be something more.*

Alone in our bedroom one day, I came across a pamphlet, a tract, with something on it called "The Sinner's Prayer." I started to read it, then I began to say the words out loud, then little by little those words became my words. I acknowledged my flaws. I acknowledged my need of Jesus. I asked Him to come into my life and be my personal Savior.

At our next Bible class, which six other players and their wives attended, I told everyone what had happened. The group was stunned. Yet when I described what it was like to turn over the reins to Jesus, I think no one thought I'd gone off the deep end.

Spring came. Donna was plump and happy. Together we signed up for some natural-childbirth classes. By the time I went to spring training in Clearwater, I was feeling great. I could tell that this was going to be my best year so far.

How wrong can a guy be?

.. ..

First I bruised my ribs and was on the disabled list for a month. Things went downhill from there. Out of 513 at-bats that year, I got only 129 hits. I struck out 103 times. My batting average was an anemic .251. The press got on my back. The "boo-birds" in the stands never let up. The harder I tried, the worse things got.

"What's this all about?" I asked Wendell Kempton in desperation. "I become a Christian and this is what happens?"

Wendell was patient with me. He knew that eventually I'd understand that being a Christian did not guarantee clear sailing all the time. And he counted on my remembering that I, after all, was the baseball player who had put the worship of God above "success." Meanwhile, Wendell gave me some advice that helped relieve the pressure.

"Mike," he suggested, "when you come to bat, tell the Lord outright that you're going to give Him one hundred percent. If you strike out, you'll strike out doing your best. If you get a hit, that'll be doing your best, too. Put the outcome in His hands."

I tried it. It was tough at first, when the "fans" were screaming for my blood and the negative thoughts crowded in. *Oh . . . I'm oh for four*, I'd think. *Fifty thousand people are expecting me to DO something.*

Then I'd pray, *Lord, clear my mind. Let Your will be done.*

It helped. It helped me get through the season, which, as it turned out, was truly the worst year in baseball I ever had.

But then, it was the best year too, because of Jessica. I was there in the hospital, suited up like a doctor in a gown and mask, watching as my daughter was born. Within minutes, they placed her in my hands. I remember noticing a fleck of crimson on her tiny cheek, where the scalpel had lightly scratched her. Today Jessica is a pretty girl of nine, and that scar is so minuscule that you can see it only if you're looking for it. But it's very dear to me because it reminds me of that wonderful moment when I first held her, and everything on earth and in heaven fell into place.

In that unforgettable moment I knew for certain that life wasn't about money or status or cars, or even baseball stardom. To this day I know it's about things like loving God, serving others; it's about families and husbands and wives loving and respecting one another; it's about having kids to raise and love.

Don't get me wrong; my baseball career is still very important to me. But nowadays I can get a home-run feeling just walking my kids to the school bus in the morning, or playing a game of golf, or hugging Donna, or telling someone about Jesus.

The simple things—they can give you a home-run feeling too.

A Fairy Tale Come True

Jahja Ling

I t's a long, long way from Indonesia to Ohio and from lead-ing a church choir in Jakarta to conducting the Cleveland Orchestra at Severance Hall. Sometimes when I think back over my long journey, I am still amazed at the way it happened. I remember my father, and Miss Lee, and Professor Munz, and the sometimes mysterious coincidences that made it possible. . . .

I grew up in Jakarta. My father, who at the time was inde-pendently wealthy, worked in civil service, first under the Dutch colonial government and then for the Republic of Indonesia. He loved everything Dutch and European—particu-larly music. My two sisters and I grew up listening to Bach, Beethoven and Chopin, and to father talking about the great pianist and conductor, Rubinstein. So because of him I devel-oped a love of music early on.

Then there was Miss Tse-Siu Lee. In those prosperous days, our mansion was so large that my parents invited Miss Lee to conduct her kindergarten class in some of the rooms. We all loved Miss Lee. I can still picture her: a tall middle-aged woman, with graying hair fixed in a bun, wearing a long, traditional Chinese dress. She was so gentle, so caring, so loving.

Miss Lee was also a devout Christian. Although my father practiced ancestor worship at a shrine in our house, he allowed Miss Lee to teach us hymns and read us wonderful Bible stories and tell us about the God-man Jesus, who had lived long ago and had died for our sins.

My parents even allowed Miss Lee to enroll us in a Chinese-Christian Sunday school. Because of her, my sisters and I eventually accepted Christ publicly; then my mother came to believe. Finally my father himself became a Christian.

By coincidence, Miss Lee came to have another important influence on me. My grandmother had purchased an expensive German Ibach piano for my older sister. After she lost interest in her lessons, it stood collecting dust for several years—until Miss Lee began playing it for our kindergarten class. I was only four, but I was fascinated by the big piano and watched Miss Lee. How did she create such beautiful sounds?

One day during class, I climbed onto the stool and played "Choo-Choo Train" by ear. I was only imitating what I had seen Miss Lee do, but Miss Lee saw something else. She went to my parents and said, "This child has a special gift from the Lord. He must have teachers."

By the time I was five, I was playing for the Sunday school and for Christmas pageants and other events. I had a tall stool in order to reach the keys. Visitors would come to watch. My parents were silent but proud. So was Miss Lee.

About this time there was an economic collapse in Indonesia. My father lost nearly everything. We had to leave our lovely big house and servants and the easy life.

A few years later, in 1959, when I was eight, Miss Lee went back to China. We were all in tears the day we saw her off. "Be a good boy, Jahja," she said in her soft voice, leaning down and brushing my hair back. "God has given you a wonderful talent. You must develop it! Study, work hard, have faith. I will remember you in my prayers."

Over the next eight years I did work hard, and I won competitions. By the time I was in my teens I was also conducting our church choir. And though piano was then paramount in my life, one day I casually asked my teacher, Rudy Laban, about studying orchestra conducting. "Forget it, Jahja!" he replied. "It's the most difficult thing to study. Impossible!"

Even before I graduated from high school, my teachers and people at church were telling me I must study abroad. One of my friends was going to Vienna to study architecture. His father urged me to go along. I rushed home and told my parents.

My father listened patiently and then said sadly, "Jahja, we just can't afford it. I'm sorry." That ended the discussion. In my culture, children don't argue with parents—ever. Or share deep longings.

I remember leafing through music-school catalogs and dreaming, especially about Juilliard, in New York. But you had to fly to America just to audition, and that was impossible.

I continued to work and study—and pray. I applied to other schools, and for scholarships. "Have faith," Miss Lee had said. I was trying. I waited. Eventually I was accepted by the Manhattan School of Music, and I received a Rockefeller grant to pay my way.

While all this was going forward, I won the Jakarta Piano Competition. As part of the prize, I would perform with the Jakarta Symphony—my "farewell concert" in Indonesia.

On the first day of rehearsal, by chance a stranger was sitting in the concert hall. He was Mieczyslaw Munz, a famous professor from Juilliard. Munz was vacationing in Jakarta.

As I rehearsed a Grieg piano concerto, he sat there without comment. But afterward he was heard to say, "Very good. I want to have him go to Juilliard."

Juilliard? It was a fairy tale come true.

In America I plunged happily into my studies and adapted myself to my new country. On Sundays I attended a Chinese-American church in Manhattan, where I began leading the choir.

About two years later I received a sad letter from my parents: Miss Lee had been killed in Communist China by the notorious Red Guards during the Cultural Revolution.

I was stunned. I cried for a long time.

In the course of my studies at Juilliard, I began to think about conducting again and took an elective in it under John Nelson. But the school kept turning me down for a major in conducting.

"Jahja, why don't you look into Yale?" suggested one of my school friends.

Yale? The very name was intimidating, but I applied, along with sixty or more others. Twelve of us auditioned for the great teacher Otto Werner Mueller, who would select only one new pupil.

The first day of the audition seemed to prove out Laban's warnings back in Jakarta—that conducting for me was impossible. Professor Mueller paced before us—all six-foot-seven of him, with bushy Beethoven hair flying out in all directions. He was a frightening figure.

"You arrogant people!" he thundered. "Who do you think you are? Do you have the effrontery to think Almighty God has appointed *you* to lead others?"

Then for two gruelling hours he tested our ear training and musical knowledge.

"In the beginning of Brahms's Haydn variations, what is the contrabass doing? Up-bow or down-bow?"

I knew immediately it was a trick question. The bow is neither up nor down. The contrabassist plucks the strings. Oh, he
had all sorts of tricky questions.

When we accompanied him, he said my playing was
"heavy." In my private interview he growled, "You're in America. Do you know how to play 'The Star-Spangled Banner'?
Harmonize it!"

Oh, that's easy, I thought. *It's in B-flat.*

"Transpose it into F-sharp major!"

And, when I finished: "Tomorrow you will conduct the
orchestra in Brahms's Haydn variations." Then, almost as an
afterthought: "And also a symphony, uh . . . Beethoven's Second, first movement. Prepare for these overnight."

Overnight? He couldn't be serious!

After hours of intense study that night, I could no longer
focus on the notes. It was too much. Sure, I had talent. But so
did others. Who *did* I think I was?

If only Miss Lee were here! I thought. *She would know
what to do!*

"Miss Lee would pray," a voice in my mind gently whispered. Of course! Her last words to me were, "Jahja, have
faith. I will remember you in my prayers."

Folding my hands on the open music and bowing my head I
whispered, "Dear Lord, I don't *think* I'm arrogant. I don't
want to be. Calm my fears. Be with me tomorrow. I can't do it
without You."

Sitting there in that dormitory room, I suddenly had a new
perspective on things. I didn't just "happen" to have a father
who loved music, and we just didn't "happen" to have a piano.
Miss Lee didn't "happen" to come to live and teach at our
home or lead me to Christ or discover my talent. And Professor

Munz didn't just "happen" to be in Jakarta when he heard me play. No, all those "coincidences" were part of a plan. They were the Lord's doing. If this was God's timing, I had to be ready. With new confidence I turned back to the music scores on the desk before me.

The next afternoon I was nervous. But once I raised my baton I lost track of time. How can I describe it? The music in both selections, in turns soft then powerful, lovely then wrenching, poured out from the orchestra and seemed to wash over me in waves—waves that I was mentally and physically *drawing* from the musicians. It wasn't arrogance. It was something mystical, almost holy.

When I brought my baton down at the final crashing notes of the Beethoven movement, I paused a moment, spent by the effort. There was a smattering of applause from the few spectators in the hall. I turned to Professor Mueller. His stern look had been replaced by something like respect, maybe amazement.

As I look back on it now, I know my audition at Yale *was* God's timing. I became Professor Mueller's student, and I embarked on a career as a musical conductor that eventually brought me to Cleveland to one of the world's best orchestras.

"Study, work hard, have faith," Miss Lee had said.

And, she might have added, if you do, God will provide the opportunities and the means to fulfill your dreams.

A Gift from Gigi

Tony Dorsett

Does God give us something very beautiful for just a short moment to let us know what Heaven is like? I think that's the way it was with Gigi.

Our paths first crossed at a social gathering. Our eyes caught for a moment and then the slim, attractive girl vanished in the crowd.

I couldn't forget her; her vivacious laughter and sparkling brown eyes haunted me and I kept watching for her elsewhere. Finally, at another party I looked across the room and there she was. I walked over to her. "Hi."

She looked up with those marvelous eyes. "Hello."

We talked nonstop all evening. For the first time I forgot my shyness. I forgot football. I was captivated by this beautiful person. I learned that Gigi Clayton was eighteen, lived at home with her parents in Dallas and was going to college.

At the end of the evening, I walked her to the parking lot where she discovered that she had locked the keys in her car. We laughed; I found help and watched her drive off, promising myself that I would never let her out of my life again.

Our first real date was on New Year's Eve when we welcomed in 1979 and wondered what the new year would bring for us. Even then there was something different, something special about Gigi, as if she were part of this world and the next.

Perhaps it was because she was so considerate. Other girls were always seeking her advice. She would always listen intently, with understanding and compassion. If a friend admired one of her dresses, Gigi would insist she take it as a gift.

Deeply religious, she tried to get me to attend church with her family. But after two busy years in professional football, I found it difficult to get back into the church habit.

"Tony, the Lord has been good to you," she would say. "He's the only One you can count on."

I'd smile and think how much she was like my mother back in Aliquippa, Pennsylvania. Along with Dad, a steel-mill worker. Mom raised us five boys and two daughters with a strong dependency on God. She always urged us children to bring our problems to Him.

"Pray to Jesus, Tony." Mom would say. "He will always answer you."

I had done a lot of praying, and He had done a lot of answering. I knew it was God who gave me my talent to play football, who inspired my great coaches in high school and the University of Pittsburgh, and brought me to wonderful team-mates on the Dallas Cowboys.

But church had somehow slipped into the background, and I hadn't found a lot of time for it lately. I blamed this on a grueling schedule of practice and making special appearances and television commercials all over the country. I still believed in God, all right, but I'd sort of left Him back home.

Now this beautiful girl was reminding me that I had my priorities wrong. I tried to laugh her concern aside, just as I would shrug off her worries about my playing football. She thought the sport too violent and was afraid I might get hurt.

"Honey," I'd say, "football is the only reason we met. It's my job, the only thing I know, and why I'm in Dallas."

I didn't know it then, but I was the one who should have been concerned—for her. We had a big cookout at my house on Memorial Day of 1979. The next day I had to go to Los Angeles on business, and she drove me to the airport. She winced a little when I helped her into the car, and I asked if anything was wrong.

"Oh, nothing," she shrugged. "My legs feel a little strange, that's all." Then she gave me that dazzling smile. "Okay, let's catch your plane."

Something gnawed at me all the way to California, and when I got off the plane, I phoned her.

"I'm fine, Tony!" she laughed, brushing off my concern. "Don't forget, I'll pick you up at the airport tomorrow."

My plane landed at Dallas in a slashing rainstorm, and when I stepped off the ramp, Gigi wasn't there. Instead her brother was waiting, his face grave.

"She's not well at all, Tony," he said soberly.

My heart lurched, and we hurried to their home. Gigi was lying on a sofa, looking wan. She tried to smile, but could hardly walk. "Oh, I'll get better," she said.

But she didn't improve at all, and the next day her folks and I took her to the hospital. After examining her, a doctor called us all in.

"It's really nothing," he said soothingly. "I think Gigi is just nervous about her college grades." We all felt relieved since Gigi was transferring from the University of Houston to a college closer to home and it was only natural for her to be concerned about her studies.

But I was still bothered. A few days later I sat down with her mother. "Mrs. Clayton, I don't think it's nervousness. Gigi doesn't worry like that."

Mom Clayton shook her head. "I know, Tony, and I've tried to get her to see another doctor, but she says she's sure she'll get better."

Each day after that Gigi grew weaker. They did take her to the hospital several times, but the doctors still couldn't find out what was wrong. I lived in an agony of worry and exhilaration, worrying about Gigi's health and exhilarated about our coming life together. I would soon go to the Cowboys' training camp. On August 8 we'd have our first pre-season game in Dallas. That was Gigi's birthday, and I planned to give her a diamond engagement ring.

In the meantime, I remembered my mom's advice and started praying again, asking God to heal Gigi. I called Mom in Aliquippa and cried on the phone. She was so upset she wanted to fly to Dallas then and there. I said, "Mom, that's not necessary, but please ask everyone there to pray for her."

Gigi's father wrote to every evangelist from Billy Graham to Oral Roberts, asking for their prayers.

But nothing seemed to help. When I visited, Gigi couldn't walk anymore, and I had to carry her from bed to sofa. Holding her limp little form in my arms crushed my heart, and I fought back tears. I couldn't look glum in front of Gigi; she was always smiling and saying she would be better soon, even though that sparkle was gone from her eyes.

Then on the night of June 8 the phone call came. Gigi had been rushed to the hospital with a cardiac arrest. There she had gone into a coma. The doctors had finally diagnosed her illness as a rare blood disease that was fatal in only five percent of the cases. Gigi was one of those cases. She died.

I collapsed in grief. I screamed at God. *Why? Why? Why?*

Why did He have to take such a beautiful, good person like
Gigi? To snatch her away like that seemed so cruel. I wanted to
run, to get away from everything. I couldn't sleep; at night my
body would start shaking. I couldn't even think about football;
the game seemed so remote, it didn't mean anything to me anymore.

For a while I wandered in a daze. Then I thought about
Gigi's mother, and how she must be suffering too. When I got
to the Claytons', I found her inconsolable; she was just shaking
apart with sobs.

My heart went out to her. Sitting down next to her, I put my
arm around her quivering shoulders. I said, "Gigi was such a
beautiful human being, I think God wanted her to be with
Him." Her shoulders relaxed a bit, and I continued talking. I
told her that there was so much corruption in this world that I
felt God wanted Gigi in a better place.

As I continued trying to console Gigi's mother, something
started to happen in me. It was as if a frozen winter brook
thawed by the sun began running again. I began to see that
even when a young person dies, God isn't being cruel. The
length of a life isn't what counts; it's the quality of it. And
Gigi's life was of the highest possible quality. Everyone she
met was affected by her—for good. In my own case, she had
changed my values in the right direction. She had pointed me
back toward God. And then she had gone on ahead of
me . . . knowing that we'd meet again someday, but also
wanting me to live my life to the fullest, not wrap myself forever in grief.

Because I knew Gigi, I'm a changed person. I have a new
relationship with God. I realize now that He is not Someone to
be tucked away and brought out only in emergencies; He's a

real, living Presence without whom I cannot be whole. I believe He has a plan for my life, and I'm trying to follow it.

No one who ever knew Gigi was a loser. Just being around her made everyone a winner.

I know.

The Big Slump

Sal Bando

Y ou know what a slump is, don't you? It happens in everyone's life: You hit a period when nothing is going right, and no matter how hard you try, you can't seem to pull out of it.

Bad as it is for some people, it's worse for us ballplayers. Our livelihood rides on what we do out on the field. And when we're failing in game after game, it's not a private hell but a public one, with thousands of people looking on. It's one of the most frightening things that can happen to a player.

I know, because it happened to me in 1975. I went from being one of the top players on the Oakland A's (always the guy who could produce the home runs and RBI's) to nothing. My fielding was terrible, my batting was worse—and I had been one of the best clutch-hitters in the game. It was eating me up inside, particularly after I read in a newspaper that the A's owner, Charlie Finley, told reporters I was the worst third baseman in the American League.

Just like an executive who's having problems at the office, the disastrous slide in my career began to affect my home life. I neglected my wife, Sandra, and our two boys. I became moody and withdrawn. When I wasn't trying to figure out what was wrong with my batting stance, I'd be worrying about an important upcoming game.

"What's wrong, honey?" Sandra would ask.

"Nothing," I'd reply.

"Sal, maybe you're trying too hard."

With that I'd stomp out of the room.

We weren't at the battling stage yet, but our marriage was showing the strain in a hundred little ways. And that only put added pressure on me. It was a vicious, descending spiral of worry and frustration.

Another thing that was bugging me was our manager, Alvin Dark. Dark was a peculiar guy. He'd been manager of the A's when I was a rookie, back in the '60s. He was short-tempered and always in hot water with the team's management. Dark left the team after a dispute, but by the time he was rehired in 1974, he had changed.

Dark and his wife, Jackie, had become born-again Christians. The difference in him was unbelievable. There were no more temper tantrums, and he actually talked about God, faith and love on the baseball field and in the locker room. Reporters began describing Dark as the "ministerial manager" and "goody two-shoes."

Nobody ridiculed him more mercilessly than my teammates and I. We laughed at the way he walked, the way he talked, the fact that he had no vices. But the worst thing was his meekness: How could a manager not fight with the front office or chew us guys out? The man wasn't human. I kept watching to see if he'd blow his cool, but he never did. Alvin Dark was a real pain in the neck to me, but under his management we won the 1974 World Series!

My troubles began the next year. Maybe losing out in a salary arbitration with management triggered it, but I went into my slump. Dark tried to help me. I would listen to him politely and then do things my way. We were on different wavelengths. Still, everything might have gone up in smoke that year if it hadn't been for Dark's persistence.

It began in a very unfunny way. In mid-season, Dark moved me from number one in the batting lineup to eighth. As team captain and a very prideful guy, I was angered by the insult. When Dark tried to explain why he had to move me, and added that he was praying for me, it was salt in the wound. My lighthearted mockery of his faith hardened into near-hatred.

Things came to a head in June when I returned from a road trip and Sandra greeted me with some incredible news: She had committed her life to Christ.

I just stared at her. We were Roman Catholics and church-goers. "I know you can't understand it now, honey," she said quietly, "but Jackie Dark lent me a wonderful book. You really ought to read it . . ."

"Jackie Dark! I might have known it!" I exploded. "Sandy, we don't need that born-again stuff! We don't kill; we don't steal; we believe in God!"

"That's not enough, Sal," she replied. Her lower lip trembled.

The nerve of that guy! I thought. *When he couldn't get to me directly, he used his wife and Sandra!* But Sandra insisted it was not that way; she had been friends with Jackie for a long time. The Darks were only trying to help—and we certainly needed help.

For a couple of days I was really irked. Then I began to see a difference in Sandra. She was more patient with the boys, and even my moodiness didn't seem to faze her. She had the same calm, unflappable quality I had observed in Alvin Dark. It was a stark contrast to my own confusion and unhappiness. And it set me to thinking.

In July, Sandra took the boys home to visit her parents in New Jersey. I had a day to kill before going to Boston for a game, and rattled around the empty house feeling lonely and depressed. Before turning in, I showered, then settled down in bed with a magazine. A book on the night table caught my eye. *His Stubborn Love* the jacket read. It was the book, by Joyce Landorf, that Sandra had been talking about. My curiosity was piqued. *Might as well see what it's all about,* I thought, idly picking it up.

There weren't any fireworks, but as I read, I began to understand what it really meant to commit your life to Jesus Christ, as opposed to simply believing in Him in a lukewarm way.

When I finished, I lay there a long time, staring at the ceiling. My magazine had fallen, unopened, to the floor.

Finally, throwing back the covers, I slipped out of bed onto my knees. In simple terms, I asked Christ to take over my life. "Please come close, Lord; be real to me. Forgive me for not loving You, for having forgotten You . . ."

At Boston the next night, I surprised myself by getting two hits, including a single to right field that brought in the winning run. After that game I went from ice-cold to being the hottest hitter on the team.

There were other changes: I found myself more conscious of my attitudes and actions toward other people. For one thing, I began making more time for my family. Sandra and I went to a Marriage Encounter group, and it helped our relationship tremendously. In the clubhouse and on the ball field, I began to share with the other players, particularly the younger guys. They had problems, too, and a few encouraging words helped. I began participating in the Sunday baseball chapel programs, sharing my faith.

.. ..

In the final weeks of the season, my batting average went up from .190 to .230. I doubled my home-run production, ending up with a respectable fifteen for the season. I played some part in getting the A's into the league playoffs. These were not terrific accomplishments on the face of them, but they were to a guy who'd been in the cellar.

What had happened? There's really nothing magical or mysterious about it. I had been tied up in knots all season, worrying about my performance, worrying about what people thought of me, worrying about *myself*. By giving my life over to Jesus, I began caring about other people and reaching *out* instead of *in*; I began to loosen up and automatically began to play better.

I had learned Alvin Dark's secret: The reason he didn't fight with the front office or scream at the players was that he wasn't overly concerned about himself or his position. His Christian faith had made him a selfless, caring person—he cared about the team, he cared about Sal Bando . . .

I'm convinced that the way to get out of a slump, whether it's on the baseball field or in the office, the classroom or the kitchen, is to stop worrying so much about yourself and your own problems. Direct your attention upward, to God, and then outward, to helping others. Be a caring person.

St. Paul put it just right when he said, "Each of you must regard, not his own interests, but the other man's." (1 Corinthians 10:24, NEB) I'll buy that advice. It worked for me!

PART 7

The Power in the Stillness

And after the fire a still small voice.
I Kings 19:12

G od has a way of catching our attention by speaking to
our hearts when we step away from the crowd and
look and listen in the quiet—of a planned retreat, a medically
forced sabbatical, or sometimes just as we lie in bed at night
waiting for sleep that won't come. Beau Bridges remembers the
first time he became aware of God—walking alone down a
street looking for a lost arrow.

The insights we receive in those quiet moments can transform the way we live the rest of our days, whether we're back
in the midst of the bustle or quiet again, looking and listening
for signs of God's powerful grace.

The Healing in Solitude

Mary Martin

When I was very young I remember going by a large estate, hidden by trees, and being told that the road behind the huge iron gates led to a mysterious building called The Retreat, where nuns lived in solitude.

Alone? I wondered. *Away from everyone and everything? How terrible?*

Many years later my husband, Richard Halliday, and I were having dinner in a restaurant when a friend stopped to talk to us. "I heard you spent two months on a freighter," he said, "just the two of you as the only passengers. And now I hear you've bought a farm where you can retreat whenever you need to. I guess you two really value your solitude."

I forget what I answered. Before my eyes was a picture of dark trees and high iron railings and the road that led to that mysterious building. For he had used those words, "solitude" and "retreat"—words that for me still evoked the gloom and terror of that childhood scene. Not once had I applied them to what Richard and I did. Days gazing out over the endless sea, not another passenger aboard; the farm where the phone never rang because there was none to ring—were these in some sense "retreats"? Was it to be alone that we chose them?

We have traveled on many freighters and spent much time on that isolated farm. I know now that these are indeed retreats, and that solitude is their essence. And I have discovered that the real thing is utterly different from what I imagined, peering through that iron fence. To my child's mind, solitude meant loneliness—that fearful state of lovelessness and separation—and retreat meant to run away. But solitude, I know now, is the very opposite, not a loss of love, but a deliberate embrace of silence and uncluttered living in order to become more capable of love.

Nor have we ever run away from anything—or anyone. Rather, we have instinctively run to a change in the rhythm of life: to refuel, to gather fresh air and sun, to rest the mind and body, to feel the blood surge as a small ship creaks and groans through plunging waves; or to hear the wind whistling from a mountaintop climbed on foot.

At the farm, up at sunrise, to bed soon after 9 p.m. To know the joy of being hungry and taking the time to savor each bite of freshly picked fruit and vegetable. To rest, to read, to listen to the music of the night. And suddenly the mind is alive with new ideas, new thoughts, new hopes, new knowledge of ourselves and where we fit into the world of other people.

Such solitude, like all things of value, has its price. If I am to be alone, I must do without many of the conveniences of life—because they depend on other people. When the sleek and ultra-automatic refrigerator in our New York apartment breaks down (as it has three times in the past fourteen months), I phone the serviceman, who finally comes and tells me the job needs a specialist—who finally comes and tells me I must order a part from the factory. And I spend my time phoning and writing letters and waiting for the experts and the part that never comes. Interdependence is the condition of technology.

But the old white icebox on our farm, like the lamps there, runs on kerosene and an old-fashioned wick. When it stops making ice, I turn it upside down to get rid of the air pocket—like burping a baby—and then it makes ice again. It doesn't deposit symmetrical cubes into a pretty container, but it does let me breathe the air of privacy.

Some years ago Richard and I decided that instead of waiting until we were at the conventional retirement age of sixty-five, we would live that sixty-fifth year now—and live it alone, on our farm. We made many discoveries, that year of preview-retirement, but the chief one was that there wasn't one dull, boring moment. The fifty-two weeks sped by like four. We both spent more hours "together" and more hours "apart" than we had ever thought possible. We knew a stillness, a quietness; we had lived with ourselves and had no fears. We felt more eager to plunge into our next undertaking than ever before. We had learned the strengths that come naturally from those moments of solitude which nature needs from us all. We had not been alone, nor known loneliness.

Nature leads the bear to hibernate. But we human beings, especially we women, have to work to learn what riches we can gain in only a few moments of drawing aside—because, of course, solitude does not have to be taken in great hunks of a year, or even a week. These are the "big solitudes" in response to big weariness and confusion. But the frictions and frustrations of every day need healing too, and for those there are "small solitudes." Just a door to shut for ten minutes between ourselves and the demands upon us, giving time for prayer and contemplation. A walk in the park. The time to hear a favorite record all the way through, with the window shades down and the phone off the hook. All those can be retreats-in-miniature, part of the ancient wisdom of life's ebb and flow.

For like the land, we have to lie fallow from time to time—

whether short or long; like the land, we must renew our strength in emptiness. For the human spirit this means solitude in order to soar again.

I learned that truth in an unforgettable manner. After doing *The Sound of Music*, I was part of a group preparing a show called *Jenny*. The author said he was writing a serious play. The composer and lyricists insisted they were writing a light, entertaining score. It was my conceit at the time that I could bring their opposing purposes together to make a successful whole. What followed was my most torturous and frightening experience.

When we opened in Boston, the critics and audiences were disappointed. New material had to be written; cast changes made, requiring rehearsals before and after performances. My body grew weary, my vocal cords strained. I needed a doctor daily and soon required a throat specialist.

Our next stop in Detroit was equally disappointing, and with a second attempt at new material and additional rehearsals, I was near exhaustion. After six weeks, we announced we would close the show and not bring it to New York.

A few hours later, we were told we would be sued for two-million dollars if I did not open with the show in New York. I had forty-eight hours to decide whether to continue to perform and ask the audiences to share my disappointment, or go to court and be forced to work the rest of my life to pay out an enormous sum of money.

I decided that I would not spend the future in lawyers' offices and courts. I would not work to pay all my earnings to men with whom I was in total disagreement.

We opened in New York, and the critics and audiences liked

the show no more than they did in Boston and Detroit. I doubted at the time that I would ever want, or be able, to appear on the stage again.

Richard and I retreated to our farm. I saw the sunny days through a haze. I slept ten, twelve, even thirteen hours a night. I was not thinking of the past or the future. I was very much living in the present. I discovered I could still be pleased with the rolls and bread I baked. I got out the ancient treadle sewing machine and made a flower-print dress. Another day I found my oil paints and started painting again.

Gradually I became aware of the world about me. A baby on the farm next to ours died, and the distraught father asked our help to arrange the burial. Two babies were born to couples living on our land. They had no milk for them. I found myself on horseback riding over the mountains as Richard and I went to buy milk cows.

And all at once I knew that I was anxious to get back to work. I was still not sure that I would ever sing again. For the first time in my life I had heard no music for three months. I had not whistled or hummed or sung a note. I think I was frightened to hear the sound that would come out of my abused voice. What was more terrifying was that I felt no music within me. I could not even recall the joy of singing.

But I was scheduled to make recordings with a group of gifted child singers soon after we returned to New York. For the first time in my life, I went to the studio without working on the music. I was strangely calm. The children were gay and beautiful to look at. The moment came for us to blend our voices together.

There was a silence in the studio. The music began. The children's voices rose.

And to my joy I felt that glorious life-giving force from within and I sang.

Like the fallow earth, my voice had rested, and I sang clearly and fervently. Like the fallow earth, the spirit within me soared.

I understand better now that building called The Retreat, hidden behind its forest. It is in solitude that we hear the voice of God.

A Break in The Music

Barbara Mandrell

All of us who try hard to be Christians know about those times when we seem to be failing, when we seem to be losing our way on His way.

Well, it happens to country singers, too. Let me tell you about one of those times in my life. But first I must explain what can happen at a typical recording session because it so well illustrates the lesson I learned.

Picture a working studio in Nashville. The singer is doing a tracking session, the first phase of recording a song. Later in the overdubbing they will add the background things like hand claps, horns and choir. Then the performer will come back to sing the vocal again, after which the engineers will combine it all into one finished recording.

The singer, who could be me, is in the little vocal booth while the eight musicians in blue-jean-and-tee-shirt work clothes—guitarists, fiddler, French harpist, pianist and drummer—get ready to run down a song. Eighteen microphones scattered among the group glisten under the studio's blue-green mood lights. The engineer is ready in his glassed-in control room: the producer (in my case, Tom Collins) gives the signal to start the song. But then, no recording session ever goes from start to finish without a hitch. It's just like life—there's always some unexpected problem—and in this case the band delivers the intro and the singer is just ready to come in, when *cree-yowl!*—an electronic amplifier breaks into a howling squall.

The trouble seems to be with one of the guitars. As the guitarist begins checking his equipment, the singer sits back on the tall stool in her booth and waits, and waits.

The guitar player huddles with an engineer in his rack of outboard sound equipment. Then the engineer calls: "I found it. Should be fixed in no time."

He holds up a small section of sound transmission wire leading from the guitar to its amplifier. Pointing to where bright copper gleams through frayed black rubber insulation, he explains that the exposed wire had touched metal, causing a short. "That's what blocked the sound from coming through," he says. They quickly switch to a new cord. "It's fixed!" he says, and the session continues.

Such a little thing, but little interruptions like that can happen in recording sessions no matter how sophisticated the equipment.

And no matter how well along the path we think we may be as Christians, there are those times when we, too, suffer a break in communication with God.

I point this out because I experienced such a break a few years ago. For several weeks something had been bothering me, and I couldn't seem to pin down what it was, or why. I had prayed time and again asking God to take away the uneasiness I was feeling, but nothing seemed to happen.

One night after rehearsal I had come home feeling particularly depressed. It had not been a good day at all. I found myself snapping at my husband Ken and being generally fretful. At bedtime I had given our baby daughter Jamie a perfunctory kiss and hardly listened to six-year-old Matthew say his prayers. Then I lay in bed unable to sleep, staring into the dark. Again I prayed, trying to listen to Him, to feel His Holy Spirit comforting and assuring me.

.. ..

"Oh, Lord," I pleaded, "please give me a handle on what's bothering me."

And slowly, almost as if some invisible engineer had checked out the intricate strands of my life and suddenly called out, "I found the trouble," it came to me. It had been there all along, the resentment that had been burning within me the past weeks—*the trouble with "X."*

There's no point in telling you who "X" was, but she was someone whose friendship I'd valued and who'd said some things about me that hurt. Hurt a lot. And I was bitter.

But now, just like a spring wind blowing dark clouds away from the sun, it became clear; just as a frayed wire can cause trouble in a sound recording studio, so had my smoldering resentment against "X" been short-circuiting my prayers.

As a serious, struggling Christian, I knew what the problem was. After all, very clearly Jesus had told us: "And whenever you stand praying, forgive, if you have anything against any one; so that your Father also who is in heaven may forgive you your trespasses" (Mark 11:25, RSV).

Of course! I had no right to ask for peace from the One who had forgiven me so much when I would not forgive others.

"Father," I breathed, "forgive me for resenting her." And then I prayed for her well-being. I visualized her happy and smiling. And, lying there in bed, I felt at last the peace I had been seeking.

Only a few days later I saw "X" again. And do you know what? I ran up and hugged her. The amazing thing was, she hugged me back. And I'm sure she was sincere about that hug. Why? Because I had forgiven her and somehow she had sensed this extraordinary change in me. And let me tell you, the power of forgiveness is mystifying but real!

The whole incident was such a little thing, really, a small moment so far as my life as a whole is concerned. But all of us who are trying hard to be Christians know that even little things can grow into big troubles. But when you face up to a problem and seriously take it to the Lord, there will come that wonderful time when you know "It's fixed!" and you can go on with the adventure of living.

My Search

Joan Fontaine

as told to Elizabeth Sherrill

Most of us move through life looking for something. For years my search was for a sense of belonging, truly *belonging* somewhere. I spent half a lifetime looking for a place where I could feel deeply at ease, accepted, part of a family, surrounded by people who cared. I had begun to believe that no such place existed. Then, in 1972 I found one.

I'm sure the origins of my search go back to my childhood when ill-health and the isolation that it brings played such a large role in my life. My mother told me that I spent the first two-and-a-half years of my life wrapped from head to toe in cotton bandages due to the eczema that covered me. My father, Walter de Havilland, was a professor teaching at the Imperial University in Tokyo, where I was born. Mother always believed that the goats' milk that is given to babies in Japan started me on my endless succession of ailments.

My parents' marriage was not a happy one. When I was two-and-a-half, Mother, my sister and I left Japan and settled in Saratoga, California, where doctors assured Mother that the climate would be healthier. It was true that my eczema got better, but just about every other conceivable illness followed. My earliest memories are of tastes—castor oil and Scott's Emulsion and the hatefulness of unsweetened licorice cough syrup—and of white-uniformed strangers bending over me with long, hurting needles.

I suppose it was no wonder that with such handicaps I found it hard to relate to other children. And indeed the life we led was different from other children's carefree existences. By now my mother had remarried. My stepfather was an investment counselor, but I'm sure he should have been a general. The bedroom my sister and I shared, when I wasn't quarantined with some infection, was modeled after a barracks: khaki spreads on iron bedsteads, khaki-painted furniture against dun-colored walls, military-style inspections morning and night. At his insistence, each Sunday we wrote out the schedule for the week ahead in precise segments:

7:00-7:15 bathe and dress
7:15-7:45 breakfast
7:45-8:15 make beds; tidy room
8:15-8:30 walk to school

and so on through the long regimented day. My stepfather was a well-intentioned man, and I respected him, but he was unable to give the warmth, the open affection, the understanding touch that I yearned for.

And yet all the illness and isolation and regimentation had their compensations, for instead of real companions, I found my friends in books and in the dramatic sketches Mother taught my sister and me to act in when friends came to visit. On days when I was unable to sit up in bed, I would weave long thrilling dramas in my head. Little did I think, at such lonely moments, that I was going through the perfect apprenticeship for an acting career.

But apparently it showed to those around me. One day a friend of Mother's who had seen our little living-room dramas, received a call from the actress May Robson. May was looking for a young girl to play the role of the ingenue in her next play.

"Joan de Havilland," said Mother's friend without hesitation. And so I found myself in the wonderful make-believe world of theater.

By now my sister was an established actress, so in order not to trade on her name I took our stepfather's name, Fontaine. Acting was a strenuous career for a girl as sickly as I was, but I soon came to know why Dame Sybil Thorndike called it "Doctor Theater." No matter how I felt or how high my temperature, when the curtains parted, a burst of energy always flooded into me, and I went on, oblivious to everything but the part I was playing.

An increasingly successful movie career had many rewards, but it did not bring me the warmth and close relationships that I kept seeking, sometimes desperately. Perhaps it was the lack of a warm father figure in my childhood that made my expectations of marriage so ridiculously high. My husband was to be everything I had longed for as a girl. All-loving, all-strong, all-wise, he would be the answer to every need. And each time he fell short of those expectations the disillusionment was keener, the depression that followed more serious. Each time I felt as if I were a wanderer with no place to go, no place to belong.

It was during one of those bleak times in 1972 that I finally realized what I had been doing. I had been idolizing human beings, trying to make of them what flesh and blood can never be. Even if a man could be the father I dreamed of, the brother I never had, he could never be God. Of course I wanted a center to my life, of course I wanted perfect faithfulness, perfect love—only I had been looking for those things in the wrong places.

I remember so well the day, sitting alone in my New York apartment, when that realization came to me. I remember because with it, quietly and clearly, came the answer I had been seeking for so long. Not far away was a tranquil place of worship called the Church of the Heavenly Rest. I began to attend services there. A few months later. I consulted the rector, Burton Thomas, and told him I needed to be baptized. With just a few friends to stand with me, and Dr. Thomas's wife Hazel as my godmother, I *was* baptized, and I knew that I had found the place where I belonged at last.

Baptism is an inrush of grace—and grace changes people. Have I been changed? I believe so. Where I was judgmental and sometimes too demanding, I now feel more sympathy for other people, more tolerance, more understanding. My friends, who seem closer and dearer, tell me that I seem closer and dearer to them. I feel stronger in myself; I'm not looking so desperately for some other human being to lean on. I belong to a church and a church belongs to me, and I feel surrounded by love and joy.

Sometimes when a bird sings in Central Park and no one else stops to listen, I feel myself overwhelmed with wonder and gratitude to the Giver of such gifts.

And sometimes I wonder why it took me so long. Then I think of that marvelous parable of the workers in the vineyard (Matthew 20:1-16), and remember that in God's sight there is no soon or late. In that story each worker received the same reward no matter when he came. For me that reward was the gift of knowing I belong.

The Scary Season

Herschel Walker

Football.

In Georgia, fall means football. It seems everyone is a football fan, that every team is someone's favorite. In Athens, sixty thousand students, parents, alumni and just plain fans will pack the University of Georgia's Sanford Stadium, wearing red, and whooping and hollering for *their* Georgia Bulldogs.

I was the Bulldogs' running back in 1982, and I could only hope at the beginning of the season that, win or lose, 1982 would not be like our previous season.

It wasn't as if our record in 1981 was bad—we won ten games and lost only two. For the second straight year, we were Southeastern Conference Champions and ranked among the top ten teams in the country. No, it wasn't the wins or losses at all that made the 1981 season so memorable. It was the way I nearly quit being a part of autumn in Georgia.

On the first day of football practice in the fall, the Georgia Bulldogs were the toast of the state. We'd gone through the 1980 season undefeated and beaten Notre Dame in the Sugar Bowl, 17–10. Everywhere in Georgia, bumper stickers and T-shirts and Frisbees proclaimed the rallying cry of the previous season—"How 'bout them Dawgs?" We had won our last thirteen games in a row, and hardly a fan could be found who didn't think we'd win another twelve in a row and the national championship again.

It had been a good year for me, too. I had run for more

yards than any freshman in the history of college football, and had finished as a runner-up for the prestigious Heisman Trophy, given each year to the nation's best college football player. I was just thankful that God had given me a gift—a strong body and a strong mind—and a chance to use that gift as best I could. Just being at the state university was special for me—it was an opportunity Mama and Daddy had only dreamed of for any of their seven children. But even as practice began, I could sense that that wasn't enough anymore. The previous year was good, so this year would have to be better. For all our fans, nothing else would do.

I was in line to register for classes with the other students a few days before our first game when someone I didn't even know patted me on the back. "We can't lose this year!" he stated emphatically to his buddy as he turned to me. "Not with ol' Herschel out there for us." I suppose it was intended as a compliment, but the comment left me strangely uneasy. The responsibility that was being heaped on my shoulders scared me.

But out on the field, with a football tucked under my arm, I just tried to do what I did best—run toward the goal line. We beat Tennessee the first weekend of the season. 44–0, an outstanding team performance. The bell on top of the campus chapel rang out fourteen times to celebrate our fourteen-game winning streak, now the longest in college football.

It rang fifteen times the next week, after we struggled to a 27–13 win over California. I gained 167 yards rushing, but had fumbled once, just part of a team effort not quite up to par.

That's when the whispering started. It was isolated at first, a few inquiring people wondering if anything was wrong. Why hadn't I broken a long touchdown run yet? Was I worried that my play might jeopardize the winning streak? I was more con-

fused, really. I had gained 328 yards in two wins. Was that
so bad?

Coach Vince Dooley worked us hard as we prepared for the
third game of the season against Clemson University. This year
the game, one of the fiercest college rivalries in the South,
would be in Clemson's Memorial Stadium, nicknamed "Death
Valley" because of the difficulty opposing teams have winning
there. Still, we were favored to win.

We won the coin toss, received the kickoff, and began moving the ball up the field. I picked up eight yards running around
left end, another four slashing right. A pass play netted us
another first down, and I carried twice more.

On second down, from the Clemson thirteen-yard line, I took
a pitchout and headed left. Just as I was about to cut upfield
toward the goal line, a Clemson lineman hit my arm. The ball
squirted loose, and a pile of orange jerseys were immediately on
top of it. I'd just fumbled away a good scoring chance.

I fumbled again in the second quarter to set up a Clemson
field goal, but by that time our whole team had begun to
unravel. Perhaps it was the noisy Clemson fans or just a bad
day, but nine times that afternoon we lost the ball on fumbles
or interceptions. We lost the game too, 13–3. The bell would
not ring that night on the University of Georgia campus.

The locker room was somber as I shuffled in. Reporters surrounded us, probing for reasons for the loss. Herschel, what's
wrong? Why aren't you playing like last year? Herschel, are
you still happy at Georgia?

The Clemson defeat and the questions dogged me into the
next week. No matter how hard I tried, I couldn't avoid it. One
afternoon, as I walked to practice, two guys stopped me. "Hey,
Herschel, how come you're not running like last year?" I

shrugged, and mumbled something about doing my best and walked on. Though I had scored only one touchdown, compared to the five I'd scored after three games last season, I'd run for more yards. Yet, instead of "How 'bout them Dawgs?" everyone seemed to be asking, "What's wrong with Herschel?"

I walked on beneath the campus trees, thinking of the criticisms that had threaded their way in from every corner of Georgia, beginning to believe them myself. *Maybe I have lost it*, I thought. I'd even heard of bumper stickers that said, "Herschel Who?" The criticisms and doubts hurt, more than I cared to admit.

I dragged through practice halfheartedly, my mind focused more on what I would tell Coach Dooley than on how to run against South Carolina, our next opponent. I'd decided it might be easier to just quit, to forget the pressure and questions, the pain that came when your best effort wasn't good enough.

I also decided to wait until the next morning to say anything about quitting. As I dragged myself back to my room that night, I'd never felt so low and alone. Inside I flipped on a small light, and flopped down on my bed. "It's not fair," I said out loud. "Why is everybody on my case? Why can't I just be me?"

That's when I caught a glimpse of it out of the corner of my eye—the picture I had hanging over my bed, a picture of Jesus. It looked different this time, somehow. As I stared into Christ's face, I couldn't help but think about the stories of His life I'd learned back in Sunday school in Wrightsville, Georgia.

Maybe it was the recollection of those Bible stories that helped me realize what was different. In Jesus' face I saw for the first time an enormous courage. I saw a courage born in His forty-day struggle in the wilderness, and tested day in and day out by people who laughed at Him and threatened to arrest Him or stone Him. I saw the courage He showed on that final night in Gethsemane, when terrible agony forced huge drops of blood from His brow. In Jesus' face was the courage of One Who kept on going no matter what the hardship. There was no quitter in that picture.

For the longest time I just looked, drawing strength from the picture. And when I got to thinking again about why I needed that strength, I realized I'd found the example I needed to follow. Whether the criticisms of me had been fair or not, it didn't matter—Herschel Walker would be no quitter, either.

I was the first one at practice the next day, attentively listening to the coaches' instructions. On the field, I ran with reckless abandon. No, the questions wouldn't stop, and the Clemson game would continue to be talked about. The fans were still expecting a lot from me. But I knew now how to cope with the pressure. By standing up to it, just as Jesus had, not running from it. I had a job to do!

That Saturday we defeated South Carolina, 24–0; I gained 176 yards and scored two touchdowns. We didn't lose again in the regular season; we won the conference title and were ranked second—behind Clemson.

At the beginning of the 1982 football season, expectations ran high. I was determined to make it my best ever, because of what I learned in 1981: that no matter what job you do, there's Someone who understands the pressure and responsibilities you face; Who's been through it Himself. Jesus will give you the strength and courage to keep going. Look for Him. And you'll see it, too.

The Wayward Arrow

Beau Bridges

When was the first time you became aware of God? For me, it happened in an odd way when I was a kid. It was the summer when archery was the craze among my friends. And, of all things, it was an arrow that first led me to think about God.

I was a boy, just twelve, growing up in Mar Vista, California. My father, Lloyd Bridges, was a film actor, and my brother Jeff, my sister Lucinda and I did the same kinds of things other kids did—like mowing lawns for extra money and playing softball. We had chores around the house, and we loved hanging out with friends.

In fact, I was hanging out with a bunch of my pals the day this strange thing happened. We had brought our bows and arrows to a field about two miles from my house. We had made our own arrows that summer, gluing colored feathers to the ends and painting the shafts so that each was unique. That day I was using my favorite arrow; it had red dots outlined in black, and I'd stuck black and red feathers on the end. There was no classier and, I felt, no swifter arrow in my collection.

We weren't using targets. Instead we were playing a game we'd created on our own—one of those crazy, "death-defying" games that boys that age seem to love. We'd played this game many times that summer, and the fact that it was dangerous only heightened the excitement.

We would stand in a tight-knit group in the middle of the

field. Each of us would put an arrow on his bowstring, then pull it back and raise the bow so that the arrow was pointing up, perpendicular to the ground. Then someone would call out, "Let 'em fly," and we would all shoot our arrows at once.

The arrows would zoom up into the sky, out of sight. Then we'd listen for their return. We knew that, having flown straight up, they would be falling straight down, and we huddled in morbid anticipation, hoping they wouldn't be hitting *us*. The object of the game, you see, was to have the arrows land as close to the group as possible, without, of course, hurting anyone. The winner was the owner of the arrow that hit the nearest.

That day when I heard the call, "Let 'em fly," my bowstring reverberated with a loud zing and I watched the polka-dotted shaft of my favorite arrow whiz up into the sun's rays and disappear. Soon we heard, *zump . . . zump, zump*, and the arrows began falling all around us. When they stopped, everyone rushed to claim his, and several of the fellows shouted. "Mine is the closest!" I looked around, but *mine* was missing. It was strange. My arrow should have landed close to the others, but there was no trace of it.

I covered every inch of the field, and my friend Chuck Bylor helped, but we couldn't find it. Doggedly, I continued searching. I was disappointed, and felt a little silly . . . and puzzled. Where was it? Mine went up with the rest. It should have come down with the rest. It made me feel, well, kind of eerie.

Earlier I had promised to help Chuck mow a neighbor's lawn. Chuck was ready to go to our job, but I wanted to search some more.

"Come on," he yelled at me, "it's time to go."

"Let's look just a few more minutes," I begged. "It's *bound* to be here."

"Look," said Chuck, "you promised to help me this afternoon. Now, c'mon, we've *got* to go!"

It's funny how something as small as an arrow can mean so much to you when you're twelve. But I felt strangely sad, as though I'd lost a kind of friend. A lot of myself had gone into making it. I had shown it to my father and friends, and everyone had complimented me and made a big deal over it.

And now it was gone. Probably buried in the matted grass. I visualized it snapping under the weight of someone's foot, and groaned. And now I had to go help Chuck; I couldn't back out of that. I had promised.

Have you ever wished very hard for something, with all your energy, even though you knew it would be incredible if it ever really happened? Well, that's how it was with me and that arrow. While I was helping Chuck cut grass, I daydreamed about finding it.

When we finished our work, I waved "so long" to Chuck and headed home. Then, for some reason I can't explain, I was suddenly bursting with energy. *I felt good!* I wanted to run. And did I ever! I raced at top speed down the street. I charged along not knowing the reason for my elation, and then, out of breath, I slowed down to a walk. Ahead of me was a great tree whose branches reached out across the pathway. My clothes were sticking to my sweaty body, and my breath was coming in great gasps; the tree offered welcome shade from the sun, and as I drew nearer, I lifted my head up slightly and felt grateful for the coolness.

My eyes rested for a moment on the tree's gnarled branches; the leaves fluttered. Something red and black fluttered, too. I glanced down along the trunk and over to the other side of the tree, but the bit of red and black pulled my eyes back. A bird? . . . No . . . My brain did a double take, and I came to a startled halt. I blinked. Yes! There it was! My arrow! *Two miles from where I had shot it!*

I felt happy and bewildered all at once. The question—how did it get there?—kept turning in my mind. Could it have been carried along on a wind current, then dropped down into the tree? That seemed unlikely. And why *this* tree, along *this* path? Could some kids have found it and thrown it up into the branches? Still, no one—not even I—knew I'd be coming down this path; there were other ways home. Why did I choose this one? How did I happen to look up just in time to see the black and red feathers?

I was stumped. The arrow couldn't have traveled two miles on the power I had used in drawing back on the bow-string when I let it fly. I knew I wasn't that strong.

"Gee," I said out loud. I reached up to grab the arrow. Something superhuman, superstrong, Something so immense that I couldn't understand it was involved here. It made me feel a little weird, a little scared. As I took my arrow in hand again, a shiver ran down my spine.

That was the moment when I had my very first intimation of God.

It was a little thing, my finding that arrow, but it was something that had happened to *me*—it was my own special mystery. For the first time in my life I had to accept something I couldn't understand, and I was in awe of it.

From that day on I began attending church and Sunday school with new interest, learning about faith, talking to God, praying the Lord's Prayer—which became a part of my daily life. As I grew older, I discovered that my experience with the arrow that summer's day was but a tiny sample of what religion is all about. Faith in God is a mixture of mystery and awe; you cannot see it or touch it; it requires only that we accept and believe.

And that has been my understanding of faith ever since. It is something that I like to talk about to my own sons. Yet I wonder if they can really comprehend my story. I wonder if faith doesn't come to everyone differently, in some mysterious way.

PART 8

The Power in a Wife's Love

If you can find a truly good wife,
she is worth more than precious gems!
Proverbs 31:10 (LB)

W ho would Roy Rogers have been without Dale
Evans? Would the trails have been happy?

And Andy Griffith, speaking of his wife, Cindi, who walked him through a devastating illness and then urged him to risk a steep path back to a successful career in midlife, says, "I don't know how I would have made it without her." That's a line that grateful husbands worldwide can say of faithful, support-ive wives whom God has used to set priorities, to give perspec-tive that reins in ambition or despair.

Journey to Health

Andy Griffith

Each of us faces pain, no two ways about it. But I firmly
believe that in every situation, no matter how difficult,
God extends grace greater than the hardship, and strength and
peace of mind that can lead us to a place higher than where we
were before. Let me tell you about one of the hardest times in
my own life, and how I found this to be true.

I had been alone for a long time when I met an extraordinary woman named Cindi Knight. She had come to Manteo,
North Carolina, to be in a production of *The Lost Colony*, a
summer play in which I had got my start several decades
before. Our relationship began as a friendship, but as the
months passed, I couldn't help but notice her strong faith and
gentle strength. Did I mention she was also quite beautiful?
Somehow she fell in love with me. Five years after we met as
friends, we became husband and wife.

When she married me in April 1983, I was not at the pinna-
cle of my career. Ageism is rampant in Hollywood, and
although I was only in my fifties, work was getting harder and
harder to find.

Cindi had had frequent and major attacks of sore throat all
of her life. So, shortly after our marriage, we returned to Los
Angeles and went to see a throat specialist, Dr. Robert Feder.
He determined her sore throats were coming from her tonsils,
and scheduled an operation. Early the next morning we drove
over to Cedars-Sinai Medical Center and Dr. Feder took out

her tonsils. While she was recuperating, I got a bad case of the flu. Not exactly a honeymoon of the rich and famous.

My illness was strange. As I got better, the symptoms of influenza were replaced by pain—terrible, searing pain that ricocheted through my entire body. Cindi and I joked about our invalid status and settled in that Saturday to watch the Kentucky Derby on television.

But after the race, when I stood up and took a few steps, I pitched headlong into a nightmare. I was overcome by pain so encompassing that I couldn't feel my feet. I had no control over them, and fell to the floor in agony.

We couldn't reach any of our doctors that weekend. Yet I was so desperate for relief from the pain that I took some of the codeine prescribed for Cindi for her throat. It barely made a difference.

On Monday my doctor met us at a local hospital. There, a roomful of doctors attempted to find out what was wrong. For four days they hadn't a clue. Finally they did a spinal tap. When the results came in, one mystery was solved. I had Guillain-Barré syndrome, a rare form of nerve inflammation. It's thought to be caused by an allergic reaction to a viral infection, such as the flu. The nerves become inflamed and begin to send erroneous and scrambled messages to the brain. In some people it causes little pain but extensive paralysis; in cases such as mine, it causes little paralysis but intense pain.

There are no drugs or surgery to treat Guillain-Barré—so the doctor sent me home. "There is nothing we can do," he said. "You've got to ride it out. I'll prescribe some pain medication, but use as little as possible. Come back in a week."

The following week he said the same thing. And the week after that.

.. ..

By my next visit I was desperate. If anything, the agony was intensifying. Cindi tried not to let me see her fear, but my physical condition was deteriorating noticeably.

Up to that point, we had seen every doctor and specialist I had ever known. Nothing was helping, and the pain had become so consuming that there was nothing else in my life.

Then an old friend, Leonard Rosengarten, a psychiatrist, asked if he could come visit. I didn't want a friend to see how bad off I was, so I took my most potent pain medication just before he arrived.

A handsome, white-haired fellow, Dr. Rosengarten had nearly died from cancer of the esophagus, so he knew a thing or two about pain. He pulled up a chair and sat . . . and sat. He waited until the pain medication wore off and I could no longer hide my agony. Then he went to Cindi. "I know Andy," he said. "He's a stoic if there ever was one. So if he says he's in this much pain, I know he is. Would you mind if I got involved?"

The next morning, true to his word, Dr. Rosengarten got me into Northridge Hospital Medical Center in Northridge, California. I was admitted onto an entire floor of people fighting their way back from auto accidents, strokes, Guillian-Barré. Here, the specialty was therapy and pain management.

I'll never forget that day. The doctor assigned to my case brought along a medication specialist. The first thing the doctor said was, "We know you're in impossible pain. We're here to help you through it." At those words, Cindi said she saw my body relax. Just to have the severity of my condition acknowledged was the first step on my journey to wellness. The druggist was there to start me on as much medication as I needed, but then I would be weaned off it as I learned to handle the pain in other ways.

The doctors at Northridge Hospital knew that treating pain meant treating the whole person, not just the body. Every day we had classes in biofeedback, which taught us how to use our minds to help control pain. For example, imagining the pain coursing down through your body and out through your toes actually releases endorphins that physically fight pain. But even though my pain was gradually diminishing, my foot still felt lifeless. It was slow-going as I shuffled around.

State of mind is crucial, we were taught. Consequently, we patients were all pulling for one another. I'll never forget looking into the day-room one Saturday and seeing a group of stroke patients in a semicircle, with a therapist behind each of them. The patients were passing a ball from one to another. Each time one successfully maneuvered the ball to the person seated next to him, all the therapists cheered wholeheartedly. There wasn't a bored or blasé staff member among them. It was one of the sweetest and most wonderful scenes I had ever seen.

One day, the therapist working on me saw one of my toes move. The whole hospital heard about it. Patient after patient and doctor after nurse stopped by my door and said, "We heard the great news! Congratulations!" I was on the mend.

So instead of lying at home, isolated, with nothing to do but dwell on the pain, I was suddenly busy, part of a team, pulling not only for myself but for the others on my floor as well. By the time I left the hospital a month later, I was taking eighty-five percent less medication than when I arrived. The pain wasn't as severe, and I was equipped to handle it.

Although I was no longer in the acute phase of my illness, we weren't out of the woods yet. It took me nearly a year to recuperate to the point where I could participate in everyday activities. And it was a rough year. My former manager told

Cindi and me that we were virtually broke. We thought life would be easier back in my home state of North Carolina, so we put our Los Angeles house up for sale. But the real estate market was bad, and not one good offer was forthcoming.

As I fought my way back from Guillain-Barré, I never stopped thanking God for the help He had provided me through Dr. Rosengarten, but especially through Cindi. Yet I couldn't help but feel bad. She had married me for better or worse and all she had got was the worse.

At the end of that year, I sat in our unsold house with no bank account to speak of and no work in sight. Not only was I old by Hollywood standards, but I had also been out of the game for a year. That alone is hard to overcome. I was getting physically stronger, but I was so depressed. We couldn't sell the house—I didn't know what to do.

Then Cindi came up with an off-the-wall idea. "Maybe it's a *good* thing we couldn't sell the house," she said. "Maybe it was God showing us grace. If we moved to North Carolina now you might indeed never work again. What we need to do is stay here and stoke the fire."

That day, and every day for quite a while, Cindi and I went over to The William Morris Agency at lunchtime and sat in the lobby. My agent and every agent in the building saw us. Everybody talked to us, invited us to their offices, some to lunch.

The upshot of it was I got roles in four TV movies that year, including *Return to Mayberry* with Don Knotts and Ron Howard, and the pilot for *Matlock*—a show that ended up running for nine years!

During this period Cindi decided to give up pursuing her own acting career and work with me on mine. I don't know how I would have made it without her.

That was more than a decade ago. Now, though *Matlock* is over, I have a new feature film, and I've recorded an album of my favorite gospel songs. Ageism hasn't left Hollywood, but I hope I'll continue to work.

Guillain-Barré has left me with permanent pain in both feet, but like an unwelcome guest, it isn't so bad when I stop paying attention to it.

Challenges and pain will continue all my life, I know, but with Cindi at my side to remind me to accept God's grace, I'll go forward and continue to work with love and happiness.

I Didn't Get Away with It

Roy Rogers

W hat's wrong with a guy who isn't scared when he nearly breaks his neck filming Western pictures, but gets the shakes when he has to make a simple speech? For years I asked myself this question.

I was shy from my boyhood days when we lived on the Ohio River in a three-room houseboat built by my father. Our family—Mother, Dad, and three sisters—later settled on a farm outside Portsmouth, Ohio. Dad worked in a shoe factory, while my sisters and I helped Mother run the farm.

We kids went to a one-room schoolhouse, which was just an even hundred yards from the Baptist Church. I know because we measured it and discovered it a perfect distance for a foot race.

Our shoes came off after the last snow and didn't go on until fall. To toughen our feet in the spring, we ran barefoot races from school to church over a course of tough corn stubbles. My feet grew skin an eighth of an inch thick on the bottom.

By the time I was ten I could call a square dance and play the guitar. But to get up and talk before a class, or just a few people, would make me take off across the cornfields.

I earned a dollar a week by ploughing corn on neighborhood farms; later quit school and went to work in the shoe factory to help out the family finances. When the family went to visit my sister in California, I fell in love with the far West.

I drove a gravel truck in Lawndale, California, for a while, then during the depression took any kind of job. I helped build a state highway from Newhall to Castaic, later joined the "Okies," and picked peaches in the California fruit orchards described in *The Grapes of Wrath*.

During my spare time I practiced on my guitar, hoping that some day I could make a living as a musician and a singer. Three of us formed a musical trio called the Texas Outlaws, but it was rough going. Often the three of us lived in one room, where sleeping was done by unique arrangement of daybed, couch and chair. In our travels we often had to go out and shoot rabbits to live.

Then, as often happens to a guy who wanders into Holly-wood, I had a lucky break, got a spot in a picture and my film career started. When my wife died during the birth of our third child, I was faced with a demanding career and the responsibilities of raising three fine children.

The story I want to tell begins several years later. Dale Evans, a film star in her own right, and I had been making pictures together for many years. With the unanimous approval of my children, we were married on December 31, 1948.

We hadn't been married but a few days when she started one morning with "It's a beautiful day to go to church!"

Now I wasn't a stranger to churches. I just hadn't time to get acquainted with very many because of other things I preferred doing. "Honey, I've gotta go see Joe Miller this morning," I said quickly. "Why don't you go ahead without me?"

This was the first excuse I could think of, but with more advance warning I could have done much better. Dale fixed a firm eye on me, and I knew her nimble mind was working overtime. She let me get away with it the first time, but going

.. ..

to church soon became the most important thing there was to do on Sunday.

One night before going to bed I noticed a new book on my reading table. "Where did this come from?" I asked, picking up a copy of the Bible.

"Since you lost your old one, I bought it for you this morning," Dale said brightly. She knew that I knew I never had a copy of the Bible, but what can you do with a woman whose mind is made up!

Grace before meals became a regular thing. Cheryl, Linda and Roy, Jr., (the three children of my first marriage) were quick to take a part. Dale introduced a type of Grace where everyone said a sentence prayer.

I would squirm in my chair a little, hoping they wouldn't notice me. So it went around the table, then "Why don't you say something, Daddy?" Linda piped up.

Dale, God bless her, is the smartest and most loving woman in the world. She didn't press me; but she never lets go of an idea she thinks is right.

Later, when I tried to explain my feelings to Dale, she would say, "The Lord gave you many talents, Roy. Some you use well for yourself, but there are some you haven't developed at all for Him. If you could learn to let God speak through you, honey, you could make a good speech every time—and not die doing it."

I didn't know what she meant at first. To some people, religion may come in one big emotional experience. I moved to it a step at a time: regular attendance at church, reading a few passages from the Bible, saying Grace. A warm quality grew into our family life. It was a spiritual kind of love that makes you want to do something for others.

A group of people in Hollywood began to get together and talk about all these things, people like Tim Spencer, Red Harper, Colleen Townsend, Jane Russell, Henrietta Meers, Connie Haines, Joyce Compton, Dale, myself and others. We would meet at different homes, some of us bringing along extra chairs. There was prayer for the problems of others; several would speak of religion out of their own experience.

I never had enough education to understand theology, but when a fellow like Tim Spencer stands up before a group like this and tells frankly how his belief in Jesus Christ helped him change from a drunk to a hard-working citizen, then Christianity comes alive to me.

One day I discovered that I actually looked forward to saying the blessing at mealtime. It may sound corny, but I could hardly wait for my turn. I began to appreciate the wholesome things that happen in each area of life when you're right with God. Not that I don't have plenty far to go.

As I said before, Dale is a mighty smart woman. She helped bring something new into our family life, but not at the sacrifice of other things we enjoyed, like outdoor sports.

The biggest triumph came when I used Dale's suggestion about speaking in public. The occasion was like many others. The music part I handled without any fear, but when it came time to say a few words, I felt the same old nervous symptoms. Then I closed my eyes for just a moment and said silently, "Lord, I'll just make a mess of things on my own. Help me to relax a little so that what I say to these people will really mean something."

I started to talk and found myself saying things I'd never said before. And they came out as naturally as though I was just standing there and someone else was talking. From that time, I've never had more than the normal amount of nervousness.

Somehow it doesn't make any difference now whether the group is simple farm folk or sophisticated New Yorkers, the things I try to say are the same. At the Rodeo in Madison Square Garden, I took the opportunity at every performance to reply to a letter I received from a boy who asked, "Is it sissy to go to Sunday school?"

Now there was a question I really enjoyed answering.

"It certainly is not," I said. "Going to Sunday school and church is one of the greatest privileges we have. I only wish I had been smart enough to know this earlier in my life."

An Unscheduled Stop

Karl Malden

Acting was the furthest thing from my mind when I got a backstage carpentry job at the Goodman Theatre School in Chicago. But one day one of the actors the director needed wasn't around, and I was hastened into a play. Suddenly everything in my life changed. All I wanted was to be an actor. A good one. I'm still working at it.

At the Goodman I met Mona Graham, a pretty girl from Emporia, Kansas. When we were married in 1938 Mona gave up her own dream of becoming a star. "One actor in any family is enough," she said. Before we set out to try to make it on the New York stage, I laid down an ultimatum: "Make it big in five years, or we go back to my hometown of Gary, Indiana."

I had some luck on the New York stage and began pushing hard. Too hard.

Suddenly I took sick with a mysterious ailment and everything came to a sharp halt. For the next six months I languished in a hospital in Denver, Colorado, all knotted up inside. Maybe Someone was telling me something, but I wasn't listening. While the doctors were trying to figure out why the health of a husky man like me had nose-dived, I was trying to figure out why my career had plummeted.

One day, feeling especially depressed, I told Mona, "I'm like an express train that's been derailed."

"Maybe we're not derailed at all," she said. "Maybe we've just made an unscheduled stop in a pleasant place we'd have never seen if we'd been barreling through. Let's get off the train and rest."

"Suppose I don't make it big?" I asked, not resting at all.

"And suppose you just get enough acting jobs to keep food on the table," Mona quickly replied. "We'll still be together. You'll still be doing what you enjoy doing. Relax, Karl, sometimes you have to stop to keep going."

Then and there I stopped my wild race with ambition. And as soon as I did, the doctors discovered an abscess on my lung, treated it successfully, and I went on with my career. Whatever part I got in a play or movie or TV, big or small, was sufficient, and I enjoyed doing it. I don't think all that was coincidence.

Since then, whenever the urge to rush ahead hits me, I slip into whatever church is nearby, and there, in the stillness, I thank God for freeing me from the frustrations of pushing too hard. It's a stop I'd recommend to anybody who wants to keep going.

Charity Begins at Home

Rosey Grier

B ack in 1978, on my way from Los Angeles to an out-of-town speaking engagement, I gave my ex-wife, Margie, a call. She asked me if I'd be coming to Parents' Night at Rosey Jr.'s school.

"Sorry," I said, "I'll be out of town."

"Again?"

"Come on. I'm the main speaker at a fundraiser for underprivileged kids."

"I see," said Margie softly. "You know, Rosey, there's an old saying you might consider: 'Charity begins at home.' "

Her remark angered me. But why, I wondered, do I feel so empty inside?

By all appearances my life seemed to be going great. When my pro football days ended, I'd made the transition from athlete to former athlete pretty smoothly. I found myself in surprising demand as a speaker for a variety of charitable causes.

On the home front, however, things weren't so good. My marriage had ended in divorce, and because I was always on the road, I hardly had time to see my son.

Early one Sunday morning I was sitting alone in my apartment, feeling down, when the phone rang. A concerned friend urged me to listen to some preacher on TV. Reluctantly I said okay.

It was the best thing I ever did.

Holding an open Bible, the preacher—Fred Price—talked

about Jesus in a personal way. And he promised that if I only believed in God and accepted His Son, my life would be transformed.

I hadn't thought about Jesus in a long time. But that morning the mere mention of His name touched me. Before the show was over I phoned Margie, asking her to have Rosey Jr. watch this show.

I began to watch Pastor Price every Sunday. He emphasized reading the Bible. So I did. And one day I noticed that the word *charity* (used in the King James Bible) is often interchanged with the word *love*. "Charity begins at home," Margie had said. Could it be, I mused, that love begins at home, as well?

Margie and Rosey Jr. started watching Pastor Price's show regularly, too. Then one Sunday we visited his church, and little Rosey and I went forward and committed our lives to Jesus. Several weeks later Margie joined us. In time, Margie and I reconciled our differences and were remarried. Praise the Lord!

Though I'm still on the road a lot talking about the life-changing power of Jesus Christ, I'm well aware that love begins at home—and spreads out into the world from there.

My Own Apocalypse

Martin Sheen

as told to *Charles-Edward Anderson*

I n the summer of 1976 I flew out to the Philippines to begin work on a film that, to my way of thinking, was a great step upward in my career. I had a leading role in *Apocalypse Now*. At last—a really important movie for this boy from Dayton, Ohio. From now on it was going to be big parts and a taste of real fame. How was I to know it would nearly be the end of me?

From its inception, *Apocalypse* had all the earmarks of success: Francis Ford Coppola, with his worldwide recognition and glittering record of box-office hits, was at the helm as director, Marlon Brando was the costar, Robert Duvall had a supporting role, and the film's financial budget was way up in the millions of dollars.

I had been assigned the role of Captain Ben Willard, an Army intelligence officer and hit man, who, although on the brink of emotional and psychological collapse, had been ordered by his superiors to travel through war-torn Vietnam into Cambodia, where he was to assassinate an American Green Beret colonel. That colonel, played by Marlon Brando, had, from all appearances, gone mad and was operating his own private renegade and bloodthirsty armies in the wilds of the Cambodian jungles.

Just before the filming of *Apocalypse* began, Janet, my wife of fifteen years, and our four children joined me in the Philippines, where movie set designers had transformed the lush, green tropical vegetation outside Manila into amazingly close replicas of all the actual photographs I had ever seen of Vietnam and Cambodia. For as long as I can remember, I have always taken my wife and family along to live with me during extended periods of time on location. I had never wanted my acting role to get in the way of my being a good husband and father. This time was to be no different.

From the first moment I read the script of *Apocalypse*, I was fascinated by the character of Captain Willard. I generally try to create a character I'm portraying in my own image. In "becoming" Willard, I had no idea how dangerous this would be, for Willard was emotionally burnt out, insensitive to those around him, uncaring, hard-drinking, overly ambitious, self-centered and single-purposed. Were these menacing attributes of this on-camera character, coupled with the intensity of my own pursuit of success, beginning to boil over into my off-camera life? Or was I really more Willard than I wanted to admit?

Janet tried to talk out the wrinkles growing in our relationship and tell me what I was doing to others around me, but I vehemently denied that *anything* was changing—least of all me. Then Janet tried to reason with me that she and the kids didn't mind making *some* sacrifices for my success, but now this role, this Willard thing, was making me lock them out. I was making them more and more miserable. Even Francis Coppola was beginning to find me difficult to deal with, but I couldn't seem to help myself.

Although I was raised in a devout Catholic home, the thought of praying about my family problems never entered my mind. And I wasn't about to go near a church—I had given that up in my mid-twenties.

.. ..

To understand where all this was taking me, let me explain where and how it all began. First, Martin Sheen is only my acting name. Born and christened Ramon Estevez, I was the seventh of thirteen children of Francisco Estevez and Mary Ann Phelan Estevez. My father, a Spaniard, met my mother, an immigrant from Ireland, while the two attended citizenship training classes in Dayton, Ohio.

I was eleven years old when my mother died. My father, a factory worker for the National Cash Register Company, never remarried, and single-handedly raised us (ten boys and one girl; two boys died in infancy) in a lower-middle-class neighborhood in Dayton. I attended Holy Trinity grade school, run by the Sisters of Notre Dame, and Chaminade, a Catholic high school for boys. Early on I served in the parish church as an acolyte. It was our life in the church that helped keep our family together.

By the time I was six or seven years old, I was spending hours alone acting out the parts of characters I read about in books. Not until movies came into my young life did I know that what I was doing had a name—acting—and I knew then that I was an actor. Right after high school I headed for New York to fulfill my dream of becoming a professional actor.

That's where "Martin Sheen" was born. The first name came from Robert Dale Martin, a drama coach and friend in New York. The last name came courtesy of the late radio-TV personality Bishop Fulton J. Sheen, whom I admired and—because of my name change—met in 1965. Martin Sheen. The name sounded good, solid, Irish. To my eighteen-year old mind, Ramon Estevez was too ethnic and would cause me to get typecast.

My career in New York grew gradually, first on the stage,

then TV and films. I married Janet, an art student at the New School for Social Research, and our family grew gradually too—three sons, Emilio, Ramon and Carlos (Charlie), and finally our daughter, Renée, all two years apart.

When the Captain Willard role in *Apocalypse Now* came along, it seemed to be the one big bright opportunity I had been waiting for. But the grueling work of putting together *Apocalypse* went on and on, often in hot, steamy days and sultry, humid nights. After nearly six months into the shooting, my Willard-born attitudes, with all the damage they were doing to my family life, had not changed. Our home was now a hotbed of intense stress and pressure.

Our kids began begging to go back to the United States to live with relatives. And finally Janet gave in and let them go. Then one day in early March 1977 Janet went into Manila for an overnight stay—to make sure we would have a decent hotel when I came the next day for a weekend there.

Late in the evening, I got back to the large rustic cabin we had rented for the duration of the filming. It was a comfortable place, perched on a mountainside and overlooking a volcanic lake. However, like all the other houses in the area, it had no telephone, radio or TV.

On that March night, I was alone and tired. Shooting the scenes of that day had drained me physically and emotionally. I looked forward to sacking out for the night, but when I went to bed I couldn't sleep.

I lay in bed for a while, then got up and paced wildly around the bedroom floor. I felt strangely clumsy and awkward, and at times it was hard to keep my balance. My breathing grew strained. When I went back to bed, sleep defiantly refused to come. I don't recall how many hours I continued in this state, but it must have been about three in the morning that I began to sweat profusely. A nagging pain crept into my right arm, and I leaped out of bed again. Something was terribly wrong, but I had no idea what.

I started to feel faint and slumped to the floor. Then came a devastating explosion of pain in my chest. It left me too weak to stand up. My breathing became rapid and difficult. I had to get outside for help, even though I was aware that outside a windstorm was raging.

I slithered slowly over to the closet and, one by one, yanked down pieces of clothing, then twisted and pulled my way into them as best I could. Another blast of pain hit my chest, and I knew what was wrong—a heart attack, the same thing that had claimed the lives of my mother, father and two of my older brothers. I knew I was dying.

I began to crawl slowly, agonizingly toward the door. The pain in my arm and chest was making me weak. Sweat poured off my body, I rose awkwardly to my feet and began taking baby steps out the front door. Just outside the house another blast of pain knocked me to the ground.

The wind was still howling. Towering palm trees were bending near the ground and lightning flittered nervously about the sky, giving the whole area the look of an eerie movie set. But this time it was definitely not a movie. Ramon Estevez/Martin Sheen was dying, and the scene was all too real.

Once more I struggled to my feet, only to find that my depth perception was failing. I reached for trees and clumps of shrubbery, only to find that they were about fifty feet away. Then my eyesight went altogether. I yelled weakly for the guards the production company had provided, tripped over something and fell again. My hearing was also weak, but I could feel the wind pick up speed. I couldn't move anymore. That's when I called to God for help.

I don't know how long I lay there before one of the security guards making his rounds spotted me and carried me to the guardhouse station. He laid flat boards across the back of a Jeep and gently placed me on them. Then he drove a bumpy mile and a half down the mountainside to a small village, where a young Filipino doctor had a small clinic. I had come to know the doctor earlier since he had often given first aid and other medical treatment to members of the cast and crew. He found my heart rate was very low and my blood pressure way up. He slipped a glycerin tablet under my tongue. Soon another blur of a figure bent over me. It was a priest. "Do you want to make your confession?" he asked in broken English. I tried to answer but couldn't. He waited a long moment, then began to intone the Roman Catholic last rites.

My last recollection before losing consciousness was of being placed aboard one of the helicopters—used as a prop in *Apocalypse*—for a daring flight through the storm to a hospital in Manila.

When I awoke, another blur of a figure was bending closely over me. This one was smiling. Janet.

"You're going to make it, Babe," she said glowingly, "and remember, it's only a movie. It's only a movie." At that very moment, all that ailed me physically, emotionally and spiritually began to heal.

Even though I did not physically die that night, the Willard character in me did. My face-to-face confrontation with death and my own human vulnerability purged the need to be an empty celluloid image bent on the accumulation of such things as fame or wealth. I had been shocked into recalling something

I had known all along but had forgotten: that love is the true foundation of happiness. Love of family, love of people, love of God.

In the years since that painful night, Janet, our children and I have grown closer and happier than ever. I have long since returned to my church. I have never forgotten that even though I turned my back on God, in my time of greatest need, He came to find me.

PART 9

The Power in an Inner Principle

The just shall live by faith.
Romans 1:17 (KJV)

"I want a principle within," wrote hymn writer Charles Wesley. A principle that helped him know right from wrong and live a life pleasing to God.

The notable men and women featured in this section tell us about the inner principles that have molded their work, their relationships, their daily decisions. As you read their stories, think about your own life: What values or phrases are so foundational to your life that they help define who you are? What inner principles has God used to change the course of your life?

A Partner with God

Stan Smith

W hen young Boris Becker of West Germany won the men's singles tennis title at Wimbledon in 1985—at seventeen the youngest player and the only unseeded player ever to win this most prestigious of tournaments—I not only saw the happiness on his face but also shared his exultation as he held the shining trophy aloft. The thought came to me that, of all the millions watching in the stadium and on TV, I was one of the very few who knew exactly how Becker was feeling, because I am one of the privileged players who have won that tournament myself—in 1972.

Now I spend a lot of my time teaching eager youngsters the fundamentals of the game. I also try to teach them Christian values, because Jesus Christ came into my life when I was still in college in California, and that has given me a peace and a purpose that has made all the difference ever since.

It's easy to see how youngsters can become confused these days, or pick up the wrong values. Sport has become big business, with enormous sums of money paid to first-class athletes. As you work your way toward the top, the pressure and ego temptations become greater. It's easy to be jealous of other athletes who are more successful. I tell my tennis students, "Can you conceive of Jesus being jealous of the rich young man who came to Him for advice? Or envious of John the Baptist because at first John was better known than He was?"

Another confusing thing for some of the kids is that Christianity stresses unselfishness and going the extra mile for others. But competitive sport emphasizes winning, and in tennis—which is often a one-on-one duel to victory or defeat—this direct confrontation can be ferocious. My advice is: Play hard, play fair and respect your opponent while you're doing your best to overcome him.

There are seven principles that I teach, principles just as applicable to life as to tennis. The first is, Set high goals. The higher you set the bars for yourself, the higher you're likely to jump.

The second is: Prepare as thoroughly as you can. No worthwhile goal in sports is ever achieved without paying the price of preparation. That means practice—endless, exhausting practice; taking care of your body; driving yourself to the limits of your endurance, mental and physical.

I remember when I was moving up in the tennis world. I used to imagine myself in the finals at Wimbledon. In this fantasy I was always in the fifth set of a grueling match against a brilliant and tenacious opponent. Games stood at five all. Tennis talent on both sides of the net was about equal. The man with the last ounce of stamina and determination—in other words the best-prepared player—was going to win. And the day came in 1972 when I did find myself in the finals at Wimbledon, playing in the fifth set against Ilie Nastase of Romania. And I won—just barely—possibly because I was a fraction better prepared than he was.

The third thing I tell young players is: Never give in to discouragement. There have been some sensational comebacks in the history of tennis, but never by a player who gave up.

The fourth is: Strive for self-control. If you blow your top, you're likely to blow the match along with it because you'll lose your concentration and you may not get it back.

Rod Laver, the Australian player whom I consider the greatest of all, knew this, and I never knew him to let his temper get out of hand. It's a hard lesson for a fiery, competitive youngster to learn, but it's really a matter of self-interest. If you lose your self-control, you aren't hurting the linesman, or the umpire, or your opponent. You're hurting yourself.

Here's the fifth thing I say to young players: Go for absolute honesty. When you're starting out in tennis, almost all your matches will be played without linesmen or umpires. You will have to call the close shots, because your opponent can't see them. Now and then there may be a temptation to call one out when you know it was in. Don't do it. You'll have to make up your mind very early not to cheat; otherwise one little deception will lead to another, and first thing you know, your self-respect—and perhaps your reputation—is down the drain. You can't carry that kind of burden if you want to be really good.

My sixth suggestion is: Choose a good role model for your life. Someone to look up to, to admire, someone who represents good values. I tell them that my own role model is Jesus, and I think they can't do any better than that. "Having Christ as a role model," I tell them, "doesn't mean you have to be a pushover. Christ faced tough decisions. He came through tough situations. He never complained. He never whined. He just did what He knew was right with a combination of love and strength and courage that has never been equaled."

Finally, I say to the kids, "Look for God's purpose in your life." If they reply, "How do I do that?" I tell them to watch for the talent in their makeup. Everyone has a talent for something, and this is God's gift. He plants it in us; then it's our job to make it grow.

"Once you've recognized your chief area of talent," I say to young players, "once you've decided that it's a sign of God's purpose for your life—even if it's not tennis or another sport—you're free to move ahead consistently and boldly. Then you feel good about yourself, because you're a partner with God in the way He wants us all to be—living life abundantly."

Team Captain, Team Respect

Harold "Pee Wee" Reese

The news about the first black major league baseball player wasn't the most important thing in my life that hot afternoon in 1945. I was more concerned with filling out a royal flush in the card game some buddies and I were playing on a Navy ship coming back to the States from Guam.

Someone hollered at the door, "Hey, Pee Wee, did you hear? The Dodgers signed a n_____!"

I shrugged and called for another card.

Then the guy added, "And he plays shortstop!"

My head jerked up. The guy was serious.

Just my luck, I thought. He plays my position.

I had been playing shortstop for the Brooklyn Dodgers since 1940 and had made the All-Star team in 1942 before joining the Navy. Though the black player, whose name was Jackie Robinson, would be playing for the Montreal Royals, a top Dodgers farm team, I figured eventually we would be on the field together.

Oh, well, I thought, picking up my card. I was confident in my abilities. And if Robinson could beat me out, more power to him. I was concerned about getting home to my wife, Dorothy, and daughter, Barbara, who was only eleven days old when I had left.

Not that I had any special affection for black people. I had grown up in the small Kentucky town of Ekron, where blacks lived on one side of town and whites on the other. I'm sure most of the kids had heard that old Sunday school song: "Red and yellow, black and white, they are precious in His sight"; but there wasn't any mixing, even in the marble games we played. (I got my nickname at age thirteen from the "peewee" I used as a shooter to play marbles.)

When I started playing baseball it was the same: The blacks had their leagues, we had ours. After high school I worked in Louisville as a cable splicer for the phone company, and played weekends on the New Covenant Presbyterian Church team. In 1937 we led the church league and got to go to New York to see the Giants and Yankees battle it out in the World Series. A year later I was playing shortstop for the Louisville Colonels and then went to the Dodgers under Leo Durocher. It wasn't until April 11, 1947, when Branch Rickey signed Jackie Roosevelt Robinson to a National League contract with the Dodgers, that I was directly affected.

I don't remember shaking a black man's hand before, but on that spring training day, I walked over to Jack and, as captain, welcomed him to the team. I knew he had something going when I saw him bat and throw.

Some of the guys weren't happy about their new teammate. Late one night while Pete Reiser and I were talking in my hotel room there was a knock on the door. I opened it to find outfielder Dixie Walker and two others. He handed me a petition stating those who had signed wouldn't play baseball with a black man. "I'm not signing it," I said. Neither would Reiser. And that was that.

I wasn't trying to think of myself as being the Great White Father. I needed the salary, and I just wanted to play the game. It didn't matter to me whether Jackie was black or green; he had a right to be there too.

It turned out Jackie didn't play shortstop. I stayed in that slot and eventually Jackie played second base. We got to be kind of a partnership. Recently a sportswriter called us "one of the brightest double-play combinations in baseball." Well, a team's got to be strong up the middle if it's going to win pennants, and that's what we did—won pennant after pennant.

But it wasn't easy for Jackie. During that first year, after I had played cards with Jackie in the clubhouse, Dixie Walker came up to me. "How can you be playing cards with him?"

"Look, Dixie," I said, "you and Stell travel with a black woman who takes care of your kids, who cooks your food, who you trust—isn't that even more than playing cards with a black man?"

"That's different," he humphed.

"Tell me how," I said.

He couldn't come up with anything and walked away.

A lot of other team members took to Jackie, like Gil Hodges, Ralph Branca and Eddie Stanky. Jackie and I developed a kind of rapport. Once while we sat in the dugout, he complained that "the pitchers are throwing at me because they're racists."

"No," I said, grinning. "They aren't throwing at you because you're black. They're throwing at you because they don't like the way you hit."

He leaned back and gave a long easy chuckle.

But Jackie did take a lot of guff on the field. There was one time when I didn't see how any human could stand what he was taking. It was on our first road trip. In Cincinnati the heckling from the fans really became brutal. It was more than boos and jeering; the whole stadium seemed to be in a bellowing frenzy. Then somebody threw out a black cat, which scampered across the field.

I looked over at Jackie standing alone, looking so sad, so vulnerable. Something in my gut reacted. Maybe I was thinking of the hanging tree in Brandenburg, a little town near Ekron. I remembered my dad pointing to a long branch and telling me black men had been lynched from it. As a little boy, it made a terrible impression on me that people would do things like that just on account of skin color. Something about the unfairness of it all, the injustice—what? I don't know. But I stepped over to the pitcher, called time out and walked over to Jackie. I said something consoling, then reached up, put my hand on his shoulder and just stood there looking at the crowd.

The jeering stopped like someone turning off a loud radio. And we began doing what we had gone there to do, play ball.

As you know, Jackie Robinson went on to greatness. He would turn the other cheek, but he also stood up for himself. He could be a tough bench jockey, and sliding into base he might plow into a guy who was in his way.

When I see the talented black players in sports today, I'm grateful for having had the privilege of playing with the man who opened the door for them. But none of us was trying to put on a show. All that any of us was trying to do was best use the talent God had given us.

One of my last talks with Jackie kind of wrapped it all up. "You know, I didn't go out of my way to be nice to you," I said.

He grinned. "Pee Wee, maybe that's what I appreciated most."

The Question That Lights My Life

Pat Boone

Whenever I mention that I go to church during the week and twice on Sundays, even preach at times if I'm asked to, it always seems to come out as if I'm some sort of a goody-goody. Or as if I say it because it would help my career.

Neither is true.

What I do, what I believe, are derived from these people: my mother, who was a registered nurse, and my father, a building contractor in Nashville, Tennessee. They were steady, decent, believing, basic people, who gave their four children a steady, decent, believing, basic outlook.

When we were kids we didn't have a car. So we'd drive to church in my father's little pickup truck. He was a deacon and Sunday school teacher at the church. It always looked kind of funny pulling up in front of the church in a truck with "Boone Construction Co." painted on it. But such things brought us all close together. We always did things as a family, the six of us, playing or praying.

I have a kind of second father too, Mack Craig. When I first met Mack, he was the principal of David Lipscomb High School in Nashville, Tennessee, as well as a teacher working then for his Ph.D. He had his own family to take care of too. Skinny as a rail, mostly because he seldom took time to eat, he was always moving at a fast trot to keep everyone around him happy.

Whenever I was worried about something or had a decision to make, I'd take a walk with him or call at his house or even wake him at the awfullest hours. And he'd always say: "Forget what it means to you personally, or what you can gain by it, or have to give up, or what someone else might think of it. Just ask yourself: 'Is it right?' "

Since we met I have always tried to apply that yardstick to whatever I do.

It isn't always easy.

Like the question of joining a high school fraternity. To presume an air of exclusiveness, some frats discriminated against boys because of their poverty or beliefs or race. My parents disapproved of that, but when I pledged, intending to join a frat, they didn't try to stop me. Something else did: the question that has come to light my life when facing any perplexity: Is it right?

When you look at life from that perspective, the decision isn't hard, and you always feel relieved.

Singing was one of those things.

If the truth be known, it was really my appetite that got me into singing. Starting when I was about ten, my mother used to take me to sing at prayer meetings and other services. Then the ladies asked me to sing at their luncheons and club socials. They wanted free entertainment and I wanted a free meal. They told their husbands about it and pretty soon I was singing—and eating—at Kiwanis and Rotary too.

Then came the opportunity to sing with a good, local dance band, something I'd never done before. But singing with a dance band meant late hours, being around drinking. Troubled, I got Mack Craig out of bed at some horrible hour in the morning, and we talked about it.

Mack said: "Suppose there are temptations. Of course there

will be in singing, as in everything. But there's nothing wrong with being a singer if you handle yourself properly."

But instead of the dance band job, he went out and helped get me my first radio show: "Youth On Parade," over at the local station. It featured high school kids. I was the master of ceremonies and sang a little too. We did it for two years, my senior year in high school and freshman year in college. No pay at all, but it was great.

While in college I married Shirley Foley, a wonderful girl. She's the daughter of Red Foley, the TV star of "Country Music Jubilee," and we were high school sweethearts. We both transferred to North Texas State College in Denton, Texas, and with marriage, eating became a definite problem. I needed a real paying job. I got one as a TV entertainer in Fort Worth, and continued in college.

Following an appearance on "Ted Mack's Original Amateur Hour," Randy Wood, the president of Dot Records, asked me to come to Chicago to make a recording of "Two Hearts." I hesitated a little. If the impossible happened—a hit record— everything might go haywire. I was making $44.50 a week on TV and radio, which wasn't much, but enough to pay our way. Besides, our first daughter, Cheryl Lynn, was already here and our second, Linda Lee, was on the way.

Was it right to leave the security my family had then on the slim chance of a hit record? And what about my schooling?

My father and Shirley felt I should take that chance—so did Mack Craig. Shirley said she was sure I'd finish school whether the record was a hit or not.

It was. And then I was asked to move to New York. That was a much bigger step than Chicago. But I could attend Columbia, something I wanted to do. Everything seemed to fall into place when Arthur Godfrey invited me to be on his show any time school permitted.

Then came the offer to make a movie, *Bernadine*. The picture was to start in January, which meant I would have had to drop out of school before the term ended.

But that presented a problem. A lot of kids I know, and a lot of others who wrote me, said that if I could work and go to school full time, they could too. But if I dropped out before the term ended just for money, wouldn't I be letting them down? The movie people said it would cost an awful lot of money to postpone the picture. What was right?

I finished the term, but agreed to skip the following term to make the movie, which meant graduating in January instead of in June.

We all usually know what wrong is. I'm not sure we all know as often what right is. Mostly right is determined for me by what the Bible says it is, and how my parents and Mack Craig and other people I admire and respect live it.

Like them, I always ask myself about anything I do:

Will it violate my conscience?

Will it have a bad effect on others?

Will it have a good effect on others?

I'm not always sure about these things but I try to be.

My co-managers, Jack Spina and Randy Wood, also asked these questions about any place I was requested to perform in, or any song I was asked to sing. Sometimes it cost us.

When we were offered a song to record once called "Roll With Me Henry," we all knew it was going to be a sure hit. But the lyrics seemed suggestive. So we didn't record it. Another singer did, under a different title and with changed lyrics, and it sold over a million records.

.. ..

Before we got the TV show we liked, we were offered many. One came from a cigarette sponsor. I don't smoke, and it would be hypocrisy to ask others, especially teenagers, to smoke. I couldn't feel honest about it, that's all. So I asked the sponsor: "Suppose I went before the camera, and said: 'I don't smoke. I don't advise you to smoke, but if you're going to smoke, smoke this brand'."

They laughed, and then said: "Why, that's a new approach. Maybe we ought to try it."

They were getting serious, so we cut it off quickly.

What all this means is that we try to act the way we believe, publicly as well as privately.

No matter how long my singing career lasts, it's given me a great responsibility not just to my family, but to the many who look to singers as their example. I owe them a lot, if not everything. The only way I can repay them is to make a day-to-day reality of the question that lights my life: "Is it right?"

What a Manager Needs

Tom Lasorda

Soon after I took over as manager of the Dodgers in 1977, sportswriters began to comment on how I'd pal around with my players and sometimes hug them unashamedly on the field in front of thousands of fans.

I started reading criticisms such as: "You can't get too close to your players and be a good manager. If you get too friendly with them, it'll be impossible to maintain any kind of discipline. They'll interpret it as a sign of weakness and take advantage of you. It's human nature."

That's the sort of talk that bugs me about sports today. Ever since Leo Durocher remarked that "nice guys finish last," it seems to me that a lot of people connected with sports have been trying to prove it's true. Well, I just don't believe it. I love baseball, and I'm just naturally enthusiastic about the game, and when the chance came at last to manage a major league team—after twenty-nine years of working and hoping—I was ready to put my theories on the line.

Now, every manager has his own way of running a ball club. Some lay down strict rules and keep tight control over their players on and off the field. I wanted to pattern the Dodgers after a family—a family that loves and respects one another, a family that wants to do things together and prays together.

I suppose this idea of "family" in baseball came from my own background. I've been blessed with my loving wife, Jo, and two wonderful kids, Laura and Tom, Jr. I don't fail to tell them how much I love them and appreciate them. I feel that's important, especially because they've had to put up with a lot from me—mostly not having me at home a good deal of the time because of all the road trips during almost three decades with the Dodger organization.

But it goes back even further, to when I was growing up in Pennsylvania, where my dad was a truck driver for a Bethlehem Steel quarry near Norristown. There were five sons in our family. Our parents were Italian immigrants and we loved them. I wasn't ashamed to kiss my father every time I greeted him, and all of his sons would have gone through fire for him. But if we got out of line, he'd lower the boom on us. Discipline, yes—but loving and caring were the things that held our family together. Why, I asked myself, shouldn't the same principle work with the Dodgers?

Well, to my enormous satisfaction the Dodgers got right off to a big lead in 1977. Then one day a cynical reporter asked me right out, "What do you mean, you 'love' your players? What do you mean, you're 'close' to them?" I could tell he wasn't buying it—he felt somebody was putting him on.

I didn't answer him directly; instead I began a rundown: "Steve Yeager's wife is Gloria, and they have no children; Johnny Oates' wife is Gloria, too, and they have a daughter, Lori, and a son, Andy; Jerry Grote's wife is Sharon and his son is Jeff and his daughters are Sandy and Jennifer; Steve Garvey's wife is Cyndy and his daughters are Krisha and Whitney. . . ."

I went through the whole roster. I think I bored the pants off him, but he got the idea—I really am close to my players. And they know the difference between feeling cared about and just being a number or a valuable property. Caring—that's the important thing.

Reggie Smith is a good example of what caring can do. Reggie had been with St. Louis and Boston, and by the time he came to the Dodgers, Reggie had a reputation as an uncooperative malcontent.

I was coaching third base at the time, and I kept hearing bad things about Reggie Smith this and Reggie Smith that. I realized he was tough—there isn't a guy in the world who can knock a tear out of him. Yet I remembered seeing him cry when he got word that his father was critically ill. I filed that away for future reference. It was obvious that he loved his father.

I began to notice other things. Reggie would bring his son, Reggie Jr., into the clubhouse to meet the other players; he was proud of that boy. And after the game he'd always greet his wife, Ernestine, and his daughter, Nicole, with a kiss, and he'd greet his brothers warmly. I said to myself, "This is a family man; he's a good man, a loving man." And I refused to believe any of the mean talk about him.

Then, when I became manager, I called him aside and said, "Reggie, I want to do a good job with the team. I need you."

Reggie put his arm around me and said, "Tom, I'll never let you down." And he kept his word. He was a super guy and a super star all season long. In fact, he broke Duke Snider's long-standing Dodger slugging record, and the fans voted him our team's most valuable player.

Reggie's super effort for the team seemed to bear out a lesson I learned from the Bible, because I believe what a manager needs most of all, just as Solomon said, is "an understanding heart" (1Kings 3:9, KJV). I kept praying to God for an understanding heart in my dealings with people. I must have been doing something right because we went right through the season, winning our division by ten games.

.. ..

I'm not naive enough to think this team won because of me. I never got a base hit for this team. I never scored a run or struck anybody out for this team. The players did that. And even though we didn't win the big one that year, we still had a very successful season.

Naturally we were disappointed that we couldn't bring the World Series championship to Los Angeles, but we didn't lose our sense of humor over the loss. In our gloomy locker room, after Reggie Jackson blasted our hopes with his three homers in the final game, I told the Dodgers, "I still think you're the best ball team in the world, and I wouldn't trade you for any team anywhere." I paused, then added, "By the way, I hear there's a great team in Red China. . . ." That broke the whole team up.

Afterward a writer cornered me and asked if I was going to change my tactics. "Look," I told him, "in spite of what Vince Lombardi once said, winning isn't the only thing. Is it wrong that I tell my players that I love them? Is is wrong that I enjoy being around them? Isn't that what Jesus was talking about when He said, 'Love one another as I have loved you'?" And the writer just stared at me, as though he couldn't believe what he was hearing. But I meant every word of it. I still do. And I always will.

PART 10

The Power in a Child's Comment

Let the little children come to me, and do not hinder them, for the kingdom of God belongs to such as these.

Mark 10:14 (NIV)

C hildren ask a lot of questions. And often their questions and comments are catalysts God uses to nudge adults to a deeper faith or more intentional service to others.

Just ask Henry Winkler, better known to a whole generation as The Fonz.

Or consider the story of Robert Young, the TV father who always knew best, but who in real life was humble enough to learn a life-changing lesson from his young daughter.

A Small, Shy Voice

Henry Winkler

For years I played one of television's most popular characters, The Fonz—Arthur Fonzarelli, also known as
Fonzie—that supercool guy on the hit series *Happy Days* who
came on like Marion Brando in *The Wild One* but was really a
street-sweet guy with a heart of gold.

Fonzie rode a motorcycle, and slicking-back his hair with a
flick of his comb, set teenagers in the audience shrieking. Kids
all around the country greeted each other with The Fonz's
familiar, "Hey . . . ay . . . AY!" In fact, Fonzie became such a
part of American life that the black leather jacket he wore on
the show is now displayed as part of the permanent collection
at the Smithsonian Institution in Washington, D.C.

Over the years *Happy Days* and all its characters and cast
became like a real family to me. And yet, sometimes there were
doubts in my mind about Fonzie. I was trained as a classical
actor at Yale Drama School, and I'd always meant to be a
"serious" actor—doing drama, not comedy. And there were
times when interviewers asked me if I felt I was "compromising
myself" by playing a character like The Fonz.

Well, I'd answer that every acting job is important if it's
conveying a worthwhile message, and you adapt the part to
your own talents and tastes. That it took every bit of my training and skill to make the character of Fonzie come alive on the
home screen—and that it was more demanding to play comedy
and bring it off successfully. I meant every word of what I said,

but occasionally I too would wonder: Was playing the character of Fonzie doing anybody any good? I'd been raised in the Jewish faith and still felt a real peace and closeness to God when I worshiped in a synagogue. Was I doing what I was really meant to do? Was I using my God-given talents in the best possible way?

I'm chairman of an annual event called the Special Arts Festival that's held at the Music Center in Los Angeles. It's sort of a special olympics of the arts, where children with mental and physical handicaps come to perform in their own amateur theatrics, to show their talents, and exhibit their artwork. The walls are filled with paintings done by the boys and girls, music rings out as they play instruments and sing songs. It's an exciting time for everyone as the kids have a chance to display what they can do and become aware of the special contributions they can make.

Children are there from all backgrounds and all walks of life, and as I walk through the crowds, I do a lot of hugging. I hold the hand of a little girl in a wheelchair. I joke with a young boy without a leg.

Several years ago there was such a racket that it's amazing I heard the voice at all. "Fonzie," someone said. A small, shy voice in all the hubbub. "Fonzie!"

A little girl with large brown eyes and dark curls looked up at me. She was perhaps five years old—just staring at me. She didn't say another word. She wouldn't answer my questions. I just figured she was simply one of those shy ones that you see occasionally.

I told the little girl how glad I was to see her, then stood up and looked into the face of the woman who must have been her mother. But why were the woman's eyes shiny with tears?

The crowd closed around us and I went on.

And then one day I got a letter—from the mother of the little girl. She told me all about her daughter—I'll call her Claire. Claire was autistic. Autistic children are locked in a world of their own and rarely speak or communicate with others. For reasons doctors and psychologists still don't understand, autistic children are so totally self-absorbed that they don't seem to realize that anyone else exists at all.

In the entire five years of her life, Claire had not spoken a single word. Until she called out . . . "Fonzie!" Somehow the character of Fonzie had broken through to her, enabling her in that one mysterious moment to make a connection. With life.

The next year Claire was at the festival again, and I eagerly went to see her. This time her voice was firm and clear. "Hi, Fonzie," she said.

"Claire's teachers say she now has a vocabulary of over fifty words," her mother told me. "They can't believe what's happened."

Just at that moment Claire tugged at my hand. "My sister," she said, pointing out the young girl standing close to us. "Hug her, too."

Sometimes we wonder if we're doing our best for God. We're not sure if we're doing what we should with the gifts He gave us. That little girl showed me that we simply have to do whatever comes our way to the best of our abilities. And trust that God will find His way to touch someone else with them.

And what is that trust called? It's called faith.

Are You Too Old to Believe?

Julius LaRosa

My wife, Rory, and our five-year-old daughter, Maria, sat in the rear of the rehearsal hall while I ran through the song with the band for that night's performance in a Miami hotel. From time to time I left the microphone to lean over the stage and talk to the bandleader. This was the first time Maria had attended a rehearsal.

When it was over she hurried up to me. "Daddy," she asked, "how is it I can hear you so loud from way back where I was sitting with Mommy, but when you talked to the band-leader I can hardly hear you at all?"

"It's the microphone, Maria, it makes the sound louder."

"But how?" she persisted.

"Well, sound is measured by what they call decibels and . . ." Her large brown eyes were growing larger with perplexity. How do you explain decibels to a five-year-old? "I could tell you, sweetheart, but you really wouldn't understand. You will when you get a little older. Right now it's too advanced for you."

A few days later Maria and I were sitting together watching the sun set. "Daddy," Maria said, "where does the sun go at night? Does it go to sleep?"

"No, sweetheart, the earth turns and it goes around and . . . Maria, I could tell you, but it's really too advanced for you now."

"What's advanced?" She was really puzzled.

I hesitated, gathering my thoughts. "When you were born, Maria, your legs were very small; they weren't strong enough for you to walk. Walking was too advanced for you. But when your legs grew bigger and stronger, walking wasn't too advanced for you and you walked."

The puzzled look was fading from her face. "And when you were very small," I went on, "you couldn't eat a hot dog because you didn't have teeth yet. Hot dogs were too advanced for you until you had teeth. When something is too advanced it means you might not understand it now, but you will at the right time. Do you understand that, Maria?"

"Mmmm . . . I think so. Thanks."

Fours years after that particular question, I was taking Maria to church one Sunday. Her mother was going through the final stages of a shaky pregnancy that kept her in bed. My wife was the churchgoer, I wasn't. I had stopped regular attendance after a storm of doubt.

As we approached the church, Maria asked, "How come you don't go to church anymore, Daddy?"

"I used to go, sweetheart, but one Sunday I was sitting in church and I felt like I didn't mean it anymore and I thought it would be more honest if I didn't go."

"But, Daddy, you believe what happens there. You do believe in God?" Then, hesitantly, "Don't you?"

"I don't know, Maria."

She looked up into my eyes thoughtfully—as if she were scratching her mind, trying to decipher my confused answer.

"Do you think," she finally offered, "maybe it's too advanced for you?"

Inside the church her question began gnawing at me. It gnawed at me for weeks afterward, not without pain. Wiser heads than mine have yet to explain electricity or coincidence or the cosmos.

In time, all the things that made me feel "I didn't mean it anymore" seemed to answer themselves. Now, when I grope for the meaning of a sad or tragic event, a friend's child dies, an elderly relative loses a lifetime job, a plane crashes, whenever I think of all the ills that flesh is heir to, I'm reminded of the innocent wisdom of Maria who believes in belief. And I know there are many, many things that are too advanced for me, as there are for all of us.

And I believe, I believe.

On the Way to Christmas

Mala Powers

In a crowded store one afternoon before Christmas last year, I watched as the salesclerk grew more and more harassed. Finally, she turned to me, and with a gasp of irritation said, "Christmas! Who needs it?"

"I do," I said softly. "You and I both need Christmas." She stopped, and I could tell that for a few fleeting seconds she was thinking about that other Christmas, the one that is far removed from the noise of holiday shoppers. She relaxed.

"It's nice to see somebody happy in the middle of all this," she said, and smiled.

That salesclerk was right; I *was* happy. Maybe I had just been lucky, but years before, I had been led into a highly meaningful season that I'd known very little about—Advent.

It happened when my son, Toren, was a small child. As an actress with a busy schedule outside the home, I was determined, as a good mother, to bring up Toren with a love for the Lord. I wanted the holidays to mean more to him than jolly Saint Nick and gifts under the tree; but this was not easy to accomplish. There was too much competition from stores and television, from bags full of toys and red-nosed reindeer. From the start, I'd told Toren about the Nativity and Baby Jesus, but if you asked him what Christmas meant to him, he always said, "Santa Claus!"

I wasn't against old Santa, but I wanted Jesus to come first. Then one day a friend gave me the gift that changed both

my Christmas and Toren's. It was an Advent calendar, something I'd never seen before: a large, decorative card with little
window flaps that opened to reveal pictures underneath, one
for each of the twenty-four days of Advent. Each night after
that, I watched Toren as he opened another window: disclosing
stars, shepherds, donkeys; then Joseph and Mary; and finally,
on the last night, the Christ Child. Each time he opened a new
one, I'd talk to him about the significance of the picture, and
gradually found myself weaving little stories around them.
Toren was delighted.

And I was curious. What was the real meaning of Advent,
anyway? I knew dimly that it was the season of preparation,
that it always included the four Sundays before Christmas.
Now I started doing some research and found that the word
itself came from the Latin *adventus* and meant the "coming"
or the "coming in"; that among the earliest Christians, Advent
had been a time of fasting and prayer; that during this season
in the Middle Ages many of the beautiful rituals had sprung
up: the Nativity plays and processions of Wise Men, the crèche
scenes, the story-telling. I also found that there were Advent
wreaths available today, evergreens with four candles apiece,
one for each week.

At the end of November the next year, I got ready to celebrate my own version of Advent. When the first Sunday
evening arrived, we turned down the lights, and with careful
ceremony, Toren helped me light the first red candle on our
wreath.

"Think of it, Toren," I said quietly. "For centuries and centuries the world was in a kind of darkness, and then God
brought to earth a new and beautiful light for everyone: His
own Son."

Toren understood. "That was the Baby Jesus," he said in an awed whisper.

Each night in the weeks that followed, we'd open another window in our Advent calendar, and I'd find a new story to tell, the one about The Night the Chimes Rang, or The Animals' Christmas, or Toren's favorite about the little girl whose parents were too poor to buy her a present, but who in full faith put her wooden shoes by the hearth, and the next morning found the gift of a shivering baby bird inside one of them.

On the second Sunday of Advent, we lit the second candle and I talked about the meaning of the evergreen, how it stood for the eternalness of God, and how the circle of the wreath symbolized His all-encompassing love for us.

Gradually, some of Toren's little friends began to come by for our nightly ritual, and before Christmas arrived that year we found that we had created our own neighborhood tradition. It's a custom that continues today, even though Toren is grown now and away from home.

The form of our little Advent observances hasn't changed much over the years. I've had to learn a lot of different stories. We've added prayers to the story-telling. And, actress that I am, I've found ways to heighten the drama of the occasion by such things as ringing a bell to attract the children's attention and bring them to a reverent hush. There aren't as many children in our neighborhood as there used to be, and sometimes there are more grownups in my living room than youngsters. But no matter what age, there's a meaning in the Christmas story for everyone.

Any night that I'm at home before Christmas these days, in fifteen minutes or so, we still try to create a mood of awe and devotion into which the Christ Spirit can enter. The children in the room learn more about the meaning of His coming, and the adults, including me, seem to derive an added benefit. I think that benefit comes partly from those few minutes of tranquility when, during the most hectic days of the year, we force ourselves to be quiet and let His Being sink into our souls. It's a quietness that I seem to take with me throughout the following day. It's a calm that often I've been able to share with others, even harried salesclerks who suddenly think, if ever so briefly, of the real Christmas, the one that began in the stillness of a night long, long ago.

What Father Knows Now

Robert Young

When our first daughter was born, my wife, Betty, and I prided ourselves on being enlightened parents. We hoped for a large family, and had decided to be very modern, very intellectual with our children. They were to have something we called "Christian Standards," by which I suppose we meant ethics, and to project the children in the right direction, we decided each would be christened in a nonsectarian church. But no church ties would be forced upon them: they were to be allowed to choose for themselves.

I realize now that it would have been difficult to offer them any other course, since we had never made the choice ourselves. I had been accepted into the Baptist church at the age of ten, but the only impressions my memory retained were the rite of immersion, the ability to recite the Books of the Old Testament, and a good attendance record at Sunday school for about two years. A flood in Kentucky had destroyed the church record in the town where my wife was born and her mother could never rightly remember whether Betty was baptized a Congregationalist or a Methodist.

As a young married couple we didn't worry about this, for we attended church only at the fashionable times of the year, Christmas and Easter. When I thought about it at all, I felt no need for constant church affiliation.

But we did want our children to have those Christian Standards!

Thus, each of our four daughters in order of their appearance—Carol Ann, Barbara, Betty Lou, Kathy—were christened in a lovely ceremony right in our living room by the minister of the Beverly Hills Community Church. And right there my ignorance was showing; had I entered the church proper, as I have since done, I would have observed on the bulletin board that the denomination was Presbyterian. But I didn't. Betty and I simply assumed that a Community Church was nonsectarian.

Once the girls were christened, we followed point two of our plan. Their mother and I tried to surround them with a closely knit, loving family atmosphere; we heard their prayers regularly, for we were praying people ourselves.

"You are," I told my daughters proudly, "free to choose your own religion." But I was as foolish as I was wrong. No real choice was being offered them, no habit of churchgoing was being developed.

Fourteen years—fourteen long years—elapsed before any one of the children decided upon anything or even mentioned a specific church. Then from boarding school Carol Ann wrote us a letter. Would we mind, she inquired, if she joined the Episcopal Church?

"It isn't sudden," wrote Carol Ann. "I've always had a tremendous respect for our chaplain, and I must admit it was his faith that made him what he is. So I began studying the service, trying to understand the words and the symbolism, and now they have great meaning for me. I truly love the service, and it gives me something I need."

A few weeks later we attended her confirmation.

During that summer vacation, each Sunday while mother and father and all her younger sisters slept, our fifteen-year-old daughter rose quietly and went to All Saints Church in Beverly

Hills. Then, out of deference to Carol Ann, Betty and I began attending with her. The younger girls, still free to make their choice, now chose to get up and go to church school.

In one short summer we became a churchgoing family!

At first I, personally, felt strange; I had not been to church in a long time. Carol Ann's return to school left us on our own, yet still we went. Why? Because it began to seem important, that's why.

Then one Sunday morning an Adult Confirmation Class was announced. Here again my ignorance was evident. Somehow, I had thought that after one reached a certain age one was too old to be confirmed . . . nor was I sure I wanted permanent membership.

I listened to the reassuring statement that the curious, the weary, were welcome, temporarily or permanently.

As Betty and I attended the class we began to learn things, to feel a part of the group, and when the instruction period ended we went right on into full church membership.

We had made our decision.

Our three remaining daughters were still offered their freedom of choice, but with this difference—our own choice had given them a real choice, churchgoing had become a reality. It was a thing you did, not something you just talked or wondered about.

How can you teach a child the necessity to make a choice if you haven't found it necessary to make one yourself? Talk does not place values anywhere. If we wanted our children to place God in the center of their lives, to have lasting Christian standards, then worship was not a question of forcing something on them but of offering them an opportunity, and of availing ourselves of the same privilege.

.. ..

Has being a churchgoing family made a difference in our lives?

We feel it has.

There has been no dramatic sinner-to-saint conversion. Fortunately we did not insist on miracles. But we have grown into a greater unity with one another and our fellow man, and there is a new steadiness and stability in our family life. It has been easier to discuss our problems in terms of our relationship to God.

The first thing it did for me personally was to rid me of a vast store of ignorance—the sly rumors I'd accepted almost unconsciously that "church people" are stuffy, no fun at a party, that Sunday school teachers and clergymen are pompous, dull. I found our church filled with people much like ourselves, a mixture of problems, good will, humor, shortcomings, but banded together to help one another, and to be helped to *do something about our difficulties*. I gained insight into my own shortcomings, and I began to overcome self-consciousness when I thought or spoke in terms of God, Jesus Christ, God's will, God's children.

Church membership has meant to me instruction and activity, theory put into practice. I found I had a lot to learn, some of it uncomfortable, but all of it invaluable.

I think what amazed me most was that I could live all those years with a real need for church and not know it. I have been a church member five short years now and I am still asking, "Why did I wait so long?" I guess perhaps the answer is that Father *didn't* know best.

Many legitimate opportunities for activity and service have come to me through church membership, and very often I've felt shy, or too new. As, for instance, when our minister tapped me to serve on the vestry.

"I don't know how," I said. "I'm a beginner at all this."

"You're on the Board of Directors of Bishop's School, aren't you?" he demanded.

"But that's different," I protested.

"Not much," he replied firmly. "Here's your do-it-yourself kit," and he handed me a neat volume called "How to Become a Vestryman."

Recently, I was asked to serve as consultant to the Radio and Television Division of the Episcopal Church. Betty has been very active with the church-sponsored Neighborhood Youth Association. Now none of this has been the dramatic, soul-saving activity I anticipated when I first joined the church, yet from every task which we have undertaken, Betty and I have gotten solid satisfaction and felt very humble to have been offered an opportunity to serve.

In taking stock, we became even more fully aware that our lives have been full of blessings and answered prayer. I think my reaction has been much like that of our youngest daughter, Kathy, who knelt to say her evening prayers with us shortly after her ninth birthday. She asked blessings for everyone—her mother, myself, her sisters, the neighbors, her school teacher, the dogs. Then she started on her request list. That was pretty long, too. It sounded like an enthusiastic letter to Santa Claus.

Suddenly there was a pause and then I heard Kathy say, in a small, meek voice: "And now, dear God, is there anything I can do for You?"

The Power in a Push to Potential

Let us not become weary in doing good,
for at the proper time we will reap a harvest
if we do not give up.

Galatians 6:9 (NIV)

C atherine Marshall told Diane Sawyer as a teen: "Above all, dream big." Sometimes that dream, of doing and being all you're meant to be, is realized only as a colleague or mentor, or even someone you haven't seen in years, says or does something that opens up a whole new world of potential. Sometimes that person gently nudges, as a man named Rich encouraged young Art Carney; sometimes it's a harder push, as John Wayne remembers of the "merciless" film director Henry Hathaway. Whichever the case, it can be just what is needed to persevere, to see a new solution to a problem. All because someone in your circle of acquaintance has taken a special interest in you—to help you realize your dream and, more, God's dream for you.

The Man Who Spoiled Me for Good

Art Carney

U nder a glass dome on my dresser is a gold pocket watch, not expensive, but very precious. It belonged to Rich. Whenever I look at it I see him, and I hear him. And I remember how he filled my youth with love and wonder and the special magic of hero worship.

His name was Philip Richardson. He was once the mayor of Woburn, a small Massachusetts city; he was an editor, and gave my father his first newspaper job. He and Dad became firm and lifelong friends with an enduring affection for each other. My mother loved Rich, too. Everybody did.

Rich had an unhappy and childless marriage, and when he was about fifty, he was alone. Naturally he came to live with us. My parents wouldn't have it any other way. He quit newspapering and, until he retired on a pension at sixty-five, worked for the American Telephone and Telegraph Company. Meanwhile, Rich gave all the love he wasn't able to give elsewhere to the six Carney sons. I was the youngest, so the relationship between Rich and me was the longest, and I like to think, the deepest.

My parents were unstinting in their love for us, but Rich added a new dimension to that love. My parents were the security, the authority, the insurance. Rich was the hero, the friend, the reassurance.

Our house was always full of frantic people. Any minor event could quickly reach the proportions of a major crisis. But

Rich had this wonderful calm that always punctured any crisis. Once, after eating a lot of junk, I got a fierce stomachache. I yelped. My brothers yelped at me to stop yelping. Amid the bedlam my mother and father sternly ordered me to take some milk of magnesia. That was for babies. Stubbornly I yelped back: "No! No! Never!" They appealed to Rich. He silenced the din with his smile, then swallowed a spoonful himself, filled the spoon again, and held it out to me. It was the gesture of an equal to an equal. I took it without a word.

He had a way of leaving anyone, young or old, with his dignity intact.

You were never conscious of his age. He was never older than the person he was talking to. He looked like a medium-sized, gray-haired General MacArthur without the severe face, but with the same meticulous air of distinction. Even when he played marbles with me he never lost that air. We had a crazy rug in our dining room with big colored squares in it and almost every day before dinner we'd play marbles on it. Then he'd go into the living room to read his paper. While he read I'd comb his hair into weird hairdos, pulling it up to points from every part of his head. He'd just go on reading the paper until I asked him to look at the hairdo in the mirror. Rich would get up, look, smile his approval, or frown his disapproval, then return to his paper. And I'd start another weird hair comb.

Rich got me my first ball, my first baseball mitt, my first two-wheeler, and my first dog. He was always at the games when we boys played baseball. He also took me to see the Woolworth Building. But mostly I remember walking with him. Long walks, in a lot of silence and always feeling his love.

It seemed that Rich never had any problems of his own. He

did. Plenty. But he never burdened anyone with them. I suspect he eased his problems by being with kids, especially me. Or maybe with painting. He was a good artist. He used oils, charcoal, water colors, or pen. And sometimes on our walks, we'd stop in a nice spot and sit, and we'd both paint or sketch.

Those walks. They were great. Every Friday we'd take a special long walk to Aunt Mabel's, a cousin of my father. Once, on the way there, I thought I smelled gas coming from the ground. I yelled "Gas! Gas!" Rich didn't think I was crazy. Anybody else would have. Not him. He went over, bent down, sniffed very seriously. Sure enough, there was part of an old gas pipe there with a strong gas smell. From then on, every Friday night, when we got to that spot we'd both stop, bend down, sniff, look up knowingly, and walk on happily, sharing our great, dark secret.

Then, coming to the hedges before Aunt Mabel's house, I'd duck behind one, then dash up the steps before Rich would catch me. I don't know if he started that or if I did. But like the gas-smelling it became a regular ritual on the Friday night walks to Aunt Mabel.

When I got older, much older, near thirteen, the walks got longer, much longer. I mapped them out to pass the house of the girl I was madly in love with at the time. Rich never protested. I knew that he knew, but he never let on.

He was at the heart of my world, really, but once, when I got articulate enough to tell him he was, he said: "I'm not the center of your universe or any universe. God is."

And whenever there was any trouble, big or small, his calm hovered over us, and we'd hear him say: "God and time will take care of it. Just ask, 'Lord Jesus, help me,' and if you really mean it, He will."

At school I spent more time in the principal's office than in my classes because of this irreverent urge I had to mimic my teachers. In one class, off in a corner, there was this bust of Beethoven, very severe-looking, very cold. One day I just couldn't resist: I rushed up, pulled out my handkerchief, and blew Beethoven's nose. The class broke up.

The principal didn't. "Arthur William Matthew Carney," she said, "you will never amount to anything."

I believed her. Rich didn't. Under his auspices I gave my first professional performance. I was nine when one day I got the idea of a one-man show. It was Rich who promptly sat down and wrote twelve invitations in his own beautiful script, mostly to relatives: "You are invited to a special evening of entertainment by Mr. Arthur Carney called 'Art by Art.'" I danced and had funny disguises, doodled on the piano as my father had taught me, and I got by on drums, slide whistle, and flexitone, a kind of musical saw.

I always wondered if I would make it in show business. Sometimes I still wonder. Rich never did. He was always there, through the years, even when out of sight, when I was knocking about the country with Horace Heidt, in night clubs, in vaudeville, when I couldn't get work of any kind. He was there in the early days of radio, and he was there when, as an infantryman, I set up my machine gun on one of the Normandy beaches and got a piece of shrapnel in my right leg before I could fire it.

And he was there, out of sight, when I drank. I once was able to drink pretty good as a young man. When I got older and had real responsibility, the remorse was worse than the hangover. I told myself I was headed for that endless lost weekend. I tried to quit. It wasn't easy. I could fool a lot of people about it. But when you talk to yourself or to Rich you have to tell the truth. He was gone when I dropped to the depths as a drinker. But at the lowest point I heard him remind me:

"Just ask, 'Lord Jesus, help me,' and He will—if you really mean it."

Hearing Rich say that, even when he wasn't there, I learned to mean it.

I try hard not to drink anymore. I don't beat the temptation every time but, whenever I say "Lord Jesus, help me," and mean it, I win, and the drink loses.

When Rich was seventy he was still playing tennis with me. When he was eighty-one he got a blood clot in his heart, and survived it. But he was never really right after that. For a time he lived with my wife, Jean, and me, and one night, when I was sitting by his bed, holding his hand, listening to his calm voice, he saw my worried look, and suddenly smiled reassuringly. He asked: "Do you think I'm going to make it?"

"Sure," I said, "you always will."

He died shortly after that. But he made it. He made it here, and elsewhere too.

Attitude!

Chi Chi Rodriguez

Chi Chi's my name and golf is my game. But when I was born in Rio Pedras, Puerto Rico, my name wasn't Chi Chi. Mama and Papa named me Juan Antonio after John the Baptist and Saint Anthony. But because baseball is very big in the Caribbean and my hero was a local player named Chi Chi Flores, I ran around asking everybody to call me Chi Chi. And they did.

As for golf, I didn't know what a putter or a driver was. As a seven-year-old all I knew was how tired I got plowing a sugarcane field behind a team of oxen all day. But it helped put food on the table for my five brothers and sisters and me. Sometimes we ate a real dinner only twice a week. Sometimes our meal was just coffee. Even so, we kids were brought up to share what we had, and as famished as Papa might be, he'd give his last plate of beans to a hungry youngster. He was that kind of man. "Jesus asks us to be compassionate and sharing," he'd tell us, "and that gives you peace of mind." Papa had that peace, even if he worked like a horse all his life.

Little by little I began hearing of other people who didn't have to work so hard. Some of my friends talked about money to be made at a fancy place nearby called the Berwind Country Club. They played a game called golf there. The game didn't interest me then, but earning money for carrying the bags of the players sounded a lot better than following those oxen.

I knew nothing about caddying. However, Mama always

taught us that when you're not sure what to do, just take the next logical step. She called this "walking in faith." And so one day I did just that: I walked down from that sun-scorched cane field into the strange new world of the Berwind Country Club.

At first I caddied just for the pay. But then the game itself started to fascinate me. I found a long piece of pipe and nailed one end of a guava limb to it. Then I invented my own game of hitting a tin can around our baseball diamond from plate to plate. Those years behind the oxen had given me forearm muscles for a vicious swing.

When not working, we caddies used to sneak onto the course, and with beat-up discarded clubs, we'd play to see who could win the most holes. Once, to my astonishment, I sank a forty-foot putt. But then the ball popped out—all by itself! I couldn't believe it. I looked again. A toad had been sitting in that hole, and when the ball rolled in, he jumped out from under it. I lost the hole. That's why, whenever I sank a long putt, I used to run and quick put my hat over the hole so the ball couldn't pop out.

As a teenager, I was hitting the ball pretty good, and some of the club members began to encourage me to think of golf as a career. They said if I really concentrated on it, I might be able to earn a lot of money on the PGA Tour.

However, at nineteen I went into the U.S. Army. About that time, some of my family had left Puerto Rico and moved to New York. On my first leave I went there, only to be dismayed by what I found. Back home I'd always thought that everybody in New York must be rich, maybe because of the way some neighbors who had moved there acted when they returned to visit. They'd put a hundred-dollar bill on top of a wad of singles and our eyes would pop.

When I saw the dismal, dirty tenement my family had to live in, I told Mama, "No, you can't stay here anymore."

I went right back to my Army base in Oklahoma vowing to get her out of that place, *somehow*. That "somehow" turned out to be golf. For waiting in the barracks was a set of clubs sent to me by one of the men I used to caddy for in Puerto Rico. I went out and hit shag balls, one after another. With every drive, I'd see the house I planned to buy for my mother. When I got out of the Army I went back to Puerto Rico and showed the club members how I'd worked on my game—and how determined I was. Those men helped me get started on the PGA tournament circuit in 1960.

It was slow-going at first, but in the 1963 Denver Open those forearm muscles of mine paid off. I won that tournament, and Mama moved into her new home.

I played in a lot of tournaments after that, though I usually ended up making more friends than money. Before every tournament, we pros usually played practice rounds with club members. On one of these rounds, I met the famous psychiatrist, Dr. Smiley Blanton, who was a member of the Sleepy Hollow Country Club in New York. A godly man who wrote many books on finding peace of mind through biblical principles, he helped found, with Norman Vincent Peale, what is known today as The Institutes of Religion and Health, which trains clergy of all faiths for pastoral counseling and also treats people who need psychological and spiritual help.

Smiley Blanton was in his late seventies and I in my twenties, but when we'd walk the course together, laughing and talking, those years between us didn't exist. He usually shot in the low eighties and could drive a ball two-hundred yards off the tee. I learned a lot from him. About life. About golf. He

.. ..

taught me that when I prepared to tee off, I must concentrate on the pin, not on the sand traps and water hazards in between.

"Be positive," he'd tell me. "Your body can do only what your brain sees, Chi Chi. If you think of the negatives, you'll be drawn to them. But if you keep your goal foremost in mind, you'll aim for it."

By the time I reached age fifty in 1985 and was eligible to join the Senior PGA Tour, I had won eight PGA tournaments in twenty-five years, a respectable record, though small change compared to the superstars. It didn't look as though I would take the senior circuit by storm either. I told friends that I was thinking about learning to hit shots off my knees. "I figure I have a better chance if I'm praying and swinging at the same time," I laughed ruefully.

I had a major problem with my putting. If anything kept me from winning big through the years, it was those last few feet before the cup. Putting is a decisive factor in winning championships. You have to drop those three- to six-footers consistently. And you must hole some of the long ones. Many a tournament is won by just one stroke.

By May of 1987 I was at a real low point. I had just blown another tournament. I mean I really blew it, missing about thirteen putts. I bogeyed and double bogeyed, shooting a forty-two on the last nine holes. I didn't even earn enough money in that tournament to cover expenses.

I felt lower than a drainage-ditch lizard in my old barrio in Rio Pedras. The next tournament was the Vantage at the Dominion Country Club in San Antonio. But I didn't have the heart for it. In fact, I was thinking of calling it quits. My wife and I flew to Dallas, and I said, "Iwalani, I'm going to put you on a plane for home, and I'm just going to sit here by myself in the airport hotel for three days and think." I wanted to just meditate; maybe God would show me something. And so I sat there in my room wondering if I should give up the game.

As I brooded, an hour passed, then two. I had never asked God for a win, only for the strength to accept whatever happened. But what *was* happening? I desperately searched for some kind of answer.

Suddenly it was as if God was talking inside of me. *Get out of here*, He said.

When God speaks, I listen. Just like when Papa would give an order, I learned to jump. With God I was even more attentive.

Get out of here.

I quickly packed my bags, and walking in faith, like Mama had taught, I took the next logical step and went to the airport. And since the next tournament seemed to be the place to head, I bought a ticket for San Antonio.

When I got to the gate to board the plane, who should be standing there but Bob Toski. My mouth fell open. Bob is one of America's top golf teachers. A champion pro player, he was on *Golf Digest* magazine's professional panel and has written books on the game.

He greeted me warmly.

After some small talk, I blurted. "Bob would you help me with my putting?"

He looked at me for a moment, his friendly blue eyes crinkling. "Chi Chi," he smiled, "I was wondering how long it would take you to ask."

On the way to San Antonio, Bob gave me some pointers.

"First, you must look at your attitude toward putting," he said. "One simple problem is carelessness. This leads to really

bad misses which then make you overconcerned. That gener-
ates more tension. And it becomes a vicious circle as you
change your style, grasping at gimmicks; your stroke becomes
mechanical, overcontrolled."

Then Bob mentioned something that reminded me of my
old friend, Smiley Blanton. "Target projection," Bob called it.
"Before you putt, always *see* the ball running up to and into
the hole," he said. "Keep doing this and your subconscious will
help you hole that putt."

I could just see Smiley's eyes twinkling behind his horn-
rimmed glasses.

When we got onto the practice green, Bob watched me.
After a bit, he suggested a small change in the way I handled
my club.

"Your putter is traveling upward at impact instead of level
or downward," he said. "That gives the ball a bad sidespin."

Bob encouraged me to hit slightly down on the ball and finish the stroke with my putter low to the ground. All it took
was to position the ball a little farther back in my stance, making it easier to deliver a downward hit.

The result? I birdied six of nine practice holes, then went on to
win that Vantage tournament. In the next three months I won
five more big tournaments, earning in 1987 more than $500,000,
plus the *Golf Digest* title of "Senior Player of the Year."

However, I gained a lot more than awards and titles from
that experience. And I pass it on to the kids I teach in Clearwater, Florida, at my Chi Chi Rodriguez Youth Foundation for
troubled, abused and poor children. I tell them it's a lesson they
can apply to any challenge they face. "First," I say, "communicate with God. *Listen* to Him, and when you feel His direction,
don't willy-wally around. *Obey.*"

The Lord sees a lot farther down the course than we do. If I hadn't obeyed Him that day in the hotel, I wouldn't have met Bob Toski at the airport.

Life is full of hazards and traps, I tell the kids. But if you keep your eye on the pin and follow through with all your might, you'll be a champion at everything you do, even if you don't win every time.

Yes, Chi Chi's my name, and through the grace of God, golf is still my game.

How to Be an Eskimo

Mariette Hartley

as told to Richard H. Schneider

Years, ago, in a group-therapy session, I heard a story
that I have never forgotten. It enlightened me to how a
Higher Power works in our lives. It went like this:

"Hey, Father," said a man talking to a priest. "You got it all
wrong about this God stuff. He doesn't exist. I oughta know."

"Why's that, my son?"

"Well, when I was ice-fishing in the Arctic far from the
nearest village, a blizzard blew up with wind and blinding
snow. I was a goner. So I got down on my knees and prayed
real hard, begging God for help."

"And did He help you?"

"Heck no. God didn't lift a finger. Some Eskimo appeared
out of nowhere and showed me the way."

It took me a while to recognize the Eskimos in my life. And
I had needed them so desperately.

I grew up haunted by my maternal grandfather, John B.
Watson, a famous psychologist who founded a movement
called behaviorism. It taught parents to resist their children's
natural bonding needs, which he considered undesirable. There
was to be no cuddling, no kissing, few outward signs of affection. As a result of this kind of treatment as a child, my mother
later learned to use alcohol to numb her feelings of isolation.
And my father, a high-powered advertising executive, also succumbed to alcohol. Despite their affliction, they loved me

deeply. I grew up with my younger brother in affluent Weston, Connecticut, where I discovered my calling. At eleven I joined the Silver Nutmeg Theatre Company with roles in plays like *Alice in Wonderland* and *Little Women* in elementary schools around the state.

Smitten by the theater, I met one of my first Eskimos, Eva Le Gallienne, the legendary actress, who was teaching at the White Barn Theatre nearby. Miss Le G. was a small, delightful woman with a tiny nose, violet eyes and translucent skin. She wore lavender cashmere sweaters and periwinkle-blue dresses. A loving, giving person, she taught youngsters like me as well as professionals. I learned so much from her—how to feel and project emotions, and to let "the sacred fire strike" by eliminating self so that the character one is playing shines through.

Miss Le G. also inspired me spiritually. Though Mom and Dad were not religious, I was attracted to church. Sunday mornings I'd hop on my bicycle and pedal to the Norfield Congregational Church, where I sang solos in the choir. My early days in a dysfunctional family were traumatic, to be sure, but it was in church that I was reminded of hope and goodness.

The power and abundance of that hope became very clear to me one beautiful summer afternoon when I was sixteen and just back from a rehearsal at a nearby Shakespeare festival. I was walking in a field, and as I stopped by a tree I suddenly had an overwhelming spiritual experience. In a family of atheists, it was hard to share these feelings, and I was lucky enough to be able to tell Miss Le G. in a letter. She wrote back from London that she, too, had had a similar experience, that there were "times, alas, when I felt so utterly undeserving that I was filled with a kind of wondering humbleness, not just humility, but the sort of thing that flings you to your knees. Try terribly hard not to fail it," she continued, "always be yourself . . . never get conceited or spoiled . . . keep brave, keep strong, do the job at hand to the best of your ability . . . know that you are being used by some greater Power and try to obey it."

It was my belief in a spiritual life that sustained me through the difficult years to come. As a teenager I suffered a short-lived marriage to an older man who beat me mercilessly. Later I was offered a leading role in the film *Come Fly With Me*, but a doctor misdiagnosed my hepatitis. Without proper treatment, I got too sick to take the role.

Then, most devastating of all, was my father's suicide. It happened after Dad, tormented by alcohol, had lost job after job and succumbed to hopelessness. Mother and I were eating lunch when a gunshot rang out from the bedroom. We dashed in to find he had shot himself in the head. For a year I kept hearing that gunshot and was barely able to work at all.

Finally, after fighting my own alcoholism, I went into therapy. I realized I had been skipping from one "answer" to another—acting, not acting, overeating, starving myself. And by grace I found a support group where I learned to admit my own faults and my own responsibility. I surrendered my defects to a Power greater than I. Only then was I able to embrace my past, make peace with it.

Gradually I emerged from my self-imposed exile. I started accepting offers to do commercials (which I had sworn I would never do as a "serious" actress). I really started living by "When you let go of the things you think you should be doing, what you need to be doing comes to you." This was what happened to me when I appeared with James Garner in commercials for Polaroid. I played the wife, and the instant we started working together there was electricity.

The TV audience loved it and we shot almost two-hundred-fifty spots. Eventually, I had to wear a T-shirt proclaiming: "I am *not* Mrs. James Garner."

In 1974, I met another Eskimo, Patrick Boyriven, who became my husband. We have two children, Justine, and Sean. I even discovered I had been an Eskimo myself, albeit unwittingly. It happened when Linda Hunt, the Academy Award-winning actress, rushed up to me at a premiere and said: "Oh, thank you! It's because of *you* I'm in the theater."

It turned out she had watched me, at age twelve, play Jo in the Nutmeg production of *Little Women* that toured Connecticut schools. She said she had never forgotten watching someone her own age act and love it so much.

What continually impresses me is the effect we have on one another. This was brought home to me in May 1991 when my family and I drove east to visit an Eskimo named Dolores Hart, an actress with a beautiful spirit whom I had known when she appeared in *Come Fly With Me*, the film I had missed so many years before.

Now she was Mother Dolores, a cloistered nun at an abbey in Connecticut. When I saw her—for the first time in thirty years—there was peace and wisdom in her kind eyes. She told me what she had learned from her years of contemplation in one sentence: "The only way to heal is to speak."

That is why I now speak all over the country. And I pass on Mother Dolores's message, telling people we all walk around wounded, but we can heal our wounds by helping others.

And when we get down on our knees, answers come, often in the form of Eskimos.

How I Found My Voice

James Earl Jones

Today I am known for my voice as much as for my acting. It has been my good fortune to receive jobs such as the speaking role of Darth Vader in George Lucas's *Star Wars* trilogy and the voice-over announcer for CNN cable television. I also narrated Aaron Copland's *Lincoln Portrait* on a compact disc I recorded with the Seattle Symphony. Perhaps my greatest honor came when I was asked to read the New Testament on tape.

But it took a long time to believe such good things could happen to me. When I was a youngster, I stuttered so badly I was completely unable to speak in public.

Since I was eight I'd had trouble speaking. It was so bad that whenever I stood up in class to read, the other kids snickered and laughed. I always sat down, my face burning with shame.

I'm not sure what caused my stuttering. Perhaps it was an emotional problem. I was born in Arkabutla, Mississippi, and when I was about five, I moved to live with my grandparents on their farm near Dublin in northern Michigan. It was traumatic moving from the warm, easy ways of catfish country to the harsh climate of the north, where people seemed so different.

Fortunately, my granddaddy was a gentle man, a farmer who taught me to love the land. He was short and he had a prodigious amount of energy. He even built a church to please grandmother, a fervent worshiper of the Lord. All sorts of people were invited to our little church; white, black and American Indian came together in a nondenominational fellowship. Granddad's Irish heritage came out in his love for language; during the week he used "everyday talk," but on Sunday he spoke only the finest English.

As much as I admired his fluency, I couldn't come close to it. I finally quit Sunday school and church, not wanting to be humiliated anymore. All through my grade school years, the only way the teacher could assess my progress was for me to write down everything I had learned.

Oh, I could talk, all right. Our farm animals knew that. I found it easy to call the pigs, tell the dogs to round up the cows, and vent my feelings to Fanny, the horse whose big brown eyes and lifted ears seemed to express interest in all I said. But when visitors came and I was asked to say hello, I could only stand, pound my feet, and grit my teeth. That awful feeling of my voice being trapped got worse as I grew older.

Then, when I was fourteen, Professor Donald Crouch came to our school. He was a retired college professor who had settled in nearby Brethren, a Mennonite community. When he heard that our agricultural high was teaching Chaucer, Shakespeare and other classics, he couldn't stand not being a part of our school. So he left his retreat to teach us English, history and Latin.

Donald Crouch was a tall, lean man with gray hair; English was his favorite subject, poetry his deepest love. He'd been an associate of Robert Frost. He held a book of poems as if it were a diamond necklace, turning pages as if uncovering treasures. He memorized a poem every day, explaining that if he ever lost his eyesight he would still be able to savor all that beauty.

.. ..

When he learned that I not only loved poetry but was writing it, we found a kinship. There was, however, one difficulty between us. Professor Crouch (we always called him that) could not stand the fact I refused to read my poems to the class.

"Jim, poetry is meant to be read aloud, just like sermons," he pressed. "You should be able to *speak* those beautiful words."

I shook my head and turned away.

Then he tricked me. I labored long and hard on a poem, and after handing it in I waited expectantly for his critique. It didn't come. Instead, one day as the students assembled, he challenged me. "Jim, I don't think you wrote this."

I stared at him in disbelief. "Why," I started, anger flooding me, "course I did!"

"Well, then," he said, "you've got to prove it by getting up and reciting it from memory."

By then the other students had settled at their desks. He looked at me meaningfully and nodded. With knees shaking, I walked up before my peers.

"Jim will recite his latest poem," announced Professor Crouch.

For a moment I stood breathless. I could see smirks and wry smiles on some faces. Then I began. And kept going. I recited my poem all the way through—without hesitation or fault! I stood amazed and floated back to my desk in a daze, amid wild applause.

Afterward, Professor Crouch congratulated me. "Aha," he said. "Now we have something here. Not only will you have to write more poetry and read it aloud to know how good it feels, but I'm sure that you will want to read *other* writers' poetry before the class."

I was dubious about that, but said I'd try.

Soon I began to discover something other stutterers know. Most have no problem singing because the lyrics' rhythmic pattern flows by itself. I found the same cadences in poetry, and before long my fellow students actually looked forward to hearing me recite. I loved the rolling beat of *The Song of Hiawatha*, especially since I had Indian blood in my veins. "By the shores of Gitche Gummee," I recited. "By the shining Big-Sea-Waters . . ."

I discovered I *did* have a voice, a strong one. Under Professor Crouch's tutelage, I entered oratorical contests and debates. He never pushed anything at me again; he just wanted all his students to wake up. He never even pressed us with religion, but figured if we did wake up we would find God, find our calling and, in so doing, find life.

As my stuttering disappeared, I began dreaming of becoming an actor, like my father, who was then performing in New York City. No one in my family had ever gone to college. But encouraged by Professor Crouch, I took exams and won a scholarship to the University of Michigan.

There I entered the drama department and after graduation fulfilled my ROTC responsibility by serving with the Army's Cold Weather Training Command on mountain maneuvers in Colorado. It was in the Army that a Jesuit chaplain helped me understand who God really was and opened the door to which Professor Crouch had led me.

Later, on the GI Bill, I signed up with the American Theatre Wing in New York and supported myself between roles by sweeping floors of off-Broadway stages. In 1962 I earned an Obie for my role in an off-Broadway production of *Othello*, and have been an actor ever since.

.. ..

Meanwhile, I always kept in touch with my old professor, by letter and telephone. Every time we talked it was always, "Hi, Jim. Read any good poetry lately?" He was losing his sight and I remembered his early explanation of why he had memorized poetry. In later years when I was doing Shakespeare's *Timon of Athens* at the Yale Repertory Theatre in New Haven, Connecticut, I phoned him. "Can I fly you in from Michigan to see it?"

"Jim," he sighed, "I'm blind now. I'd hate not to be able to see you acting. It would hurt too much."

"I understand, Professor," I said, helped in part by the realization that though my mentor could no longer see, he was still living in a world vibrant with all of the beautiful treasures he had stored.

About two years later I learned Donald Crouch had passed on. I thanked God for all the professor's help and friendship.

And so, when I was asked to record the New Testament, I really did it for a tall, lean man with gray hair who had not only helped to guide me to the author of the Scriptures, but as the father of my resurrected voice, had also helped me find abundant life.

True Courage—Now I Know What It Means

John Wayne

Long before I ever made the movie *True Grit*, people would talk about my screen characters in terms of courage, firmness, stamina—true grit. But what about the man who played those characters?

Certainly I have never thought of myself as a timid type. Even as a child I know I had a certain brashness. I remember two incidents in particular when I was a little boy and my family was homesteading in the Mojave Desert. The four of us—my mother, father, younger brother and I—had come from a little town in Iowa where dad had been a pharmacist, but because of his health the doctors had told him he should move west. At first he had thought about going to Montana, but my grandfather wrote and said, "Why not come to California and starve?" We did both.

Dad found some isolated land in Antelope Valley, not close to anything, yet not too far from Lancaster. He built a house for us, which was hardly more than a shack, and he tried to grow corn on the land as though we were back in Iowa, which clearly we were not. We had a pretty desperate time of it. I was hardly aware of it, because I was happy—especially, I recall, because I had my own horse which I took care of and rode back and forth to school. Her name was Jenny, and I loved her.

One Halloween night out there in the desert, my brother

Bob and I had just come to the table when my mom brought out a bowl full of weenies, a special treat since we didn't have meat very often. Just at that moment we all heard an eerie sound.

"Who-o-o-o. Who-o-o-o-o."

It was my dad standing outside the screen door with a sheet over his head, but I thought it was the bogey man. I grabbed the bowl of weenies and flung it at the apparition. It broke up dad's performance.

As I look back, hurling that bowl of weenies at the bogey man came as natural to me as a knee jerk. Not too long after that, though, I was asked to do something that required a different kind of courage. My horse Jenny began to get so thin that people in town accused me of not feeding her. Finally the vet told us that for her own good we should destroy her—which was like destroying me. I didn't want to do it, but it had to be done. So it was done.

Those things were way back in my childhood, but years later, in the fall of 1964, I came face to face with a different kind of demand: the Big C. In October I'd gone down to the Scripps Clinic in La Jolla for my very belated yearly checkup. I knew I'd been coughing a lot more, but I wasn't in any kind of pain.

The doctors kept taking X rays, and I was getting impatient. When they sent me back for the fourth set of pictures, I said to the X-ray doctor, "What's the deal?"

"Well, it's positive, of course, but beyond—"

"Wait a minute. Positive? What are you telling me?"

"I'm sorry," the doctor said, "didn't you know?"

When I left the clinic that day, I realized I must have a lung operation as fast as possible and that there were a lot of arrangements to make, but for the moment I was dazed. I'd promised Senator Goldwater, who was running for President then, that I would appear at a rally in San Diego, and I headed there. I sat in the back of the audience instead of on the dais. I don't know why. I wasn't trying to escape attention; I think I just wanted to be close to people.

Before the end of the rally, they had hauled me up on the stage and the crowd cheered, and I remember thinking how odd it would be if they knew what was happening in my head, that I was standing there a bewildered man in the first flush of fear.

I'm a big man physically and I was lucky to have been born with an unusual amount of strength and stamina. All my life I've been grateful for those physical gifts. They shaped my career. They made it possible for me to play football for the Southern Cal Trojans, which led directly to my getting a summer job as a prop man with a movie studio; and a bit of muscle wasn't exactly a hindrance for the rest of my career in pictures either. But any dim-witted thug knows that physical strength is not the same as courage. And that night in San Diego, I needed courage.

Obviously there was no bludgeoning one's way out of this one; there was nothing to hurl at the bogey man. My very helplessness gave me awful twinges of fear. Mark Twain wasn't being humorous when he wrote that, "Courage is resistance to fear, mastery of fear—not absence of fear." If I was going to do battle with cancer bravely, I knew what it was that I had to conquer first.

In this struggle I had a lot of allies—my family and friends, of course. And prayer. I did a lot of praying in those few shaky days before the operation, and this I know: There is a Man

Upstairs holding all this world together, including you and me. You cannot believe this, and believe it firmly, without drawing the strength, the courage, to master your fears.

The operation was successful, thank God. They cut away a lung, but they left me alive and grateful, and ready to learn something more about adversity. Overcoming trouble can be like skidding in a car on a slippery road. There's the first skid which, if you can control it, you feel pretty relieved about. But there is an after-skid waiting to surprise you from the other direction. My after-skid was getting back in harness again.

With all that vaunted energy of mine, I was surprised at how much the operation had slowed me up. I began to think about it, and worry. My conscience hurt me because I had been scheduled to make a picture with Dean Martin called *The Sons of Katie Elder*. Everybody had been most considerate about the postponement, but now time was wasting, careers were being interfered with, money was going down the drain. Finally I made up my mind to do the picture, but I had misgivings about myself, about my strength. Those reservations were taken care of by that tremendous old director, Henry Hathaway.

Hathaway had directed me in a number of films, and luckily he had the assignment on Katie Elder. It was he, really, who got me going again, though not with tender loving care. That man was merciless. The film was shot on location in Durango, Mexico, which is eight-thousand feet above sea level, not the best place for breathing—even with two lungs. It didn't take me long to figure out what Hathaway was up to. He was being deliberately tough on me. He had me getting soaked in the river, jumping out of rigs handcuffed, always testing me. I was determined not to let him get the best of me.

One evening we had a night shot in which I was supposed

to come riding down a street on a horse carrying a rocking chair in one hand, a Bible in the other and a basket over one arm. I was supposed to stop, dismount and walk into a girl's domicile. The horse I was riding had never worked at night before and he was fractious and hard to handle. I kept doing the scene over and over, mounting, dismounting and mounting again with all those encumbrances. Hathaway watched me carefully, but no more carefully than I was watching myself, for I was getting tired. At last when he finally called out, "Print it! Let's go to bed," I knew for sure that not only had I beaten Hathaway at his game, but that I had also won my fight with cancer.

Why had Hathaway chosen to take such a rough tack with me? Why did I let him? Because more than ten years before, he had undergone an operation for cancer far worse than mine. He knew me well. He knew just how far he could push me and he used the courage he had shown in his own recovery to help bring about mine. Nowadays it's one of the rewards for me that I am able to tell people that simply because they have cancer doesn't mean they're at the end of the road.

It is good and it is helpful to have physical strength; but looking back, I am certain that the truest part of true grit is not physical—it's moral. It's making a decision and standing firm in it, whether it's submitting to an operation or putting an ailing pet to sleep. It's doing what must be done. After all, if you think about it, that's the root of all morality, for no moral man can have peace of mind if he leaves undone what he knows he should have done.

Daring to Dream Big!

Diane Sawyer

Many of us, I think, can look back and recall certain
specific moments in our lives that take on greater
importance the longer we live. "The past has a different pattern," T. S. Eliot wrote, when viewed from each of our changing perspectives.

For me, one of those moments occurred when I was seventeen years old. I was a high school senior in Louisville, Kentucky, representing my state in the 1963 America's Junior Miss
competition in Mobile, Alabama. Along with the other young
contestants, I was doing my best to hold up under the grueling
week-long schedule of interviews, agonies over hair that curled
or wouldn't, photo sessions, nervous jitters and rehearsals. In
the midst of it all, there was one person who stood at the center—at least my psychological center—someone I viewed as an
island in an ocean of anxiety.

She was one of the judges. A well-known writer. A woman
whose sea-gray eyes fixed on you with laser penetration,
whose words were always deliberate. She felt the right words
could make all the difference. Her name was Catherine
Marshall.

From the first moment I met Catherine Marshall, I was
aware that she was holding me—indeed all of us—to a more
exacting standard. While other pageant judges asked questions
about favorite hobbies and social pitfalls, she sought to challenge. She felt even seventeen-year-old girls—perhaps especially

seventeen-year-old girls—should be made to examine their ambitions and relate them to their values.

During the rehearsal on the last day of the pageant, the afternoon before it would all end, several of us were waiting backstage when a pageant official said Catherine Marshall wanted to speak with us. We gathered around. Most of us were expecting a last-minute pep talk or the ritual good luck wish, or at most an exhortation to be good citizens, but we were surprised.

She fixed her eyes upon us. "You have set goals for yourselves. I have heard some of them. But I don't think you have set them high enough. You have talent and intelligence and a chance. I think you should take those goals and expand them. Think of the most you could do with your lives. Make what you do matter. Above all, dream big."

It was not so much an instruction as a dare. I felt stunned, like a small animal fixed on bright lights. This woman I admired so much was disappointed in us—not by what we were but by how little we aspired to be.

I won the America's Junior Miss contest that year. In the fall I entered Wellesley College, where my sister, Linda, was beginning her junior year. I graduated in 1967 with a B.A. degree in English and a complete lack of inspiration about what I should do with it.

I went to my father, a lawyer and later a judge in Louisville's Jefferson County Court. "But what is it that you enjoy doing most?" he asked.

"Writing," I replied slowly. "I like the power of the word. And working with people. And being in touch with what's happening in the world."

He thought for a moment. "Did you ever consider television?"

I hadn't.

At that time there were few if any women journalists on television in our part of the country. The idea of being a pioneer in the field sounded like dreaming big. So that's how I came to get up my nerve, put on my very best Mary Tyler Moore girl journalist outfit, and go out to convince the news director at Louisville's WLKY-TV to let me have a chance.

He gave it to me—and for the next two-and-a-half years, I worked as a combination weather and news reporter.

Eventually, though, I began to feel restless. I'd lie awake at night feeling that something wasn't right. I'd wait for the revelation, the sign pointing in the direction of the Big Dream. What I didn't realize is what Catherine Marshall undoubtedly knew all along—that the dream is not the destination but the journey.

I was still working at WLKY when, in 1969, my father was killed in an auto crash. His death—coupled with my urge to make a change—spurred me in the search for a different job, and also seemed to kindle my interest in the world of government, law and politics. I racked my brain. I put out feelers. And then one of my father's associates said, "What about Washington?"

Several months later, in the autumn of 1970, I said good-bye to my mother and Linda and to the good folks at WLKY, and boarded a plane for Washington, D.C.

Now, I know this may sound incredibly naive, but when the plane landed at National Airport, I got off with a very firm idea of where I wanted to work. At the White House. True, in the eyes of official Washington I might be right off the equivalent of the turnip truck, but working in the White House was exactly what I had in mind!

Thanks to a few kind words of recommendation from a friend of my father's, I was able to obtain an interview with Ron Ziegler, the White House press secretary, and I was hired.

Those were heady days. The Press Office, located in the West Wing of the White House, was the hub for information flowing between the White House and the media. I worked hard and I worked long and loved every part of it.

Then came Watergate.

In the summer of 1974 the President resigned. Immediately I was appointed to his transition team in San Clemente, California.

My assignment on the West Coast was supposed to last only six months. But a few days after my arrival the President made a request that I was totally unprepared for. He asked me to consider staying on in San Clemente—along with several other writers and aides—to assist him in researching and writing his memoirs. I had to make a choice, and a choice that I knew would have consequences.

"Career suicide," mumbled some of my friends.

But I had worked for this man and he had been good to me. Now he was asking me for something that I was in a position to give. I have never regretted the decision. I stayed.

One day in the long exile, Catherine Marshall and her husband, Leonard LeSourd, called to say they were nearby. They came for a visit, and once again I felt the searching gaze and, implicit in it, the words, "What is next?" Again I came to appreciate the immense power of someone who is unafraid to hold other people to a standard. And again I realized the way a single uncompromising question can force reexamination of a life.

After three years as coanchor on the CBS *Morning News*, I

became co-editor of CBS's *60 Minutes* television news-magazine. We worked at a breakneck pace with long hours and constant travel thrown in. I kept a suitcase packed at all times so that I could be ready to fly out on assignment at a moment's notice.

When I go out into the world again—and who knows where I'll be flying next?—I can almost hear a wonderful woman prodding me with her fiery challenge to stretch further and, no matter how big the dream, to dream a little bigger still. God, she seems to be saying, can forgive failure, but not failing to try.

Ready? Set! Now!

Chris Evert Lloyd

The court was still wet from an early morning drizzle as Tracy Austin and I began warming up for our semifinal match in the 1980 U.S. Open tennis tournament. I was worried, nervous. Not only was Tracy the top seed in the tournament, but she had beaten me the last five times we had played each other. And as I tentatively returned one of Tracy's slashing backhands, I didn't feel any confidence that today would be different.

Earlier that spring, after a grueling series of matches, I'd taken some time off from the tennis circuit. But when I resumed playing, even though I won some tournaments, I didn't feel at all like the same player who'd been number one in the world five of the previous eight years. I'd lost the confidence I needed to play boldly and make the snap decisions so necessary in athletics. Instead, I was continually replaying the past. Poor shots would often trigger memories of past matches, where I'd made wrong decisions in similar situations. And that would make my play even worse.

By the fourth game of the first set, all my worst fears had materialized. Tracy was ahead, 4-0, and I was playing terribly.

Suddenly a loud voice boomed, "The match is starting *now*!" I whirled around and saw my good friend Ron Samuels standing next to his wife, television actress Lynda Carter. He was cupping one hand around his mouth—and shaking his fist at me! It made me smile—I knew Ron wasn't mad at me. It was his way of reminding me what had pulled me out of the doldrums months before, when I'd rejoined the tennis circuit. "If you decide things are going to be different," he had said, "you've made a new beginning. You don't have to worry about the past anymore." And that's what he was saying now with his clenched fist. So what if you're down 0-4. You can still turn things around. **Now is the beginning!**

Ron's words seemed to spur me on. I broke Tracy's serve in the next game, and even when she won the first set with a brilliant cross-court forehand, I felt my lost confidence surging. I came back to win that match, 4-6, 6-1, 6-1, and went on to win the tournament.

That U.S. Open match really did turn my tennis game around—I won fifty-nine of my last sixty-two matches that year—but it taught me an important lesson, too. You don't need to let the disappointments and defeats of the past get in the way of what you're doing now. Now isn't then. Now is the beginning.

PART 12

The Power in Scripture

Princes have persecuted me without a cause:
but my heart standeth in awe of thy word.
Psalm 119:161 (KJV)

Over the course of history, millions have known the life-changing power of Scripture. A line of a love song, "And suddenly nothing is the same," says it all. A New Testament writer says that the Word of God is "sharper than any two-edged sword, piercing even to the dividing asunder of soul and spirit" (Hebrews 4:12, KJV). Some, like Lionel Hampton, have found hope in the Book of Psalms. Others, like Ernest Borgnine, have been transformed by the words of Christ. Hostage Terry Anderson, clung to any number of biblical passages in his captivity. And . . . the last story in the book is one of the best: the unique experience of Charlton Heston filming *The Ten Commandments*, taking on the character of Moses, a man mightily used by God to change the course of history.

The Rock of My Life

Lionel Hampton

When my wife Gladys died in 1971 I said to myself, "Hamp, you got to call it quits too." Gladys was such a big part of me that when she was gone, I swore I'd never play another note. For the thirty-five years of our marriage she was my business manager, my accountant; she arranged my bookings, my recording dates and gave me every kind of guidance I needed. Then, suddenly, she was gone.

For a while I didn't care much about anything. I'd just stare at her photograph all day while my vibes collected dust. I felt totally helpless without her. I didn't want to do anything and even felt like chucking away the biggest dream of my life—a housing project and music school I wanted so much to build in New York City.

This dream had really begun back in the 1940's. I had left Benny Goodman's band and had a group of my own. We would be playing a lot of one-nighters on the road and when we'd go into a southern town, I made a point of going to the presidents of the black colleges and asking why they had no courses in black music and its place in American history.

"That's all behind us," was the usual answer I got.

Well, to me it may have been behind us, but I knew the importance black songs had on this country, and I wanted people to understand how the gospels and blues rose up out of the cotton fields and plantations. I wanted to tell how blacks, through their music, had created an identity for themselves.

CHANGED LIVES

While the college presidents weren't interested, my idea
stayed with me for the next twenty years. In the 1960's, I managed to get together some pretty important cats to rap seriously
about my dream. They included the presidents of several colleges and the head of the New England Conservatory of Music.
I told them I wanted to teach not only the works of Bach and
Mozart but also have students study great black musicians like
Art Tatum, Fats Waller, Fletcher Henderson and, of course,
Louis Armstrong. The school, we decided, would be built in
New York's poverty-stricken Harlem section, an area that I had
lived in for thirty years. I was also going to teach there and
later we would expand into law and business programs.

When I first took our idea to the Harlem community lead-
ers, their response was, "We need housing first, man. Get us
this, and you'll get your school."

Spurred on, I immediately went to work. About $750,000
was raised from local sources. The governor offered his help
and so did the federal housing authorities. But, much more
money was needed, for the plan called for three apartment
towers—over 355 apartments in all, plus a day-care center, a
clinic and then my school. On paper it was something I could
really dig, like something dropped from heaven.

I kept working on the plans and the money, right up until
Gladys died. Then I shelved it. It didn't seem to hold me anymore—nothing did. All I could seem to do was think of her
and how I missed her. I turned into one sour song.

Then, to add to my woes, the housing project began to run
into trouble. Many of the Harlem residents were unhappy that
whites were going to do much of the construction work, and
that even some whites would be going to the school. The hatred
started to rise and I didn't know how to deal with it. We needed

the knowledge of the whites and we needed them at the school. Harlem, though, can be a bitter place—some residents were even threatening to tear my complex down if it was ever built.

One evening I sat at home, alone and discouraged. I wondered what Gladys would have advised. How I wished she was there to give me some answers! Then I thought about how close Gladys and I were, and how in our closeness we had shared many things—tastes in music, food, friends, shows. We would also share our worries. In fact, that evening I remembered what Gladys usually said when I had a problem.

"Dear," I could hear her say, "let's forget our troubles tonight and rub them out by reading the psalms."

We often shared the reading of many of the psalms. Gladys' favorite was Psalm 40, the second verse in particular, and there were several nights when she would read it to me and vice versa. There was such a great pleasure in that psalm for me that I turned to it on a night when I thought I couldn't possibly go on. I took my Bible and went over and sat on the sofa that Gladys had recovered herself, and read the second verse. I read it over and over: "He brought me up also out of an horrible pit, out of the miry clay, and set my feet upon a rock, and established my goings" (KJV).

This seemed to be a turning point. Soon after that I got what seemed like some new burst of energy. I was strong all of a sudden, like after a four-bar rest. I wrote letters to all sorts of people, pushed the architects, and gave talks on my dream. Soon, money began pouring in. We were nearing our goal.

One day I found myself up near the building site, talking with Harlemites about the racial trouble on the project. "Look," I told them, "it's just like in music—you got to have the white keys as well as the black ones to make harmony."

Somehow they bought this, and the hatred began to fade, maybe because, as one fellow said to me later, "It was your enthusiasm, Hamp, that hooked us." Black workers were now eagerly looking forward to getting some great on-the-job training there from whites.

Finally, on November 21, 1971, I knew I had, through God's help, pulled myself out of the horrible pit I had been stuck in.

On that day we held a ground-breaking ceremony in Harlem. I jammed on for a big audience that morning and made some speeches and got a lot of tears in my eyes. It was all too good to be true. What made me proudest though, was telling everyone that when the buildings were completed there would be a motto nailed up out front. The motto, I said, was one that was very close to me now. It was that old second verse of Psalm 40: He "set my feet upon a rock, and established my goings."

At the Foot of the Cross

Ernest Borgnine

Back in 1975 I was offered a part in the film *Jesus of Nazareth*, which through the years has been shown at Easter time on NBC television. Our cast, directed by the renowned Franco Zeffirelli, included Anne Bancroft as Mary Magdalene, and Olivia Hussey as Mary, mother of Jesus. I played the part of the centurion who was present at the crucifixion, the one whose servant had been healed by Jesus.

Much of the film was shot in Tunisia on the Mediterranean during January and February of 1976. A cold, damp wind continually knocked over floodlights and stung us with desert sand. I was uncomfortable in my thick leather uniform. My neck ached under a ponderous metal helmet, and I even began to pity those ancient Roman soldiers who were called centurions because they commanded one-hundred men.

When it came time for my scene during the crucifixion, the weather was chill and gray. The camera was to be focused on me at the foot of the cross, and so it was not necessary for Robert Powell, the actor who portrayed Jesus, to be there. Instead, Zeffirelli put a chalk mark on a piece of scenery beside the cameraman. "I want you to look up at that mark," he told me, "as if you were looking at Jesus."

"Okay," I said, moving into position and looking up at the mark as instructed.

"Ready?"

I hesitated. Somehow I wasn't ready. I was uneasy.

"Do you think it would be possible for somebody to read from the Bible the words Jesus said as He hung on the cross?" I asked.

I knew the words well from the days of my childhood in an Italian-American family in Connecticut, and I'd read them in preparation for the film. Even so, I wanted to hear them now.

"I will do it myself," Zeffirelli said. He found a Bible, opened it to the book of Luke and signaled for the camera to start rolling.

As Zeffirelli began reading Christ's words aloud from Luke 23, I stared up at that chalk mark, thinking what might have gone through the centurion's mind.

That poor Man up there, I thought. *I met Him when He healed my servant, who is like a son to me. Jesus says He is the Son of God, an unfortunate claim during these perilous times. But I know He is innocent of any crime.*

"Father, forgive them; for they know not what they do." The voice was Zeffirelli's, but the words burned into me—the words of Jesus.

Forgive me, *Father, for even being here*, was the centurion's prayer that formed in my thoughts. *I am so ashamed, so ashamed.*

"Verily I say unto thee, Today shalt thou be with me in paradise," said Jesus to the thief hanging next to Him.

If Jesus can forgive that criminal, then He will forgive me, I thought. *I will lay down my sword and retire to my little farm outside of Rome.*

Then it happened.

As I stared upward, instead of the chalk mark, I suddenly saw the face of Jesus Christ, lifelike and clear. It was not the features of Robert Powell I was used to seeing, but the most beautiful, gentle visage I have ever known. Pain-seared, sweat-stained, with blood flowing down from thorns pressed deep, His face was still filled with compassion. He looked down at me through tragic, sorrowful eyes with an expression of love beyond description.

Then His cry rose against the desert wind. Not the voice of Zeffirelli, reading from the Bible, but the voice of Jesus Himself. "Father into Thy hands I commend My spirit."

In awe I watched Jesus' head slump to one side. I knew He was dead. A terrible grief welled within me, and completely oblivious to the camera, I started sobbing uncontrollably.

"Cut!" yelled Zeffirelli. Olivia Hussey and Anne Bancroft were crying, too. I wiped my eyes and looked up again to where I had seen Jesus—He was gone.

Whether I saw a vision of Jesus that windswept day or whether it was only something in my mind, I do not know. It doesn't matter. For I do know that it was a profound spiritual experience and that I have not been quite the same person since. I believe that I take my faith more seriously. I like to think that I'm more forgiving than I used to be. As that centurion learned two-thousand years ago. I too have found that you simply cannot come close to Jesus without being changed.

* * *

Faith and prayer have been a part of Ernest Borgnine's life ever since he was a boy growing up in Connecticut. His grandmother taught him a little prayer in Italian that began with the words *Signore, ti ringrazio per il giorno che mi hai datto* (Lord, I thank You for the day You have given me), which he repeated every morning and evening.

Prayer continued to be part of his life—during ten years in

the U.S. Navy (which included serving as a gunner's mate in World War II), and in the postwar years as he labored in warehouses, attended acting school and appeared in plays and television dramas. It was especially important to him during a lonely moment in 1951 when he was desperate for work. He'd heard that a film company was casting, so he showed up for a screen test. But there were forty people ahead of him, and so the casting director said, "Go and lose yourself for a couple of hours."

With only fifteen cents in his pocket, he walked down Fifth Avenue and came to St. Patrick's Cathedral. He climbed the wide stone steps and sank down in a back pew. "Please, Father," he prayed, "I need the work. If You can possibly help me, I would appreciate it very much."

He got the part. It was Ernest Borgnine's first movie, *The Whistle at Eaton Falls*. That launched him on a career that saw him play the part of villainous Fatso Judson in *From Here to Eternity* and the lovable hero in *Marty*, for which he won an Academy Award in 1956.

Small Graces

Terry Anderson

At the time it was a mystery. Why was I led to that old church?

It had happened in the fall of 1984 when my fiancée, Madeleine, and I were visiting her family in Sunderland, a town in northern England. I had looked forward to peace and quiet, a respite from my hectic career. After six years as a Marine Corps correspondent for Armed Forces Television and Radio Service in Vietnam, I had joined the Associated Press, reporting disasters, plane hijacks, rebellions, and, for the past several years, covering the ongoing violence in Lebanon.

I was so dispirited that it took me some days to settle down, even in the pleasant atmosphere of this English hamlet. As we strolled its neat streets, inhaling the crisp, early winter air, I noticed a church steeple outlined against the pale blue sky. Although I had been brought up in the Catholic church back in Batavia, New York, I had drifted far from God and considered myself an agnostic. Why did that tall gray spire keep catching my eye?

After a few days in Sunderland, I finally decided to walk over to the church. When I got there I pulled open the heavy oaken door, stepped in and settled in a worn pew. Looking up at the altar and cross gleaming in the shadows, I suddenly had a strong sense of coming home. This was where I belonged. I believed in God the Father, His Son, Christ Jesus, and His Holy Spirit.

For the next six months back at work I tried to sort through this revelation. What did it mean in my life? What was I required to do? I was beginning to sense a closer relationship with God when, one morning on a street in Beirut, I was shoved at gunpoint into the back of a green Mercedes. My face was pressed to the floor and a blanket thrown over me as the car accelerated. It was March 16, 1985.

I lay on a cot for twenty-four days, eyes covered by a blindfold, chains painfully tight on my wrists and ankles. Finally, as shoes scraped the floor nearby, I gasped in Arabic, "Hey, *chebab*" ("mister").

The footsteps halted.

"You can't do this to me," I said. "I'm a man, not an animal. I'll go crazy."

"What do you want?"

"A Bible."

He left without another word. The next day something thudded on my cot. My chains were loosened; I sat up. The blindfold was removed, but the blanket was pulled over my head so that I couldn't see anything except the book on my lap.

It was a Bible, the Revised Standard Version, red cover.

In the past I had read parts of the Bible on an intellectual level. Now I scoured its pages, book by book. I read it through, ten times, twenty, fifty. Each time, I found something new to sustain me. A verse that inspired me one week filled me with even greater illumination the next. *Why haven't I seen that before?* I wondered.

I read the Old Testament along with the New, flashing back and forth, finding fascinating correlations and insights. And after a while, a marvelous thing happened. The Bible characters came to life! I knew them as living beings: the hopeful,

poetic Isaiah; the stentorian Jeremiah; the holy, pure, young
Mary of Nazareth.

Amid the filth, the beatings, and the chains that shackled me
to a wall, I felt so close to the long-suffering Job. I cried out to
God with him: "I'm a good man. Why are You doing this to
me? It's not fair!"

God answered: *It doesn't have to be fair. I'm going to do
what I want and you have to accept it.*

So it was that I began to learn acceptance.

And can anyone speak better to a man in chains than Paul,
who wrote so often from a prison cell? I sensed the hidden
worth in his suffering: "I want you to know, brethren, that
what has happened to me has really served to advance the
gospel" (Philippians 1:12, RSV).

I found Paul both fascinating and frustrating. He has such a
beauty, a sense of Christ's presence, and then he says something
that irritates me, revealing him as a difficult and tortured man.
And in this I found solace too, knowing this saint.

One of my worst ordeals was looking back on my thirty-
seven years to see things I was ashamed of. Peter helped me
here. I had come to know him as the stumbling saint. He kept
getting it wrong, and Jesus kept patting him on the back, saying, "It's okay. Don't worry about it." Like Peter, I could rec-
oncile myself to the fact that I had done some bad things and
would probably do more in the future. But that need not pre-
vent me from finding forgiveness in Christ. God doesn't ask us
to be perfect, I felt, but to try to live better than we do.

Months and then years ground on, each dismal day a dull
blur of boredom, punctuated by cruelty, bad food and sickness.
Most torturous of all was the deep aching I felt for my family
and loved ones.

.. ..

My captors moved me from one secret location to another, wrapped like a mummy head to toe in plastic tape, with only my nostrils exposed. I was transported in a car trunk or, worse, in a hidden compartment under a truck. As we bumped along potholed pavements, exhaust fumes filled the narrow compartment, burning my nostrils; I was overcome with nausea, and struggled to keep from throwing up, knowing I would strangle on my vomit. I calmed myself with the rosary's hypnotic repetition: "Hail Mary, full of grace . . ."

When I learned of my father's death, and then my brother's, I could only pray with David: "Why hast thou forsaken me? Why art thou so far from helping me, from the words of my groaning?" (Psalm 22:1, RSV).

Then God sent me a mouse. It arrived one day when some of us captives were kept in a dank, dark subbasement. I learned that if I placed a piece of bread on my shoulder and kept still, he would come up and nibble it. The mouse became a friend, showing up quite regularly. Eventually he disappeared, but not before my spirits were lifted.

Again and again amid our grinding ordeal, small graces came, which helped us survive. Among the hostages was Father Martin Jenko. We conducted worship services twice a day in what we wryly called the Church of the Locked Door. Communion was performed with water and scraps of stale bread.

In 1987, I was so stricken at not being allowed to send a Christmas message to my loved ones that I began madly pounding my head against the wall. With blood running down my forehead, I was pulled away by a guard, who chained me to a wall. In another moment of darkness, I prayed for hope. My guard brought me a newspaper. It carried a photo of some schoolchildren presenting my sister, Peggy, a birthday card they had made for me. The glimpse of those children was a great comfort.

To help preserve my sanity I saved matchsticks and wire to make a crucifix. When guards tossed me a set of Muslim prayer beads, I rethreaded them into a rosary.

Some of my captors were noncommittal, others cruel. But there was one sadistic man I shall never forget: Ali. The pain he inflicted was mental. One night he announced, "You're all going home." In delirious excitement we began putting on the new clothes and shoes that were handed to us for "the bus waiting downstairs."

Nothing happened. Our captors took the clothes away, and we were left dumbfounded.

After almost seven years came my true day of release: December 4, 1991. Reporters asked if I could ever forgive my captors. I hesitated a moment. But then I remembered the Lord's Prayer: "Our Father . . . forgive us our debts, as we also have forgiven our debtors."

I answered, "Yes, as a Christian I am required to forgive, no matter how hard it may be."

I learned so much in those 2,455 days. For I believe pain can help us grow. Before my capture I was a brusque, arrogant, restless man. Now I like to think I have changed. I don't know what lies ahead; but whenever I need to know where my help will come from, I will recall an old church in an English town, and a worn red Bible. And I will remember what Joseph said in forgiving his brothers, who had sold him into captivity: "You meant evil against me; but God meant it for good" (Genesis 50:20, RSV).

Where Do You Get Your Energy?

Kathie Lee Gifford

Our neighbors in Connecticut must think we're a bunch of nuts. In the morning when two-year-old Cassidy comes up to me saying, "Hosanna Mommy, hosanna," I say, "Okay." And out we traipse onto our deck where we march around singing. "This is the day the Lord has made. Let us rejoice and be glad in it! Hosanna! Hosanna!" I'm sure people all the way in New Jersey hear us.

But I don't care what they think. I believe worship should be fun and exciting so children can embrace it. After all, David leaped and danced before the Lord with all his might, and sang out with joy.

We Christians don't do that enough. Often we're all so terrified of what somebody's going to say. But if you love the Lord, you should *show* it.

The joy of the Lord is your strength. That's Nehemiah 8:10 (NIV), a verse that has always been important to me. People ask me where I get my energy. But what most people perceive as energy is really strength of spirit. It comes from the joy of knowing God, loving Him, and being loved by Him. It's so simple we sometimes stumble past it.

I first began my walk with Jesus at age twelve, when I came home and found my mom and my little sister, Michie, crying together in the living room. Immediately I sensed these weren't tears of sadness, but of some more momentous emotion. Mom had been flipping between TV channels when she came across a Billy Graham crusade. She had always scoffed at this sort of event before, but that night as she watched, she had spontaneously fallen to her knees and asked God to come into her life. My sister joined her. Then I arrived and was deeply affected as well. Not long after, I saw a Christian film called *The Restless Ones,* and at its conclusion the pastor asked us to come forward and receive Christ. It was an electrifying and life-changing experience.

In the teenage years that followed, my commitment only deepened. God seemed to be saying to me, "Kathie, everyone has to make choices. Choose *my* way and I will help you make something beautiful of your life." By then my dad was a Christian too, and over and over I got the message: Shine in the light of God's love; be a blessing, not a burden; and love others. I was taught to bloom where I was planted, to find joy in whoever I was or whatever I became, and to spread that joy generously and enthusiastically.

My husband, Frank, says I get too enthusiastic sometimes. "I can just see your motor overheating," he says, laughing. But I think if you love the Lord and love others as yourself, the Holy Spirit gives you a natural exuberance in which you say the right thing at the right time. Scripture tells us that perfect love casts out all fear. If I believe God loves me perfectly, then I won't be afraid of life. I won't be afraid to try new things, to look foolish, or to fail. And if I do sometimes fall on my face, so what? Even though we make mistakes daily, the Bible says that God's mercy is fresh for us every morning.

In 1985 when I first started working with Regis Philbin, who was hosting WABC-TV's *The Morning Show,* I knew he had a reputation of teasing his cohosts. But I repeated to myself, "The joy of the Lord is my strength," and it kept me from feeling intimidated. I was able to relax and throw wise-cracks right back at Regis.

My life hasn't been all fun. Michie, my sister, almost died at the age of twenty-three from acute ulcerative colitis. She had an ileostomy and lay in a coma. As I sat at her bedside, I silently cursed God for the unfairness of it all. Why should my sister have to go through such agony? At that moment Michie opened her eyes, looked right at me and said, "Kathie, don't curse God; thank Him. This bag means I get to live!" It was one of the most humbling—and elating—moments of my life.

In 1994, I learned a disturbed man had threatened to harm me. Even in jail and serving two life terms for another crime, he continued to write me letters. From the start I decided I was not going to worry and let this spoil my life. I have to hand certain things over to God. It's the living out of my faith that makes me a believer. God doesn't just get rid of hardship or suffering, He heals in the midst of it.

My reading of the Scripture has taught me that people who love the Lord don't automatically rise to the top in business or beat cancer overnight. At times, faith means enduring surgery or chemotherapy or any number of other difficult experiences; it means tapping into a deeper dimension when loved ones suffer terrible illness or misfortune.

One of the lowest points of my life was when I went to Hollywood in the 1970s, trying to carve out a career for myself. One gloomy afternoon, sitting in my apartment after many rejections, I realized I was down to my last few dollars. "Lord," I prayed, "if I don't get a job by this time next week, I'll go home to Maryland and be a florist or an interior designer."

That week I was offered parts in five commercials. I took that flurry of activity as my answer.

.. ..

Some people say to me: "What's a nice Christian girl like you doing in show business?" My reply is: "Aren't nice Christian men in the plumbing business?" We can't all be ministers or priests or rabbis. But we are supposed to be the sweet fragrance of Jesus wherever we are, whatever our occupation.

I've never felt apologetic about my faith or my career; it's the Lord I want to please, not critics or "religious" people. And when asked, "Don't you find it hard to be a Christian in the entertainment business?" I answer, "No, I would find it impossible *not* to be one. How does anyone get through the day without the Lord?"

That's why I jump in wholeheartedly to join Cassidy and her brother, Cody, when we march around the deck doing our hosannas. They are learning from their earliest days that God loves them and has a plan for their lives. The joy of the Lord is *their* strength too.

Heartache

Loretta Lynn

I f I'm anything in this world, I'm a wife and mother. I do enjoy performing and my musical career, but it's my family that means the most. We had six kids, and their daddy and I have a special, mystical bond with each of them. And that bond is the only way I can explain what happened with me and my boy Jack.

The strange story started with my mystery illness on a summer Sunday a few years back. I'd done a concert at the Kansas City Opera, the last stop on the tour. We were on the bus heading home for Tennessee when out of the blue I started feeling bad and went to lie down. Early the next morning, my friend Lorene Allen woke up with the feeling she should check on me, and it was a good thing she did: I was having trouble breathing. The bus had pulled into a truck stop in Illinois, and Lorene got off, hollering, "Call an ambulance!"

At the emergency room they thought I was already dead, but the doctors didn't give up. They worked till I started breathing again, then admitted me to intensive care.

I hardly remember anything in intensive care until the fourth day. My husband, Doolittle, had come up from Tennessee to tell me what had to be told. "I got news, Loretta, and it's bad," he said. "Jack's dead."

And it was like I died all over again. There's no pain on this earth like losing a child.

Jack was different from my other kids in one way. The others all wanted to follow me in singing careers. But Jack's main interest was farming. He had the same love I do for planting and doing with my hands. Jack, who'd married a pretty little girl named Barbara. They had a girl and a boy—and had a new little redheaded baby girl named Jenny. They lived on Barbara's grandmother's farm just up the road from our ranch, so Jack was over at our place often, helping out with the planting or in the stables.

To this day I believe the moment I collapsed on that bus was the moment my boy died. And when Jack died, a piece of me left with him.

On the Sunday I got sick, Jack had been visiting campers on our ranch. By the time he was ready to saddle up and ride home, it was dusk, so he decided to take the shorter way back and ford the river. But there'd been heavy rains and the Duck River was swollen. Jack and his horse never did make it across.

They didn't find my boy for three days after he drowned.

Little things came back to me, like the honeybees when Jack was just a tyke. Back then we lived in Washington State in a house that was real tiny. It had two bedrooms and the bathroom was back outside. I mean country. Jack was two then, and Betty, our oldest, three, and those kids loved to play outside. The man we rented the house from had honeybees. Well, those kids were fascinated, and so Betty took a stick and stirred up those doggone bees. I was in the kitchen when I heard the commotion. And here comes those two little kids across the yard, lickety-split, hollerin' and cryin'. Jack's little legs weren't long enough to get moving right. So he got stung up the worst. Thing is, I felt those stings worse than Jack did.

If, thirty years later, I could still smart from those bees, how could I ever get past the sting of knowing my boy had suffered and died all by himself?

I tried hard to remember the good times, how Jack was no trouble growing up. He did good in school. He liked football, but baseball was his favorite. He was big and strong and happy. Just like his daddy. The spittin' image. In fact, in some ways, he and his daddy were too much alike. Sometimes they'd just butt heads.

I couldn't help but remember the bad times too, like when Jack got older and he began drinking too much. When I tried to talk to him about it, he said, "Momma, I just drink till it stops hurtin'." It made things real hard for him and for the people who loved him.

Finally I just had to leave Jack and his alcohol problem in the hands of God. That's where I'd learned to leave problems ever since I was little, going to a Baptist church in the Appalachian Mountains of Kentucky. And I do believe God was watching Jack carefully, because his life changed. For one thing, he met Barbara. But it was more than that.

Shortly before he died, Jack had a doctor's appointment in Nashville and I drove in with him. On the way, I remarked that he seemed different and happier. His eyes sparkled and he said, "Momma, I've quit drinking. I've been sober for nine months and I'm never gonna have another drink." That was part of my pain. Things were going so good for Jack. He was just starting to live. How could he be gone?

They flew me back to a hospital in Nashville. The doctors said I couldn't get up to go to Jack's funeral, but I did. But it wasn't me who was there, really. I went through the service in a haze.

Even after I got out of the hospital, it was like I wasn't living my life, just going through the motions. The one conscious thing I did do was reach for my Bible. It was like a life pre-

server floating in the water. As I said, I grew up going to a little
Baptist church. We didn't have a proper church in Butcher Hollow, but my daddy's first cousin preached in the little one-room
schoolhouse that my great-grandfather built. We all went, and
we all were raised on the Bible, and I've always carried one
with me everywhere I went.

So after Jack died, when I was reaching for answers it made
sense to reach for my Bible. Only then did I realize that
although I'd read it, I hadn't really *searched* it, asking the
hard questions and listening to the answers. So I started
searching.

One verse that stood out for me was, "You are not your
own; you were bought with a price" (I Corinthians 6:20, RSV).
If *I'm* not my own, it's pretty clear my *kids* aren't mine either;
they're God's. Or put another way, children are loaned to us;
they really belong to God.

So if Jack was God's, was God looking out for him? Jesus
said: "Are not five sparrows sold for two pennies? And not one
of them is forgotten before God. Why, even the hairs of your
head are all numbered. Fear not; you are of more value than
many sparrows" (Luke 12:6-7, RSV).

As I thought about these things, I became more certain than
ever that Jack was in God's care, and gradually I began to find
more proof of that. I began to remember things that had passed
over me before; like the minister, Elzie Banks, who told a
strange story at Jack's funeral. He was a pleasant-looking man
from a little church there in Waverly, Tennessee, and he told
how, about nine months before Jack died, he'd been out on a
sick call. Waverly isn't that big, and there aren't many roads to
choose from, but he got lost. When he drove over the Duck
River, he knew for sure he'd taken a wrong turn and he'd better

ask directions. So he pulled up at a little house and went to the door.

It was Jack who opened that door and invited him in for coffee. As the two of them sat talking, Jack told the pastor he'd been raised in a church and baptized, but he'd been away for a while.

When it came time for the pastor to leave, he said, "Let's pray, Jack."

And Jack said, "I don't know how."

So the pastor prayed, and Jack prayed after him.

Looking back, I know what the meaning of the minister's story was. It was no coincidence that Jack had stopped drinking when he did. Although that minister thought he'd taken a wrong turn and he was lost, he was right where God sent him to be. God was looking after His boy Jack in ways that I never could.

It's been around five years now since Jack died. And I'll tell you something: The bond I have with him is still as strong as the bond I have with my living children. Anyone who knows me will tell you that Jack's death has changed my life, and the biggest way is this: My dreams are not here on earth anymore. Why spend precious time running around chasing after money or fame when we're not going to be here that long? A blink of an eye and we're gone.

There are wonderful things here, all right.

But my biggest dream is living with God and what happens when we get there, the time we're gonna have! Whether you're ill or crippled or have emotional problems, you'll be whole there. Momma and Daddy and Patsy Cline and Jack . . . the parts of me that have been missing won't be missing anymore. And best of all, we'll see God, who we really belong to, face-to-face.

The Bible tells us to store up our treasure in heaven, "For where your treasure is, there will your heart be also" (Luke 12:34, RSV). When the time comes for me to cross that ol' river myself, don't fret too much for me. It'll be an easy trip— 'cause you see, I've sent my heart on ahead.

Let Someone Else Be the Judge

Jean Stapleton

W hen I was growing up in New York City, there was one thing that I disliked with a passion and that was calf's liver. My father, an outdoor advertising salesman, loved calf's liver, and so my mother saw to it that it often appeared on our dinner table. I would rather go hungry—and often did—than eat it.

The interesting thing is, I never even tasted calf's liver until I was an adult. I simply disliked the looks of it and knew, beyond all argument, that I would despise it. Today I adore calf's liver.

It wouldn't surprise me at all if Archie Bunker hated calf's liver. If you know Archie from *All in the Family*, the television comedy series in which I played his dingbat wife, Edith, then you know what I mean. Archie's a bigot, a super bigot, and we got most of our laughs from his outrageous points of view, his rantings against other races and almost anything new or strange to him. If it's true that the bravest man who ever lived was the first fellow to eat an oyster, you have some idea of where Archie would rate for courage—and how he'd camouflage his fear with a loud tirade.

By being extreme, and therefore ridiculous and funny to us, Archie has made millions of people aware of the absurdity of prejudice. I have confessed to my own absurd dealings with liver because it points up something that I was aware of long before Archie came along: Prejudice is an assortment of deceptively small personal judgments—deceptive because of their great cost in our daily lives.

No one will ever know, for example, how many families have been racked by stubborn arguments over long hair. Is prejudice involved? Partly, I think, for at its root, prejudice is a matter of judging—of prejudging really. We have preconceived opinions that long hair means something about a boy (and therefore about ourselves, since he is our offspring) that may or may not be true.

For myself, I have seen how my own niggling, personal prejudgments often have robbed me of pleasure and peace of mind. There have been times when I have tried to cure these prejudices, and I recall one time in particular when a conscious effort at healing resulted in a crucial breakthrough in my acting career. It happened a long time ago, in the late '40s, after a good many bleak years trying to crack Broadway. Those had been years of constant work, of having a job as a secretary in the shipping department of a railroad company by day; typing manuscripts late at night in exchange for drama lessons; begging time off for summer stock; making precious little progress.

Then one day the chance came to read for one of the Equity Library Theatre productions—shows that our actors' union puts on to give us a chance to work and to be seen. The play was *The Corn Is Green*, and there were two roles in it I felt confident I could handle. One of them was so minuscule, however, that though I knew it meant a job, there was some doubt as to whether it would be a good showcase. Naturally the tiny part was the one I was offered.

I thought about it awhile. "I'll do it," I said finally, irritated that they hadn't given me the larger part.

Ten days before the opening, the actress rehearsing Mrs.

Watty fell on some ice and broke her leg. I assumed that I would inherit her role and I wasn't surprised when Ted Post, the director, came to talk to me. He asked me if I would fill in until he could get somebody else.

"*Somebody else!* But what about me?" I protested. "I can play her."

"No," he said, "you're too young."

I didn't believe him. He just was not being fair. He had it in for me.

I got angry. I got so mad that I couldn't even sit at the same dinner table with my parents that evening. I had to get up and go to my room and try to collect myself. I had to do something about this injustice or I would burst.

In those days—as well as today—I had my own way of finding help when needed. I took out my Bible. After all, I had been going to Sunday school classes in our church since the age of two. And I also took out my concordance, that remarkable compilation of all the key words in the Bible and where they appear. I flipped through the pages of the concordance to the "J's," mumbling theatrically all the while, "Justice is what I need, justice. . . ." But before I could find "justice" my eyes fell on "judge."

"For the Lord is our *j.* Isa. 33:22."

I picked up the Bible and sped to Isaiah. I had explored Scripture in this fashion many times before, sometimes losing myself for hours in random adventure. Now, chapter 33 . . . there it was: "For the Lord is our judge, the Lord is our lawgiver, the Lord is our king; he will save us" (KJV).

What was this I was asking about justice? Had I jumped to some emotional conclusion about Ted? Should I pray about this and try leaving justice to the Lord?

I prayed; I relinquished the matter to the Highest Power. My anger disappeared. I was back in the dining room for dessert.

The next day at rehearsal I was no longer driven by an ambition to play Mrs. Watty. I read the part as well as I could and enjoyed doing it, and when Ted found somebody he thought was the right age, I retired with genuine grace.

But that wasn't the end of the story. Three nights later, the producer called me at home and said that the new Mrs. Watty hadn't worked out. If Ted should ask me, would I be willing to take over? Very quietly I told her I'd be delighted, and the next day Ted said, "You're too young for it, Jean, but the part's yours."

It's still not the end of the story. Just as all show business sagas ought to unfold, an important agent saw me at the opening. She wasn't fooled by my makeup. She saw me as a young woman, just right, she decided, for the role of the niece in a touring company of *Harvey*. Out of that came my first good job in the theater; I was on my way.

Today, when I get emotional about something I think somebody has done to me, I try to think back to that experience before I start hurling a few hasty, bigoted thunderbolts. I recall that I never succeeded in changing the director's opinion of me; nor did I change my own opinion. I had simply left the judging to the Lawgiver, and He decided for both of us.

A friend once sent me a sermon entitled, "God and Archie Bunker," written by the pastor of the Brentwood Presbyterian Church here in California. In that sermon, Dr. Spencer Marsh Jr., who enjoys Archie, nonetheless noted his self-centeredness, his cliché-ridden bravado, his imprisonment inside his own narrow opinions. He quoted some dialogue from the show, from the night Archie was talking to "our" son-in-law saying,

"I've been making my way in the world for a long time, sonny boy, and one thing I know—a man better watch out for number one. It's the survival of the fittess."

Doctor Marsh said that Archie is out of position, that Archie is a mixed-up person "because the number one slot, which he claims, is reserved for God." He sees Archie as the elder brother in Christ's prodigal son parable, the one who stands outside the house grumbling about his rights while the welcome-home party is going on inside. The walls that separate him from the party are self-imposed, self righteous, judgmental ones.

That's one reason I worry about prejudice. It could keep me from the party. It could keep me from enjoying the company of other people and what they have to offer, just as surely as it almost kept me from the simple pleasure of calf's liver or, more important, the big break of my career.

And poor Archie, like a lot of us, never listens, never learns. He'll never know that by blindly pushing away the oyster, he might be missing its pearl.

What's the Worst You Can Imagine?

Mary Ellen Clark

D iving is my passion, my life. I've been doing it since I was a kid, starting out with somersaults on the trampoline in our backyard in Newton Square, Pennsylvania and quickly graduating to the springboard of our neighborhood pool. My dad, who worked for IBM, had been a diver at the University of Pennsylvania. I attended Penn State, where I became a platform diver. A ten-meter platform is as high as a three-story building. You hit the water like a bullet. My first time on the platform it took me a half hour standing at the edge before I got up the nerve to dive. I've never looked back. The exhilaration of arcing out into thin air, turning a three-and-a-half somersault, then slicing into the water is nearly indescribable to anyone who hasn't done it.

If you asked a scriptwriter to concoct the worst condition to afflict a competitive diver, a really imaginative scenarist might come up with vertigo. Of the three divers I've heard of who've battled vertigo, none was able to continue diving. In 1995, with the Atlanta Olympic Games fast approaching, I was diagnosed as vertiginous, and I was scared.

It had first happened in 1988 at the Southern Cross meet in Australia. During one of my preliminary dives, I knifed into the water only to find myself disoriented. I had hit fine, my classic rip entry; it had been a good dive. But while thrashing around in the green murk, I wasn't able to determine which way was up, I wear contacts, so I have to keep my eyes closed underwater. I swam, not knowing which direction I was going. Finally I broke the surface, gasping. When I hoisted myself out of the pool, everything was spinning like a carousel. What was happening to me?

Contrary to popular impression, vertigo is not necessarily caused by fear of heights. Dizziness and loss of balance are the symptoms, and there can be many causes and triggers. But vertigo is the last thing you want to suffer while standing on the high-dive platform. I struggled with it on and off for five months, not even knowing what was wrong or what the name for my problem was, before it mysteriously cleared up. I said a prayer of thanks and tried to forget about it. It returned in 1990, disappeared in a couple of days, and I thought I was through with it forever.

By then I had graduated from Penn State, earned a master's in physical education from Ohio State, and, with Dad's encouragement, moved to Florida to train with legendary diving coach Ron O'Brien. Coach O'Brien said I stood a chance of making the 1992 U.S. Olympic team that would compete in the Barcelona summer games. It would be a dream come true. "I know you can do the work," Coach O'Brien encouraged me.

Training is grueling. You can't dive off the platform every day. The impact of hitting the water at high velocity again and again takes its toll on the body. But all the training was worth it. When I was named to the U.S. Olympic Diving Team I called back to Newtown Square immediately: "I made it, Dad!"

Though I had good news that summer, Dad had some bad. He was scheduled for open heart surgery. My first impulse was to skip the Olympics so I could stay with him. Dad wouldn't hear of it. "After all, Mare," he reassured me, "isn't this what I got you started on? Remember?"

Through all my years of competition, one image I kept close was that of my dad bending me into the proper dive position on the springboard when I was little.

Now, hugging me good-bye before I left for Barcelona, my dad said, "I'll be watching you on TV, Mare." Dad, who had taken all seven of us children to church every Sunday, kept a strong faith that would sustain him through whatever lay ahead. On the plane I prayed and received the strong impression he would be all right.

Soon I was faced with another dilemma: The opening ceremonies were scheduled to take place between 8:00 P.M. and 1:00 A.M. the night before my first event. I would get only a few hours sleep if I marched with the other U.S. Olympians. "We can always watch it on TV back at the Olympic village," Coach said.

I recalled my Dad's words: "I'll be watching you on TV." I had got word he had come through his surgery nicely and was recovering well. It would make him so proud to see me with the other Americans. So I marched, the only platform diver at the ceremonies. After the next day's competition I was in second place, a dark horse for a medal. The Russian and Chinese divers had been heavily favored. At twenty-nine, I had been written off by most people as too old to win.

"Maybe you should march before all your events," Coach joked.

But my next-to-last dive was a disaster and plunged me into fifth place. I had one final shot at a medal. As I stood on the platform ready to take my last dive, I paused a bit longer than usual to savor the moment.

A gentle Mediterranean breeze ruffled the air. The crowd

.. ..

was silent. I patted myself dry with a chamois as the announcement came over the loudspeaker. "Mary Ellen Clark of the United States, doing a backward one-and-a-half somersault with two-and-a-half twists."

I tossed the chamois away. It wrapped itself nicely around the railing of a lower board. *Good shot*, I thought. I stepped up to the edge of the platform and turned my back to the water. With a quick prayer and an incredible sense of lightness I was airborne, arcing out over the pool, twisting and tumbling, the Barcelona skyline flashing by. A micro-instant later I ripped into the water. I knew I had nailed the dive. When I shot back to the surface Coach O'Brien was yelling, "Bronze, Mary Ellen, bronze!"

As I stood on the awards platform to accept my medal, I knew Dad was watching. *This is for you, Dad*, I thought. What an incredible feeling!

In 1995, I was training again with Coach O'Brien for the '96 Summer Olympic Games in Atlanta. January 18 was just another practice day at Fort Lauderdale's International Swimming Hall of Fame. I had kept up a full schedule of competitions since I won the bronze in Barcelona, and I was in the best shape of my life. I took a quick springing step off the one-meter board and did a simple practice dive. As soon as I hit the water I knew something was wrong.

This time I consulted a slew of specialists. An EKG ruled out an organic brain disorder. One doctor thought it was an inner-ear problem. Another suspected a virus. One thing was agreed on: I had vertigo, and it would be madness to continue diving. I had to withdraw from the Pan-American Games that winter.

I was confused and distraught. Would I ever dive again? For a while I slept with a cervical collar, sitting up in a chair. I tried acupuncture. I saw a nutritionist. I tried Eastern remedies like

ginkgo biloba, rhubarb, cinnamon twigs, oyster shell and gin-
seng, not to mention any number of Western pharmaceutical
drugs. Still, I got horribly dizzy. Sometimes it even happened
when I stood up too fast. Then *Sports Illustrated* magazine
reported that "the best female diver in the country cannot dive
because she is dizzy."

One night I found myself wailing out my problems on the
phone to Steve DuVall, a friend whose spiritual strength I
greatly admire. Finally Steve cut me off. "Mary Ellen," he said,
"what is the worst possible scenario you can imagine?"

"That I'll never dive again."

"Can you accept that?" he asked.

I hung up without arriving at a definite answer. As I leaned
back in my chair I thought of the Apostle Paul's words: "I have
learned the secret of being content in any and every situation,
whether well fed or hungry, whether living in plenty or in
want. I can do everything through him who gives me strength"
(Philippians 4:12-13, NIV).

The question was, could I *not* do something through him
who gives me strength? Could I not dive again and find contentment? And at that moment I realized my father and mother
had given me something more important than diving—they
had given me faith. It was a part of me that went all the way
back to when I was a little girl and was taught trust in God is
the most important thing of all. Isn't that what faith is? Trusting in God? As much as I loved my sport, I knew I could go on
without it as long as I had my faith, as long as I trusted and
persevered. The rest was up to God.

Eventually I found relief from vertigo with the Upledger
Institute's Craniosacral Therapy. In a strange way vertigo, I
think, has made me a better diver, a calmer and more focused

athlete. It's given me a greater appreciation for the blessings I've had in my sport, and helped me see that life is more than competition and medals. Diving is still my passion, but it is tempered. Each time I leap off that thirty-three-foot platform I am reminded what trust and faith really mean.

Editor's note: *At the Summer Olympic Games in Atlanta in 1996, Mary Ellen Clark won her second bronze in the high dive; at thirty-three, she was the oldest diver ever to earn a medal in that event.*

Dear Dad . . .

Carol Lawrence

I t was the last straw. I had just returned home from doing a
television special out of town. Mother and Dad, who'd
come out to California to take care of my two boys while I was
away, met me at the door.

As soon as I stepped into the house, mother wrapped her
arms around me. "Oh, Carol, we saw the special. You were
wonderful!"

As she went on I watched over her shoulder for Dad, who
was standing with the boys. *He* was the one I so wanted to
please. He had always been a cool and distant man, but I
thought this time, just maybe *this* time, he would give me the
support I needed. But no. He simply said, "Nice show, Carol,"
then turned back to the boys.

I bit my tongue while we put away the luggage. Then I
stormed into the kitchen, where Mother was doing what she
loved most, cooking for the family. The kitchen was filled with
the aroma of sautéed calamari. A lobster sauce simmered on
one burner and fresh pasta boiled on another.

"It's still a vendetta, isn't it?" I snapped. "He's still bitter
because I didn't become a lawyer!"

Mother looked up from stirring her caramel tapioca pudding and sighed: "No, no, Carol, he's forgotten that long ago.
You know your father; he is a quiet man. He finds it hard to
show his feelings."

"Then I won't show mine either!" I retorted, slapping the

counter. That, I determined, would be it. I had tried too long and hard to get close to the man. It was like trying to get a hug from a lamppost.

It had been that way while I was growing up too. Ours was an old-fashioned Italian family in Melrose Park, a suburb west of Chicago. My father, Michael Laraia, was a strict man who could devastate me with a look, a word of disapproval or, worse, of disappointment. Yet my younger brother and I knew he worked very hard to provide for us. He was village clerk and controller for Melrose Park by day and an insurance man at night. His ambition had been to be a lawyer, but he had been brought up by a tyrannical father. Though Dad had won a full scholarship to college, where he intended to take prelaw, his father refused to let him take it. So it was only natural that Dad had definite plans for Joey and me: We would both become lawyers.

Yet as soon as I could walk, I loved to dance. Mother gave me patent-leather tap shoes and lessons at a local dance studio. From then on I constantly tapped all those shuffles, flaps and ball changes, wearing out the kitchen linoleum. Then I danced in the garage, leaving the automatic garage door half open for fresh air. At the sound of footsteps on the sidewalk, I'd flick the switch, the door would rise like a theater curtain, and I'd sing and dance at full power. Passersby would stare open-mouthed at the funny little kid with top hat and cane pouring her heart out. By age thirteen I began performing during summer vacations in local social clubs and later danced in the ballet corps of Chicago's Lyric Opera.

My father tolerated it. "That is all right for now, Carolina Maria," he said one Saturday morning as I accompanied him to a local gas station, where he did the owner's accounting.

"But I will be so proud when I can point you out in a court-room and say, 'That is my *figlia*.' "

I smiled and looked out the window. These Saturday mornings with Dad were so precious that I did not want to break the spell.

When I graduated from Proviso High School with a scholarship to Northwestern University, he was ecstatic. He expected me to take prelaw. Instead, I was named freshman of the year in drama.

The following summer on a family vacation to New York, I found a spot in a Broadway chorus line. My mother was delighted; my father was crestfallen. He hardly said a word to me. After I found a room, they immediately left for home.

In 1957 I got my big break, singing the lead role of Maria in *West Side Story* on Broadway. From then on life was a whirl of musicals, television specials and dramas.

In the meantime my brother, Joey, became a successful lawyer. I married Robert Goulet. Two sons came along. And even though it seemed my father had finally accepted my career, conversations with him were stiff and formal.

Even during the heartbreak years, when my marriage crumbled and I struggled alone to raise my boys, working harder than ever to make ends meet, Father and I remained coolly polite. It was Mother who heard my anguished cries. Yet even she could not fill that empty space within me. More and more I felt that God had stopped loving me because I had not done everything right. I desperately sought some kind of forgiveness, some kind of relief from the guilt that burdened me.

Though I had drifted away from God through the years, I was suddenly drawn to a local church. There I found a warmth and spontaneity I had never known before. Instead of warning me about God's displeasure, the pastor talked about His unconditional love and reminded us that Jesus told us to love thy neighbor *as thyself*. And I began to understand I couldn't love anybody in a healthy way until I learned to love and accept myself. I joined a women's prayer group, where I could unload my guilt in confidence without fear of being judged.

Knowing finally that God had forgiven me with all my faults, I began to look outward. And I experienced the unexpected joy of devoting time and effort to understanding others. One morning I was inspired to do something I had never considered before.

As I waited at a gas station, the pungent odor of gasoline triggered memories, and once again I was sitting at my father's side in that Melrose Park gas station long ago. A warmth filled me, and I thought of all those unfortunate people I knew who, estranged from a friend or relative, awaited the other person's gesture of reconciliation. So often it came too late. And I remembered a pastor's telling me that when Jesus asked us to forgive others seven times seventy, He meant we should swallow our pride and take the first step. I knew what I must do.

That night I wrote Dad a long letter. Into it I poured all the love of a skinny little girl. I told him how I'd idolized him and followed him around like a puppy because he epitomized patience, wisdom, understanding and uncompromising truth.

"Dad, you always had the answer I needed," I wrote, "or knew how to mend whatever I had broken." I told how I marveled at his struggle from the poverty of immigrant status to the success of a highly respected official and businessman.

"Dad, I'm proud to be your daughter," I wrote, "and everybody else, including Mom and Joey, knows how much I really love you. I just wanted you to know it too." I mailed it that night with a profound sense of relief at having done something I should have done long ago.

Later I booked a concert just outside of Chicago for one special reason: Mother had phoned that Dad's health had become critical. He had been living with cancer for some years, but now it was devastating him. The concert would be the second part of my letter. I prayed he'd be well enough to attend.

When I called home to let my parents know when I would arrive, I asked Mother if I could talk to Dad. He got on the phone.

"Dad, did you get my note?"

"Yes," he said, "thank you for a lovely letter."

A lovely letter? Couldn't he at least . . . ? But no, I couldn't let such a thought deter me from reaching for reconciliation. I had no right to expect an emotional outpouring.

While waiting in the auditorium the night of the concert, I was terribly nervous. I had front-row seats set up with special cushions for Dad. Would he be there? I felt like I was six years old and performing for the very first time. Then I saw him coming, with Mom and Joey. His frail frame was bent slightly forward, his thin white hair shining in the auditorium lights. They sat down in front of me.

The comedy numbers were easy, but when I sang ballads, I had to watch the catch in my throat. The most difficult was the close. I was to blow a final kiss to the audience.

"This has been a special time I'll always cherish and keep deep within my heart," I told the people, "and so until next we meet, please remember that"—the orchestra began to play—"you will be my music."

My father looked into my eyes and nodded his head approvingly.

"You will be my song."

He nodded again.

"You will be my music, to fill my heart with love my whole life long."

And then I saw Dad lift his glasses to brush away a tear, and I had to look away for a second. Then Joey helped my father to his feet, and Dad stood clapping and smiling, tears streaming down his face. As I watched him, I was thankful I had taken that first step toward reconciliation. I threw him a kiss and felt my heart whole.

Finally, after Dad died, I learned how complete that reconciliation was. My sister-in-law told me, "You'll never know how much your letter meant to your father. He was so proud of it and would read it to us over and over again. In truth, he had it memorized." Then she added, "We found your letter in your father's pajamas shirt pocket where he always kept it, right over his heart."

I bowed my head. Just where I had always wanted to be.

My Three Meetings with Moses

Charlton Heston

I f you're like me, the name "Moses" summons up a stern, God-like figure with a long white beard. At least, that's how I used to think of Moses. Then something happened which for an instant whipped away the white beard and left me staring into the face of a flesh-and-blood man. It happened not once but three times. I'd like to tell you about the man I met on those three extraordinary occasions.

My first glimpse of Moses came on Mt. Sinai, where we went to film scenes for the picture *The Ten Commandments*. It took us two days to drive to the mountain from Cairo over country so desolate that half way there all pretense of a road gave out and the drivers had to pick their way among the rocks.

Then, suddenly it was there against the horizon: Mt. Sinai— to our Arab drivers, "Gebel Musa," the Mountain of Moses.

What was there about the brooding shape that brought a sudden chill to the stifling day? Certainly it was the loneliest mountain I had ever seen: a vast rock against the desert sky.

But there was something else about it, something that made me half-afraid to go nearer. In Moses' day, men believed it was certain death to set foot on Sinai—because, they said, it was the dwelling place of God.

I told myself that modern men knew better. But as we lurched toward the foot of Gebel Musa, I could not rid myself of the feeling that in some mysterious way that mountain belonged to God and not to men.

We camped that night at its base, and the next morning set off on foot for the summit. After a few minutes of climbing, my breath was coming hard and my heart was thumping. The slopes were even steeper and more savage than they had looked from below. Sudden chasms dropped away to nowhere, ragged volcanic cinders slashed my boots and the hot desert wind filled my lungs.

And all the while I had the haunting conviction that I was alone. It was nonsense, of course; there were a dozen men toiling up the mountain with me. But the mountain was all around us now, until I felt that I was alone here with the crumbling rocks.

It was around one of these that I first met Moses.

I saw him struggling up these same cliffs—sandals torn, hair blown by the desert wind, eyes wide with fear. Yes, Moses was afraid as he climbed this mountain; if it filled me with a nameless awe in this unbelieving century, what must it have done to the man who knew he was trespassing on the holy place of God Himself?

In that instant the stately law-giver with long white beard was gone, and Moses was a man, panting for breath as I was, heart hammering with the cruel climb—and hammering with something more terrible still. For Moses, as he climbed, was caught in the uncanny presence which still surrounds this mountain. And suddenly I knew that he had climbed in terror.

This was my first glimpse of Moses. A week later, I imagined I saw him again, at another moment in his life.

One of the hardest things about motion picture acting, I think, is that you don't play your part straight through from beginning to end, the way it actually happened. In this movie, the first scenes I played were the ones on Mt. Sinai. Now, a week later, I was to act a sequence that took place many years earlier in Moses' life: the scenes that show him fleeing from Egypt across the desert.

For three days I walked, stumbled and crawled through that desert while the cameras rolled and the layers of dust on me caked to a solid crust.

Our Arab drivers were dumbfounded by this new turn of events. One of them in particular watched me anxiously as I slumped to my knees in the sand. It was a scene where Moses roots up a tiny green plant and scrabbles in the soil beneath it in search of water. He watched us run through several takes, until he could stand it no longer.

"Why we not give this sad man some water?" he cried in great compassion, "then all go back to Cairo!"

But the sad man struggled on, all that day and the next, over the blazing red rock. And here in the desert I met Moses for the second time. It wasn't a sudden, breathtaking meeting, like the time I rounded a rock on Mt. Sinai. This was a gradual acquaintance, a knowledge that grew in me as I walked, hour after hour, over the most forlorn landscape I've ever seen.

It was simply this: Moses knew what it meant to fail. His flight through this desert came at a time in his life when he had no faith; he had not yet met God and received his divine commission. He was just a man running for his life. He was fleeing Pharaoh's death sentence, only to find a far more hideous death awaiting him under the pitiless sun.

He kept going simply because there is one thing more horrible than walking in that desert, and that thing is stopping there, where the heat closes around one like a shroud. He kept going, but he could not have hoped to cross this wasteland alive. Simply to look at it is to forget all hope. Despair rises from the dry wadies* like the rippling heat, and the very hills are built of dust.

Here again, Moses the patriarch was nowhere to be seen. Here was only an exhausted man, a man who, this once at least, had hit rock bottom.

My last glimpse of him came nearly two weeks later. At the edge of the desert not far from Cairo, our stage crew had reconstructed the gates of a city and here, on a Saturday morning, seven-thousand Egyptian extras assembled for the Exodus scene.

I got into my make-up and wardrobe hours early and walked out onto the set. There I stopped short. I had known there would be seven-thousand people there, but how many that was I didn't know until I saw them. For a mile in front of me stretched a solid mass of people and animals. They filled the avenue of sphinxes that led into the desert, and spilled out over the sand on either side.

After a while, I began to pick out individuals. Right in front of me, six dusty camels belched as their driver prodded them into position. Next to him a fly-ridden little girl guarded a few scrawny geese. An old Bedouin beside her tugged at the carcass of a dead donkey. A shiny new foal and a week-old infant pulled for milk from their mothers. Few of these people had ever seen a movie; none had more than the vaguest idea why they were paid to gather here.

For two hours I walked, inching my way through the sweaty swarm of people and animals, haltingly trying out my two Arabic phrases: "Greetings" and "As God wills." And

*Watercourse which flows only during rains

everywhere I walked, people recognized the tall staff and the Levite robe. Moses is as great a figure to Moslems as to Christians and Jews. Everywhere their warm murmur followed me: "Musa! Musa!"

I was lost now, not in space, but in centuries. Surely, on the morning of that long-ago Exodus, these were the same eyes that followed Moses. The same skinny animals, the ragged clothes, the stink of poverty.

I squeezed through the farthest rim of the crowd and out into the desert. Lifeless and endless it stretched to the horizon, while behind me the voices faded and swelled, "Musa, Musa!" These people had trusted Moses, they had followed where he led—and where had he led them? Into this waterless desert? Into this unspeakable wilderness?

I turned and looked back at the sea of old men, half-starved women, tiny children. Moses could not have led them into this desert! Not the Moses I had seen—not the man who had crawled on his knees through this very wasteland. Not the man who had struggled, panting and terrified, up the slopes of Mt. Sinai; that man was capable of doubt. Could he now walk into this desert with the little girl and her geese?

The moment had come for Moses to lift his staff and signal Exodus. I walked slowly to where they waited, twisted and tangled back through the cool sphinxes. What had Moses felt as these eyes turned to him in trust? The man I had glimpsed on Mt. Sinai had been afraid.

I had met Moses on Sinai, yes, but Moses had met God. And then I knew what Moses had felt, he had been confident, joyous, unhesitating.

Of course Moses could not lead these thousands across the desert. He never would have tried. But God could do it. And

.. ..

Moses, this all-too-human man, this man so much like the rest of us, had simply turned himself into the instrument through which the strength of God moved.

With joy I cried out the words that Moses cried:

"Bear us out of Egypt, O Lord,

As the eagle bears its young upon its wings . . ."

Then I lifted Moses' staff and saw the multitude heave into a vast shudder of motion, and walk out from bondage.

A Note From The Editors

This original Guideposts Book was created by the Book and Inspirational Media Division of the company that publishes *Guideposts*, a monthly magazine filled with true stories of hope and inspiration.

Guideposts is available by subscription. All you have to do is write to Guideposts, 39 Seminary Hill Road, Carmel, New York 10512. When you subscribe, each month you can count on receiving exciting new evidence of God's presence, His guidance and His limitless love for all of us.

Guidepost Books are available on the World Wide Web at www.guidepostsbooks.com. Follow our popular book of devotionals, *Daily Guideposts*, and read excerpts from some of our best-selling books. You can also send prayer requests to our Monday morning Prayer Fellowship and read stories from recent issues of our magazines, *Guideposts*, *Angels on Earth*, and *Guideposts for Teens*.